War on Autism

D1569293

Corporealities: Discourses of Disability

Series editors: David T. Mitchell and Sharon L. Snyder

War on Autism

On the Cultural Logic of
Normative Violence

ANNE MCGUIRE

University of Michigan Press
Ann Arbor

Published in the United States of America by the
University of Michigan Press
Manufactured in the United States of America
⊗ Printed on acid-free paper

2019 2018   2017   2016   4   3   2   1

A CIP catalog record for this book is available from the British Library.

Library of Congress Cataloging-in-Publication Data

Names: McGuire, Anne, 1981– author.
Title: War on autism : on the cultural logic of normative violence / Anne
    McGuire.
Description: Ann Arbor : University of Michigan Press, [2016] | Series:
    Corporealities: discourses of disability | Includes bibliographical references
    and index.
Identifiers: LCCN 2015048906| ISBN 9780472053124 (paperback) | ISBN
    9780472073122 (hardcover) | ISBN 9780472121922 (e-book)
Subjects: LCSH: Autism—Social aspects. | Violence. | Sociology of disability. |
    BISAC: SOCIAL SCIENCE / Disease & Health Issues. | SOCIAL SCIENCE /
    Discrimination & Race Relations.
Classification: LCC RC553.A88 .M385 2016 | DDC 616.85/882—dc23
LC record available at http://lccn.loc.gov/2015048906

An accessible ebook version of *War on Autism* is available for readers with
print disabilities.

For those advocating otherwise

Contents

Acknowledgments

———◦◦◦———

The process of researching, writing, and publishing this book has taken place over the course of a decade and with the support of a great many people and organizations. I am grateful for the financial support I have received from the University of Toronto, the Ontario Ministry of Training, Colleges and Universities and the Social Sciences and Humanities Research Council of Canada.

The ideas for this book began in my early academic years at what was then the Department of Sociology and Equity Studies in Education at the Ontario Institute for Studies in Education (OISE), University of Toronto. My time at OISE deeply influenced my understandings of disability culture and the politics of justice, and I remain indebted to my OISE friends and colleagues. First, to my supervisors, teachers, and dear friends, Tanya Titchkosky and Rod Michalko, who have read and listened to countless drafts of this book over the years and whose trailblazing work in cultural and interpretive disability studies has inspired me greatly throughout this process. Your work and mentorship has shaped me academically, politically, and personally. To my disability studies friends and collaborators at OISE (and beyond!)—Katie Aubrecht, Eliza Chandler, Sarah Snyder, Patty Douglas, Jiji Voronka, Sam Walsh, Isaac Stein, Jan MacDougall, Chris Chapman, Laura Thrasher, Devi Mucina, Sheila Stewart, Kelly Fritsch, Ryan Parrey-Munger, Chrissy Kelly, and so many others—and to the other members of my doctoral and defence committees, Kari Dehli, Sherene Razack, and Dan Goodley: your comments, critiques, and provocations remain very present in the work that follows.

I could not have written this book without the support of faculty, staff, and students in my new home with the Equity Studies Program at New College, University of Toronto. Thank you to New College Principal Yves Roberge and Equity Studies Program director June Larkin for their work sustaining disability studies scholarship and pedagogy at U of T and for giving me the institutional space and support necessary to complete this project. I would like also to express a debt of gratitude to the Equity Studies students in the disability studies stream: you have taught me so much about the practical and political complexities of living with difference and continuously remind me of the possibility of novel and creative forms of resistance.

Thanks to LeAnn Fields and the University Michigan Press for the support, patience, and guidance you offered this new author along the way. I also wish to express my deep respect and gratitude to my anonymous reviewers who engaged so deeply with this work and became essential interlocutors throughout my manuscript revision process. Early versions of some of the chapters in the book have appeared elsewhere. Thanks to the journals, reviewers, and editors involved in each of these publication processes. In particular, to Jay Dolmage, editor of the *Canadian Journal of Disability Studies*, to Shelley Tremain, editor of *Foucault and the Government of Disability*, 2nd ed. (University of Michigan Press), and to Katherine Runswick Cole, Rebecca Mallett, and Sami Tamimi, editors of *Critical Autism Studies* (Jessica Kingsley Press). Thanks also to my phenomenal indexer, Paula Durbin-Westby, for your deep engagement and expert guidance.

Finally, to my family: Thanks to mom and dad and Stephen and James, who taught me so much about the social and political dimensions of disability long before I had ever heard of a social model of disability. To Eduardo, whose sharp insights and artful interventions have sculpted the possibility of this work and whose love has gathered me and held me close throughout this publication process and beyond. And to Mateo and Noé, for filling all the space between the lines.

One of the most profound and humbling insights that I have gained during the process of writing and revising this book is that autism advocacy is not one thing and that, indeed, it never can be. I would like to say one final word of thanks to all those whose life and work continue to bravely and fiercely demonstrate new and alternative possibilities for speaking, thinking, writing, fighting, and caring for ourselves and others.

Introduction

———— ⚭ ————

"The ongoing constitution of disability as-a-problem condition
is accompanied by writing, reading and otherwise acting as if
embodied differences can appear purely—as if they are outside
of cultural influence, untouched by political and social organization, as if dominant discourses are not organizing our past,
present, and future relations to disability, to impairment, to
embodiment."

> —Tanya Titchkosky, *Reading and Writing Disability Differently:
> The Textured Life of Embodiment* (2007), p. 38

"My point is not that everything is bad, but that everything is
dangerous, which is not exactly the same as bad. If everything is
dangerous, then we always have something to do."

> —Michel Foucault, "On the Genealogy of Ethics: An Overview
> of Work in Progress" (1983), p. 231–32

On the 27th of September 2009, an unnamed eleven-year-old autistic
boy was murdered by his father in the basement of their family home
in Edmonton, Alberta, Canada. The boy's father then killed himself. I
read about the murder-suicide a few days later on the Canadian Broad-
casting Corporation's (CBC) newsfeed, though details surrounding the
events and those involved were remarkably thin. Those details that were
circulated through the popular Canadian news media told the story of
a boy's 'severe' autism and his 'violent' outbursts, a 'desperate' father
and 'costly' care.[1] The reports told of a child who was living in a group

home and who was making some 'progress' there. However, the care he had been receiving had become too expensive and his family was told he would be moved to another facility ("Man despaired over moving autistic son," 2009, para. 7). According to a CBC news report, this move "pushed [the father] over the edge" ("Man despaired over moving autistic son," 2009, para. 10).

Police discovered the lifeless bodies of the father and child in the basement of the father's bungalow in northeast Edmonton on September 27th 2009. News media reported that police made the decision to not release the names of the dead "in order to protect the privacy of the family" ("Dad in murder-suicide had sought help for autistic son," para. 5). While the situation was labeled a murder-suicide, no cause of death was released to the public. The boy's name, revealed in an inquiry years later, was Jeremy Bostick.

Three provinces east and less than a month later, another Canadian autistic boy was killed by his parent. On the 25th of October 2009, fifteen-year-old Tony Khor was murdered by his mother, Seow Cheng Sim, in a hotel room in Mississauga, Ontario. Strikingly similar stories circulated through the media. Reports told of a 'severely' autistic boy—diagnosed at age two—who had grown 'progressively worse' (Mitchell and Wilkes, 2009). Tony's parents were described as 'devoted,' the situation that ended in his murder as 'heartbreaking' and 'tragic' ("Mother charged with autistic son's death," 2009, para. 6; Tambar, 2009). Tony lived at home with his family, though according to neighbors his parents had been arguing about whether to send him to live in a care facility. "Their son had become more difficult to handle over the past few years" write Toronto *Star* reporters Bob Mitchell and Jim Wilkes (2009); "the stress of raising him had become extremely hard for [Sim], who mostly cared for the teen" (para. 8). Indeed, the couple had been arguing the day of the murder, and it was following this argument that Sim took Tony, drove to a nearby hotel, and killed him. While police said that the boy's body showed "obvious signs of trauma," they did not officially release the cause of Tony's death (Tambar, 2009, para. 3).

I begin this book by retelling the stories of these two murder cases not because they are particularly unusual or rare but because, disturbingly, they are not. The West has a long and violent history of targeting autistic people in particular and disabled people in general (Snyder and Mitchell, 2006). In contemporary times, such acts of violence are occurring with

an aching frequency; we are continually and even routinely encountering resonant stories of violence against autistic people as these stories circulate through our news sources, through our culture, and through our
lives. Such acts of violence seldom go unnoticed by disability advocates
and activists. Autistic self-advocates and their allies, for example, have
long been watching the headlines, marking and mourning the surging
numbers of autistic victims of violence, and demanding political action
(Smith, 2006; Cevik, 2012; Brown, 2013; Chew, 2009; ASAN, 2012). As
with other forms of ableist violence, instances of autism violence are typically framed as isolated events, encoded as random individual tragedies.
They are, in other words, seldom understood by mainstream society as
pointing to a troubling sociocultural phenomenon.

As the reports of these two Canadian murders surfaced and
circulated—first the one and then, so soon after, the other—some
mainstream advocacy organizations did identify some resemblances
between them and even declared these to be related acts of violence.
Following the murder of Tony Khor, the Canadian provincial advocacy organization, Autism Ontario, released a media statement entitled
"Ontario Community Grieves Loss of Boy with Autism" (Autism Ontario,
2009) (Fig.1). "Yesterday, a mother [Cheng] took the life of her son
with autism," the statement begins. It continues by explicitly connecting Khor's murder with the murder of Bostick: "in Canada, this is the
second time in a month that a parent has taken the life of their child
with autism" (Autism Ontario, 2009, para. 1). Two Canadian children
were murdered by their parents in under a month and such violence
called for advocacy as a response. In the violent deaths of fifteen-year-old
Tony Khor and eleven-year-old Jeremy Bostick, advocacy (Autism Ontario) heard a call to action and such a call, in turn, called advocacy into
being. Yet, in the midst of urgent calls of violence and the immediate
necessity of a responsive advocacy, it is seldom asked: what (or whose)
call is attended to and what kinds of responses are, thus, generated and
privileged? As advocacy is called to action and, so, called into being: what
is the meaning of the being of autism advocacy today? This book is an
attempt at thinking through such multifarious questions.

The Crisis in Crisis

For Autism Ontario—a mainstream, professional/parent-led autism
advocacy organization—the central call issuing forth from the deaths of

AutismONTARIO
see the potential

Media Release
Ontario Community Grieves Loss of Boy with Autism

October 26, 2009 (Toronto, ON) – Yesterday, a mother took the life of her son with autism. In Canada, this is the second time in a month that a parent has taken the life of their child with autism.

The need for supports and services is keenly felt across Ontario. Families of individuals with Autism Spectrum Disorder know that autism services can be challenging to access. When a crisis occurs, this is often more pronounced.

Studies show that raising a child with autism is more stressful than raising a child with any other disability. Many parents are stretched beyond what they feel they can possibly cope with. In this situation, the outcome was the unthinkable.

"When a child with autism is in crisis, the whole family is in crisis, says Dr. Yona Lunsky, a clinical psychologist and Research Section Head in the Dual Diagnosis Program at the Centre for Addiction and Mental Health.

Dr. Lunsky continues, "Parents need to be able to access crisis supports to help their children but also to help them, the parents. No parent should feel so alone in a struggle that she or he thinks there is only one way out. At the very least, we need responsive crisis services for every child and family. But what are really needed here are appropriate supports prior to the situation developing into an emergency."

Autism Ontario offers support and information to families dealing with autism across the province. Executive Director, Margaret Spoelstra acknowledges that crisis intervention services can be a challenge to access for many families, but says, "Taking the life of your child should not be an option. If you are a parent or an individual in crisis, you need to contact your local crisis line."

1 in 150 children are now being diagnosed with an Autism Spectrum Disorder. Autism is a developmental disability that prevents individuals from properly understanding and responding to what they see, hear, and sense. This may result in severe problems of social relationships, communication and behaviour.

Since 1973, Autism Ontario has been providing information, supports, and advocacy to families, professionals and individuals dealing with Autism Spectrum Disorders.

For more information on autism, and Autism Spectrum Disorder, visit www.autismontario.com.

Fig. 1 Autism Ontario (2009) media release following the deaths of Tony Khor and an unnamed boy from Edmonton. Press release originally published on Autism Ontario's website, 2009. Image reproduced with permission from Autism Ontario.

the two boys was the call of desperate parents/families needing better access to autism services and crisis supports: "The need for supports and services is keenly felt across Ontario," the media release states; "families of individuals with Autism Spectrum Disorder know that autism services can be challenging to access. When a crisis occurs, this is often more pronounced" (Autism Ontario, 2009, para. 2). Out of the deaths of Tony Khor and Jeremy Bostick, Autism Ontario heard the call of many families living with individuals with autism facing significant social barriers preventing access to much needed autism services and supports.

The problem identified by advocacy is clear: inadequate supports for *parents and families living with autistic people.* What is made equally clear is the necessary response of advocacy: the ensuring of more services and better access for families. As a response to this problem, advocacy itself was called into being as that which works to secure more and better access to services and supports—a reason for being clearly reflected in a press release from Autism Ontario, in which it defines its mission as such: "since 1973, Autism Ontario has been providing information, supports and advocacy to families professionals and individuals dealing with Autism Spectrum Disorders" (Autism Ontario, 2009, para. 8).

However, a careful examination of the terms and targets of the press release reveals subtle indications that the call to which advocacy is responding is a multisonorous one. The problem-in-need-of-response identified by Autism Ontario is not simply inadequate supports and services but rather inadequate supports and services in relation to an underlying 'crisis'—"when a crisis occurs," the statement tells us, the lack of access to supports and services is "often more pronounced." Lying beneath and coming before the call for more access and better services is the call of parents and families in crisis. The media release goes on to provide us with informational facts regarding the nature of such crises. It tells us, for example, that the crisis at hand is a crisis born of the invariable stress of raising an autistic child: "studies show that raising a child with autism is more stressful than raising a child with any other disability. Many parents are stretched beyond what they feel they can possibly cope with" (Autism Ontario, 2009, para. 3). In contradistinction to the taken-for-granted (normal) stress of raising just-a-child, raising a child with a disability is remarkably stressful, say empirical studies and mainstream advocacy organizations in chorus. And, more stressful still, we are told, is the task of raising a child with autism. In addition to the task of raising just-a-child, parents of children with a disability and/or children with autism must also raise that which (we are told) is not inherently 'of' the child but rather comes 'with' the child: an individual biological condition of disability or, in this case, autism. As it is made and kept separate from just-a-child, disability is inscribed by advocacy as the source of parent stress and autism as that which catalyzes even more stress still. Framed in this way, autism becomes commonsensically understood as some 'thing,' an undesirable and extraneous appendage that has simply and as a matter of biology or nature come to be 'with' some people and their families, and this 'with' of autism is, often times, too much with which to cope (for a compelling discussion of the problematic notion of autism as an appendage, see Sinclair, 1993).

The notion of autism as the originary source of undue stress in family life is secured and supported in the advocacy statement as Autism Ontario provides us with an overview of autism's biological origin in individuals and a description of its pathologically deviant signs:

> 1 in 150 children are now being diagnosed with an Autism Spectrum Disorder. Autism is a developmental disability that prevents individuals from properly understanding and responding to what they see, hear, and sense. This may result in severe problems of social relationships, communication and behaviour. (Autism Ontario, 2009, para. 7)

The primary call attended to by advocacy—the call framed as a 'crisis' underlying and exacerbating the need for greater access and better services—is the existence and persistence of a medically and morally organized autism that is located in growing numbers of individual bodies, a pathologically disordered autism that prevents some individuals from 'properly' seeing, hearing, and sensing, and that causes 'severe problems' in relating, communicating, and behaving.

The statement suggests that the developmental 'impropriety' of autism is, clearly and naturally, located and locatable in individual bodies and nowhere else: the '1's' in '150's,' as it were. However, the crisis described does not end with the individual. Autism's characteristic potential for 'severe' relationship, behavior, and communication 'problems' is framed as the core of a collective crisis that begins with the individual but that, in the absence of autism services and crisis supports, leaks outward, enveloping parents, families, and communities. The press release above quotes a statement from Dr. Yona Lunsky of Toronto's Center for Addiction and Mental Health (CAMH) that speaks to this leaky crisis: "When a child with autism is in crisis," she reminds us, "the whole family is in crisis" (Autism Ontario, 2009, para. 4). Autism, taken for granted as nothing more or less than a biological disorder—some pathological 'thing' that prevents good/proper responses and incites bad/improper behaviors—is naturalized as the originary site of both individual and collective crisis, an identification that, in turn, orients and shapes the necessary response of advocacy. Lunsky continues by offering us a prescription for advocacy:

> Parents need to be able to access crisis supports to help their children but also to help them, the parents. No parent should feel so alone in a struggle that she or he thinks there is only one way out. At the very least, we need responsive crisis services for every child and family. But what are really needed here are appropriate supports prior to the situation developing into an emergency. (Autism Ontario, 2009, para. 5)

In relation to the call of individuals and families in crisis, a call that is naturally and singularly understood to be as born of a pathological autism, advocacy is called into being as that which must mitigate 'autism crises' (i.e., through the generation of autism services and crisis supports) before things turn violent (i.e., "[develop] into an emergency").

I am in full agreement with Autism Ontario that the violence perpetrated against Tony Khor and Jeremy Bostick—and, I add, the many other overt and covert acts of violence that are being perpetrated against autistic people today—represents a pressing crisis. I also agree that such a crisis is exacerbated by inadequate social services and supports and that such a crisis requires advocacy as a response. Yet, the crisis on which I focus might be best understood as a crisis of a different order, and it has much to do with the question of advocacy itself. It resides in the common, taken-for-granted understanding of autism as, simply, a naturally occurring unnatural (pathological) biological disorder, a state of 'too slow' development causing non-normative—transformed, so quickly, to morally 'improper'—ways of understanding and responding, as well as 'problem' relationships, behaviors, and means of communicating. This is a crisis tied to the ways in which a strictly biological version of autism— one that is most often secured and supported in and through contemporary performances of autism advocacy—presupposes autism to be some extraneous 'thing' that comes 'with' some people (i.e., people 'with' autism) thereby prohibiting it from being, in some intrinsic way, a 'someone' (i.e., a valid and valuable way of seeing, hearing, sensing an identity, an *autistic person*). And so, unlike Autism Ontario, the primary crisis call

I hear issuing forth from the violent deaths of these two boys (and the many others like them) is not the call of an individualized biological or biomedical crisis, nor is it the call of a crisis of inadequate supports and services designed to respond to autism as such. The call I hear is that of a cultural crisis, born of a relentless collective commitment to understanding autism as some 'thing' medically pathological and morally undesirable—some 'thing' that some people 'have' but cannot 'be,' and so as some 'thing' that we all must be against. Such a conception of autism has important and potentially dangerous consequences for how we (all of us, autistic and nonautistic) understand and perform responsive acts of advocacy.

The cultural crisis I am identifying here, and throughout this book, is not a new crisis per se, and I am certainly not the first to identify it. Autistic activists, academics, self-advocates, and their allies have long demonstrated the danger inherent in dominant autism advocacy narratives, particularly those that frame autism as an undesirable biological pathology in need of treatment and/or cure (ASAN, 2012; Brown, 2012; Yergeau, 2013; Bascom, 2012; Sequenzia, 2012; Autism Women's Network, 2012). Jim Sinclair's iconic piece, "Don't Mourn for Us," for example, was instrumental in first articulating the material danger in separating conceptions of autism from personhood. "Autism is a way of being," he writes. "It is not possible to separate the person from the autism" (Sinclair, 1993, np). Ari Ne'eman's work—his academic work as well as his activist/organization work as founder and president of the Autistic Self Advocacy Network (ASAN)—continues to mount powerful political critiques of mainstream autism advocacy organizations (Ne'eman, 2010). As a prominent autistic blogger, public speaker, and community organizer, Lydia Brown has been influential in mounting a significant challenge to oppressive public policy and violent institutionalization practices (www.autistichoya.com). The work of scholar-activists like Melanie Yergeau and Ibby Grace critically teach us how dominant, contemporary rhetorics of autism come into contact with the materiality of the autistic body. As Yergeau writes, "my body is a site where theory is actualized" (Yergeau, 2013, n.p.). The proliferation of online writings of autistic people and published collections such as Julia Bascomb's *Loud Hands* and ASAN's *And Straight on Till Morning: Essays on Autism Acceptance* center autistic perspectives and critiques. Taken together, these forums provide new and multiple vantage points from which to glean autism and advocacy as contested and profoundly sociopolitical phenomena. In solidarity with the important political, cultural, academic, and activist work that is already being done, this book pays particular attention to dominant stories of autism and advocacy and reads them against a broader cultural, historical, political, and economic backdrop. I do this work with the hope that it might offer a means of further understanding—and further contesting—the ways autism violence is normalized as reasonable and even necessary.

Thinking the 'Unthinkable'

Attending to the re/production of autism as a *cultural* crisis allows for new ways of critically engaging with the risks and possibilities of relating to and across difference. It permits a careful analysis of autism advocacy in contemporary times and, in so doing, positions us to better understand how performances of advocacy—exemplified in the Autism Ontario media release, but certainly not limited to this—can function to produce and sustain crisis, even while making appeals to quell it. The crisis the Autism Ontario media release fails to attend to is the crisis of the naturalization of the association between autism and stress-induced crisis and the normalization of violence that such crisis is understood to, inevitably, invite.

The press release offers us an explanatory story for the violence that was enacted against Khor and Bostick. It provides us with a way of thinking—to borrow from the language of the statement—the 'unthinkable.' Put differently, it helps us to make sense of murder. Vis-à-vis the murders of the two boys, Autism Ontario offers a clear story of the nature of the problem that led to their deaths and the kind of advocacy response needed to address this problem. Autism Ontario's advocacy narrative tells the story of a biological autism that can cause such high degrees of stress in the home that, in the absence of intervening services, 'unthinkable outcomes'—violence and even murder—may very well result. As acts of advocacy frame the deaths of the two boys as 'unthinkable outcomes' of stressed out parents 'coping with' disordered children, we are dissuaded from attending to how such acts of violence against autistic people are rendered *absolutely thinkable.* The persistent move to locate autism violence outside the bounds of reason dangerously obscures the persistent and deadly ways in which autism violence is being rendered, absolutely, thinkable, reasonable, and even normal. We are dissuaded, in other words, from attending to the complex interpretive processes that move us so quickly from disability to crisis to violence and that lead us to the conclusion that parents and families 'dealing with autism' are, as a matter of nature and not as a matter of culture, stressed out and strung out to the point where violence is precisely possible, if not inevitable.

Raising a child with autism is stressful, suggests the media release, and the source of the stress is clear: the 'problem' behaviors and 'improper' responses of individuals 'with' autism. Firmly rooted in biology, the anguish of parents and families is understood by advocacy to be unrelated to a dominant culture—of which acts of advocacy are, invariably, a part—that repeats over and again that autism is nothing more than a problem in need of a solution; some 'thing' undesirable and unwelcome, some 'thing' that is sometimes tolerated, questionably accommodated, seldom celebrated, some 'thing' to be (at least) rehabilitated and (at best) eliminated. The dominant and near monolithic story of autism as a series of improper responses of the individual that generate significant stress for families functions to normalize the understanding that violence is a reasonable or even 'proper' response (albeit an undesirable one) of those 'dealing with autism.' Understood in this way, autism is positioned by advocacy as the underlying cause of its own demise. Such a conclusion, however covert, overtly fails to advocate *for* autistic people. It is, perhaps, not surprising then that a close examination of the Autism Ontario media release reveals no acknowledgment of the pressing crisis faced by autistic people as they are routinely made victims of violence. Indeed, let us note how the two victimized autistic people—the murdered children—were barely mentioned in the Autism Ontario media release, their lives and deaths left unreckoned with, evoked only insofar as they served as an occasion for the contemplation of the crisis of underserviced stressed out parents and families dealing with a biological condition of autism.

Attending to the normative and normalizing nature of such stories of autism and advocacy enables us to ask difficult and important questions about the premises and practices of acts of advocacy and, more broadly, about the culture in which we live. Critically attending to such stories allows us to ask, for example, the following: How do dominant versions of autism that characterize it as a condition of human life instead of a lived human condition—a some 'thing' and not a someone—allow for and even catalyze a collective cultural failure to recognize violence against autistic people as a significant and pressing sociocultural problem? How are dominant cultural understandings of autism as some 'thing' pathological and so as some 'thing' to be against—cultural understandings that are sustained by dominant acts of autism advocacy—creating the

conditions of possibility that render some lives more vulnerable to murder and other forms of normative violence? And how are these same
understandings providing for a doubly violent space where the lives and
deaths of those violated can be radically forgotten: where it becomes
possible for dead children and those who killed them to go unnamed
by the media, where the violence delivered to their bodies leaves a mark
that, to borrow from Judith Butler, "leaves no mark," a mark, moreover,
upon which dominant forms of advocacy seldom remark (Butler, 2004a,
p. 36)? Ne'eman (2010) reminds us of something that should perhaps
be obvious. He states: "The object of autism advocacy should not be a
world without autistic people" (n.p.). As advocacy is called into being
as that which *advocates against* an undesirable biological condition of
autism, how are dominant acts of advocacy failing to *advocate for* (or even
acknowledge) the crisis faced by autistic people whose lives are rendered
relationally more vulnerable to violence and violation in and by a culture
that commonsensically understands autism as some 'thing' we, collectively, would rather live without?

Narrative and Power

Philosopher Ian Hacking (2009a, 2009b) argues that the stories of
autism being produced in and circulated through contemporary west-
ern/ized culture are not so much providing descriptions of an autism
that already is. Rather, according to Hacking, such stories are "contributing to the formation of the discourse of autism" (p. 514). Contemporary stories of autism are, in other words, functioning to constitute what
autism is and can be. He writes:

> I believe that the [autism narrative] genre is helping to bring into
> being an entire mode of discourse, cementing ways in which we have
> recently begun to talk, and will talk, about autism. It is developing
> a language, or, if you will, a new language game, one that is being
> created before our eyes and ears. This speech is, in turn, creating or
> extending a way for very unusual people—namely autistic ones—to
> be, to exist, to live. (Hacking, 2009a, p. 501)

Hacking (2009b) does place limits, however, on what he does and does
not count as an autism story. The genre of autism narrative, for Hacking,
does not comprise "expert reports by clinicians or reflections by theo-

rists," but is rather made up of "stories about people with autism, told by the people themselves, or their families, or by novelists, or by writers of stories for children" (p. 1467).

In chorus with Hacking, I too hold the assumption that the stories we have—those given to us and those we share—are contributing to the formation of an historically specific autism discourse and that such stories are shaping what autism is and can be in contemporary times. Yet, while what autism is is no doubt being constituted by autobiographical narratives written by autistic people, parents' stories of living with autism, and narratives featured in novels about autism, I contend that it is also and at the same time being constituted by the stories told in clinician reports, for example, and in educational policies and practices, in advocacy awareness campaigns, scientific studies, and, of course, in the reflections of theorists. As he tells the story of an autism that is undergoing a "social and cultural evolution" but that is undergirded by "a family of definite biological conditions," or as he makes sense of autistics as "very unusual people," Hacking's theorizations too are involved in the constitution of what autism is and can be (Hacking, 2009b, p. 1467). What is more, the multiple, diverse, and proliferating stories we have of autism are not separate from one another, nor can they be. Hacking (2009b) does acknowledge this. He writes: "different kinds of item influence each other in complex ways. Novelists study autobiographies, whose authors learn from theorists. Parents pick up ideas from novels when they are thinking about their children" (p. 1467). As they circulate in and through culture, stories impress meanings upon one another; indeed, they are enmeshed in an intricate, complex, and ever unfolding web of meaning that allows for such hybrid possibilities as, for example, parent biographies that read and function as clinical reports, describing healthy and pathological behaviors, providing checklists of signs and symptoms of biomedical disorder, and prescribing therapeutic intervention (for one of many examples, see Jenny McCarthy's 2010 book— cowritten by autism specialist Dr. Jerry Kartzinel—*Healing and Preventing Autism: A Complete Guide*).

With this in mind, Hacking's methodological act of delimiting the autism narrative to include certain kinds of stories of autism (e.g., autobiographies by autistic people, parent biographies and reflections, fiction novels and storybooks about autism) but not others (e.g., clinician reports, reflections by theorists) not only represents an artificial divide (as all divides invariably are) but a divide that makes it too easy for us to forget that what autism is and can be today has everything to do with the ways in which stories appear against a cultural backdrop that privileges the telling of some stories over and against others. This methodological move of drawing the divide, in other words, dissuades us from thinking about power. It moves us away from, for example, questioning the ways in which the words and autobiographies of autistic people are always and differentially left open to the authoritative gaze of (mostly nonautistic) *young mind* autism 'experts'—professionals and nonprofessionals alike—and so are always at risk of being delegitimized and discarded as inauthentic, inaccurate, or nonauthoritative.

In her 2013 article, "Clinically Significant Disturbance: On Theorists Who Theorize Theory of Mind," Melanie Yergeau traces the ways power operates on autistic narratives. She argues that "denying the rhetoricity of autistic people and questioning the reliability of their narratives are tropes that permeate scholarly literature" (n.p.). Drawing on the work of leading developmental psychologists Frith and Happé, Yergeau demonstrates how autistic autobiography—or "autiebiography," to use her term—gets stripped of its testimonial legitimacy and transformational power, reframed as nothing other than evidence of disorder or lack. According to Frith and Happé, autistic autobiographies are inherently limited insofar as they are (pathologically) focused on the self: "typically in the autobiographical accounts, we find relatively little about other people's feelings or attitudes [. . .] In this respect, the genre of autobiographical writing is the perfect niche for the talented writer with Asperger Syndrome. One might say the self is not only central to the world they describe, but it is that world" (p.18). For Frith and Happé, autistic autobiographies are nothing other than a symptom of social impairment, evidence of a kind of pathological autistic narcissism. What is more, the authors go on to make the insidious argument that even autistic *self*-understanding is itself disordered: "Autism," they write, "is a devastating disorder because it disrupts not only understanding of others and their social relationships, but also understanding of self" (p.18). Thus, Yergeau observes: "to lack a theory of mind is not simply to lack a theory of other's minds—it is also to lack an awareness of one's *own* mind" (n.p.). As autistic narratives are naturalized as nothing other than symptomatic of an underlying pathology, they are politically neutralized and, ultimately, rendered dismissible. "There are," suggest Frith and Happé, "grave limitations to this type of material. While the accounts are intriguing, it might be a mistake to take what is said at face value" (p. 18).

Concludes Yergeau: "And so, I am writing this essay, presumably unaware of my reader and my (non)self. This is just my autism talking, spewing like a ruptured sieve" (n.p.).

The systematic delegitimization of autistic narrative and subsequent effacement of autistic perspectives is, of course, not limited to the realm of scholarly literature. Operations of power were evident, for example, in the fallout after autistic self-advocate and blogger Mel (then Amanda) Baggs's appearance on CNN where she was interviewed by the network's chief medical correspondent, Dr. Sanjay Gupta, and offered some personal/autobiographical insights of her lived experience as autistic (Gupta, 2007). Following her appearance, Baggs was widely scrutinized by various 'experts,' some claiming she was 'not autistic enough,' others disregarding her autobiographical story altogether by casting it as a hoax (e.g., the "Amanda Baggs Controversy" blog). Clearly, some autism stories are told more easily then others, relationally endowed with greater power and so more legitimacy. This, of course, was also exemplified in the Autism Ontario media release where parents' stories of autism as crisis were so clearly centered while the stories of autistic people in (mortal) crisis were, in fact, not attended to. So powerful are some stories even that they are widely understood to not be stories at all. For Hacking, for example, an autobiographical account of living with autism is a story engaged in the constitution of what autism is and can be, while an etiological origin story of autism as a biological condition remains a taken-for-granted (natural or unstoried) fact.

If the proliferation of autism narrative is "helping to bring into being an entire mode of discourse," as Hacking suggests; if it is involved in the constitution of the limits and possibilities for talking about and understanding autism today, then we must address the sheer force of the underlying power structures involved in governing contemporary autism discourses. I am in complete agreement with Hacking that there are autism narratives that are transgressively functioning to create new ways for autistic people "to be, to exist, to live" (Hacking, 2009a, p. 501). And yet, as I show in this book, there are also a great many dominant and dominating autism narratives that are repeatedly telling us that autism is not a way of being or existing, and it is no way to live. Work in the field of disability studies provides the grounds upon which I can build an analysis of the many ways power operates in the cultural production of autism and advocacy. I turn now to a consideration of some key political and scholarly ideas in disability studies and discuss some of the critical conversations and contestations emanating from the field.

Disability Studies

There are very dominant, very powerful, and very limited sets of cultural scripts that we collectively have, ready-to-hand, when it comes to thinking and speaking about disability. Indeed, in the contemporary West, disability is near monolithically understood as an individual problem, in need of an individualized response/solution (Mitchell, 2002). In this cultural imaginary, disability is ushered into intelligibility as nothing other than lack, dysfunction, pathology, inability, danger, tragedy. It is that which must be intervened upon in some way—prevented, stopped, cured, overcome, if not altogether eliminated. Disabled people and their allies have long resisted such narratives for their demeaning, damaging, and dangerous effects and for their failure to account for the multiple ways people identify with and experience disability (Oliver, 1993; Barnes, 1998; Garland Thomson, 1996; Shapiro, 1994). Born of an ongoing history of disability activism, and shaping it in turn, the field of disability studies provides an intellectual space to analyze disability as a cultural, geo/political, historical, and economic construct; a social category to be considered alongside and in tandem with other social categories including race, class, gender, age, citizenship, and sexuality (see, for example, such varied disability studies work as Davis, 2002; Erevelles, 2011; Hughes and Patterson, 2007; Garland Thomson, 1996; Goodley, 2010; Kumari Campbell, 2009; McRuer, 2006; Michalko, 2002; Snyder and Mitchell, 2006; Oliver, 1996; Titchkosky, 2007; Kafer, 2013; Tremain, 2008; Yergeau, 2013; Chen, 2012).

The formulation of the social model of disability was a watershed moment in the evolution of disability rights and studies. With its key distinction between impairment (physical, mental, or sensorial difference) and disability (ideological, environmental, or attitudinal barriers to participation), the social model provides a framework for understanding disability as a state of social oppression and material disadvantage (Oliver, 1993; Barnes, 1998; Finklestein, 1998). While individual and biomedical understandings of disability naturalize the association between the impaired body/mind and oppression through discourses of tragedy, loss, and lack, sociopolitical perspectives emphasize that the material disadvantages and instances of violence that are routinely faced by disabled people are neither natural nor inevitable. The social model thus offers a powerful critique of normative social and environmental structures and the ways they work, systematically, to privilege certain ways of being (i.e., moving, thinking, feeling, behaving, sensing) over and against others.

While the social model is generally recognized by disability studies scholars and activists as having political utility, many have critiqued the model for its rigid separation of the material (i.e., impairment) and the social (i.e., disability) (Wendell, 2006; Corker and French, 1999; Michalko, 2002; Tremain, 2001). Feminist scholar Iris Marion Young (2001) writes:

> While the social model of disability destabilizes the assumption that the 'problem' with some people has to do with attributes of their bodies and functions, it nevertheless continues to presume a certain fixity to these bodies, and thereby understands many of the experiences and self-conceptions of persons positioned as disabled as grounded in such bodily facts. (Young, 2001, p. xiii)

Acknowledging the political power of the social model, Magrit Shildrick and Janet Price (1998) issue call for "an unsettling of its certainties, of the fixed identities with which it is bound up" (p. 243). As with disability, interpretations and experiences of impairment are embedded within a tangle of social relations. Shelley Tremain (2001) argues: "it seems politically naïve to suggest that the term 'impairment' is value-neutral, that is 'merely descriptive,' as if there could ever be a description that was not also a prescription for the formulation of the object (person, practice or thing) to which it is claimed to innocently refer" (p. 620). Impairment is always an effect, argues Tremain. It is, she elaborates, "an historically specific effect of knowledge-power" (Tremain, 2001, p. 617).

Insofar as it is an effect, and thus a reflection, of our relations of power, the (disabled/impaired) body thus becomes a key site for intersectional analysis and social change. Eli Clare (2001) writes:

> Sometimes we who are activists and thinkers forget about our bodies, ignore our bodies, reframe our bodies to fit our theories and political strategies. For several decades now, activists in a variety of social change movements, ranging from black civil rights to women's liberation, from disability rights to queer liberation, have said repeatedly that the problems faced by any marginalized group of people lie, not in their bodies, but in the oppression they face. But in defining the external, collective, material nature of social injustice as separate

from the body, we have sometimes ended up sidelining the profound relationships that connect our bodies with who we are and how we experience oppression. (Clare, 2001, p. 359)

Feminist, queer, and race perspectives in disability studies have taught us that disability oppression does not bear down on all impaired bodies in the same ways (Bell, 2006; Erevelles, 2011; Meekosha, 2011; Wendell, 2006; Razack, 1998; Titchkosky, 2007; Kafer, 2013). Furthermore, not all disabled people are striving for the same kinds of dignity, recognition, and justice. This is all too evident when we consider the vast and variegated array of physical, sensory, cognitive, and mental impairments that are put in touch with one another under a rubric of disability; when we consider disability's fluidity—how it can appear or disappear, be noticed or remain hidden—as we move through different physical, sensory, and social spaces, and as we find ourselves in different political and historical moments; when we consider how anyone can become disabled at anytime; or how systems of ableism come into contact with racialized bodies, queer and trans bodies, classed bodies, gendered bodies, bodies that already have been touched by other (and perhaps multiple) systems of oppression and violence; when we consider the ways in which disability provokes complex and even contradictory embodied feelings of comfort and discomfort, pride and shame; when we consider how disability can be the basis of community and the effect of communal violence. Vis-à-vis this diverse expanse of disability identity and experience, Marian Corker and Tom Shakespeare (2002) argue: "the global experience of disabled people is too complex to be rendered within one unitary model or set of ideas" (p. 15). The social model is, like all models, reductive and thus is in effect normative. It fails to account for such material/embodied realities as divergent and even contradictory experiences of impairment and the existence of multiple, intersecting oppressions.

It is important to emphasize that the move to center the body as a site of meaning making is by no means an attempt to revisit individualized understandings of disability. To the contrary, critical theories of the (disabled) body theorize the disabled body as the site where multiple social categories, narratives, and relations of power converge (Shildrick and Price, 1998; Tremain, 2001; Corker and French, 1999; Garland Thomson, 2011; Erevelles, 2011; Kafer, 2013; Titchkosky, 2007; Goodley, 2010; Yergeau, 2013; Patterson and Hughes, 1997; Chen, 2012). The disabled body, here, becomes a relation: an embodiment that is not singular but multiple, not bounded but fluid. It is at once ideological (i.e., discourse and power, marginality and resistance) and material (i.e., life and death, flesh and bone, mind and senses). The understanding that disability is constituted relationally inherently makes room for multiple, complex, and contradictory experiences of disability/oppression by localizing ableism within other systems of power (e.g., racism, hetero/sexism, classism, and so on). Thinking the disabled body as a relation also implicates us all, and does so irrespective of our individual disability identities. While particular bodies experience disability in intimate ways, and while certain people are, by virtue of their embodiment, made more vulnerable to material inequities and ableist violence, disability is not so simply in some bodies and not others. "The meaning of a body resides between bodies" writes Titchkosky (2007), "between those who live through them, in them and those who bring them to mind" (p. 126, my emphasis). Disability—its meaning and thus its very materiality—is made and remade, rhetorically and interactionally, between all of us who have a body, all of who live and participate in the making of culture.

Of course, this question of relatedness—of how we relate to and with each other, of how we relate across disability and difference—is also a primary question of (autism) advocacy. It is a question that has been taken up, in many different ways, by a burgeoning group of autism scholars and activists, whose work emanates both from in and out of the academy (see, for example, Biklen & Attfield, 2005; Yergeau, 2013; Baggs, 2012; Sinclair, 1993; Douglas, 2013; Davidson and Orsini, 2013; Ne'eman, 2010; Mallett & Runswick-Cole, 2012; Durbin Westby, 2012; McGuire, 2013; Murray, 2008, Murray 2011; Nadesan, 2005; Bascom, 2012; Sequenzia, 2012b; Brown, 2013; Dawson, 2008b; Seidel, 2005a and the archives of online writing at autismwomensnetwork.org, autistics.org and neuroqueer.blogspot.ca). Autistic perspectives in disability theory are reconfiguring how autistic difference is perceived and, indeed, how it can be imagined. For example, narratives and theories authored by autistic people and their allies work to disrupt and thus challenge normative assumptions about the spaces between us: human interaction and interpretation, agency, behavior and communication (see, for example, Savarese, 2010; Baggs, 2007; Heikler and Yergeau, 2011; Dawson, 2011; Biklen & Attfield, 2005; Bascom, 2012; Broderick and Ne'eman, 2008). These disruptions, which can be found throughout the chapters to follow, are also invitations. They invite us (all) to urgently attend to and work against the normative cultural infrastructure that makes possible various forms of material inequities and violence against autistic people. They invite us, in other words, to work toward creating a more habitable world.

Heeding this invitation and drawing on critical theories of disability and autism, I analyze autism throughout this book as a shifting, unstable, transnational, and transhistorical category. Autism can and must be theorized as a relational space: an interactional, historically contingent, socially mediated, and geo/political space; a space of questions and of power relations that invariably provides the terrain for encounters across race, gender, class, sexuality, disability, and identities, at this moment, I am failing to imagine. In this space, upon this terrain, we—all of us—are making sense of the social category of 'autism' that is many and shifting and endowing it with particular and sometimes conflicting meanings. This next section aims to give the reader a sense of some the dominant meanings of autism that circulate in and through in contemporary Western/ized culture.

A Cultural Logic of War

My research for this book did not start out as research. It started inadvertently—a clipped newspaper article here and an informational pamphlet there. After a while, I found that I had collected reams of autism artifacts that were being produced in and circulated through contemporary Western/ized culture: autism information pamphlets, awareness campaign materials, newspaper reports, images, posters, speeches, public service announcements, statistical reports, webpages, educational materials, government texts, fundraising appeals, policy documents, documentary films, biographies, corporate brandings, self-help books, and various consumer goods. Some of these sources I actively sought out while others I stumbled upon, quite by accident, as I was going about my day.

Collected over course of the first decade of the twenty-first century, these cultural artifacts came to fill a great many of my file folders, both physical and virtual. Files collecting and uniting seemingly disparate, random pieces of material culture provided a unique surface upon which to glean the repetition of very organized and very limited cultural scripts. Time and again the artifacts represented autism as a pathology of the mind and body; a grueling cost; a life draining epidemic; a dangerous threat; a biological problem necessitating a biomedical solution; an illness needing to be stopped, cured, fixed, eliminated. Such limited scripts reveal an even more limited cultural imaginary. Autism is some 'thing,' the artifacts seemed to repeat, it is not 'someone'—some 'thing,' they lamented, we (collectively) do not want to have around. The proliferation of these artifacts in the early 2000s is evidence of a clear cultural turn 'against' autism. They are remnants of a culture that understands itself to be living with autism but that wishes to—and works to—live without it. And, as I show throughout this book, these artifacts are also in turn producing this culture. The sentiment that we (as a culture) are or at least ought to be 'against' autism forms the backdrop out of which all contemporary Western/ized stories of autism appear and against which these are read. In this way, it provides the power-laden grounds that privilege some ways of storying (thinking, talking, understanding) autism, while marginalizing others.

Reading across my archive of autism artifacts, I took notice of two rather glaring trends or patterns. Firstly, I noticed that the stories of autism circulating in the mainstream were most often stories told by individuals and organizations engaged in what might broadly be described as the work of autism advocacy. My use of the term autism advocacy here is therefore rather specific. Distinct from the *autistic* self/advocacy and activist work being done by autistic people,[2] *autism advocacy* denotes the advocacy work of parents, family members, professionals, politicians (and their groups and organizations) who do not identify as autistic and who understand themselves as speaking on behalf of autistic people. As we will see throughout this book, instead of disrupting the dominant cultural orientation *'against' autism* by advocating *'for' autism*, mainstream autism advocacy work, most often, supports and sustains it.

The second thing I noticed while reading across the artifacts was the militaristic rhetoric that permeated these autism representations. Indeed, contemporary forms of autism advocacy have become one of the most powerful and influential ways of representing and making sense of autism as a threatening and pathological enemy in need of military-style interventions aimed at normalization (Gross, 2012). Throughout the first decade of the twenty-first century, we saw many different kinds of advocates—doctors, celebrities, politicians, journalists, parents, school teachers, and shop keepers—come together in the 'fight against autism.' This rhetoric of war continues to mediate our encounters with autism. To this day, autism is commonly narrated as a terrifying and terrorizing enemy, threatening innocent children and destroying the 'good life'. That autism must be 'combated,' 'fought,' 'defeated,' 'smothered,' and ultimately 'eliminated' is written into US law, institutionalized in public policy, and sung throughout popular culture. While such examples are overt and glaring, there are many other, more covert examples of advocacy's militaristic discourse: the everyday rhetoric of 'red flag' signs and symptoms, biological invasion and 'ticking time bombs' are but a few examples.

The War on Autism analyzes the relationships between isolated acts of autism advocacy and traces their continuities so as to make legible an underlying logic: a powerful and ubiquitous logic that casts autism as a pathological threat to normative life, and advocacy as that which must normalize, neutralize, or otherwise eliminate this threat. This logic works dangerously to limit the role of the 'good' autism advocate to one positioned 'against' autism. Throughout this book, I show how dominant, contemporary discourses of autism advocacy that narrate autism as some 'thing' to be fought, combated, or otherwise warred against function to shape life as conditional and cast autism as one such condition. I demonstrate how this understanding of the conditionality of life provides the conditions of possibility for normative acts of violence.

Autism as an Interpretive Category

The vast majority of academic work on autism to date is empirical in character. By contrast, I do not endeavor to uncover any one true meaning of autism, nor do I think this to be possible. I write this book with the not-so-common theoretical presupposition that autism is not—as least in any clear or static sense—a knowable, find-able (and thus fixable) 'thing' in the world. Drawing on inter-/transdisciplinary theories/ methods in disability studies, cultural studies, feminist studies, critical race theory, and queer theory, I treat autism as an object of interpretive analysis, one that is produced in and through culture, and that is producing it in turn. I orient to autism, in other words, as a relational construct or artifice, albeit a *very real* one that, as I show in the latter part of this book, generates equally real, material effects, particular for those who identify or are identified as autistic. This rejection of empirical methods, itself a methodological move, invariably, opens up the possibility of new, alternative, and potentially subversive ways of approaching and theorizing autism, as well as the question of embodied difference more broadly.

As I see it, this project does not represent a moral appraisal of contemporary autism advocacy work per se: I am not interested in gauging whether particular representations of autism are inherently 'good' or 'bad,' nor do I offer a prescription for new or better ways of advocating on behalf of autistic people—autistic activists, academics, and self-advocates are already doing this work (see, for example, Sinclair, 1999; Baggs, 2012; Sinclair, 2012; ASAN, 2012; Brown, 2012; Yergeau, 2013; and the many other examples throughout this book). Instead, I engage in a project of examining the particularities of a culture—a culture that has declared itself to be at war with autism—and seek to understand the governing frameworks that hold this culture together. I analyze fragmentary pieces of dominant autism culture so as to uncover the underlying logics that connect these pieces, make them make sense. This work is thus closely in line with Foucault's assertion in the opening epigraph of this chapter. In writing this book, my aim is not to show how a particular something (or someone) is 'bad' but rather to demonstrate how and in what ways dominant, contemporary autism discourse can be, and indeed is, 'dangerous.'

I have often been asked about how it is that I came to be a collector of such autism artifacts. What is my relation to autism? I have at least two possible answers to this question. The first is a personal relation: I am invested in the ways autism is represented and understood because I have an autistic family member. This particular personal relation has certainly pushed me to be more acutely conscious of autism representations and narratives. And, of course, it also mediates how I interpret these. My relation to autism, however, does not end or even begin with the personal. As I have already suggested and will continue to suggest throughout this book, the meaning of autism (how it matters and thus how it materializes) is produced in and through *cultural* relations. The understanding that autism is a social category forged in and through cultural contexts confirms that we all are involved in its production. I find myself in relation to autism precisely because I belong to and participate in a culture in which autism appears.

To suggest that we all relate to autism is not a move to universalize our experiences of autism or to suggest that our relations to autism are equivalent in any way. To identify/be identified as autistic in a culture that understands itself to be 'against' autism is a materially meaningful difference, one that renders some people relationally more vulnerable to structural and/or physical forms of violence. By asserting that we all relate to autism, I am suggesting that we are collectively accountable for the oppressive and dangerous meanings of autism that are produced and circulated, cultural meanings that work to value and privilege certain ways of moving, thinking, feeling, communicating, and living over and against others.

Lastly, in reading and writing the premises and practices of autism advocacy, I want to be clear that I am not calling for an abandonment of the project of advocating. Of course, I too am engaged in this act. The *War on Autism* represents the risk with which all advocates are faced as we find ourselves in the midst of social and political differences: the risk of speaking, writing, representing, defending, condemning, protesting, championing, fighting, and supporting difference from within relational systems of power. Advocacy is risky. To acknowledge this risk is not to suggest that we should stop engaging in acts of advocacy. It is rather to bring into focus the necessity for critical engagement with the historical, geographical, and political dimensions and power relations that invariably structure what it means to advocate, and what it is that we are advocating for. If to speak up, speak out, speak-on-behalf-of is one crucial, if not inescapable, function of living with others—and I believe it is—it becomes necessary to trace acts of advocacy along the lines of our (power) relations, to attend to the ways in which acts of advocacy are producing and governing ourselves and others. The chapters that follow represent the belief that by attending to the organization and management of the discursive spaces of autism advocacy and the constrained production of the subject positions of 'advocate' and 'advocated for' within these spaces, we might begin to imagine new ways of advocating otherwise.

Overview of the Book

The book begins by looking at the construction of autism within contemporary discourses of autism advocacy and at how the interpretive categories of autism and advocacy are governed in and through relations of power. In chapter 1, "Delivering Disorder: Historical Perspectives on the Emergence of Autism and Advocacy in the West," I look to the emergence of autism as a discursive category and to the historical underpinnings that made possible particular and contingent understandings of autism and autistic people. I demonstrate how autism and advocacy have been and continue to be bound together in discourse. The emergence of historically particular versions of autism has shaped very particular versions of advocacy. Chapter 1 shows that, far from being simply a response to a disorderly autism, advocacy has become a productive force that has and continues to govern what autism is and can be.

The tangled relationship between autism and advocacy is made ever more explicit in chapter 2, "Raising the Red Flags of Autism: Advocacy's

Call to Arms." Placing autism within the historical context of an enduring biomedical tradition of discrediting and dehumanizing particular
bodies—racialized bodies, for example, colonized bodies, queer bodies,
classed bodies, women's bodies, and so on—through discourses of developmentalism, I examine how notions of autism as improperly or not 'fully' developed work to create autistic bodies as both deviant and as always
and already in need of development. I show, moreover, how the conceptualization of autism as a not-yet-developed-human inaugurates an advocate who must become literate in reading particular autistic behaviors or
ways of communicating as red flag warning signs of deviancy and who,
ultimately, must take up the normalizing role of a human developer.

Chapter 3, "Act NOW: The S/pace of Advocacy in a Temporality
of Urgency," extends earlier analyses by looking to and 'getting with'
neoliberal times and their normative and normalizing understanding
of developmental time. I examine a multitude of cultural artifacts both
mundane and spectacular and treat these as prolific, productive, and
powerful discursive sites. I show how such sites of meaning-making shape
collective experiences of the passing of time (i.e., as either 'too slow' or
'too fast') as well as our understandings of bodies in time (i.e., as being
either 'on time' or 'late'). As autism is narrated as a growing threat to
the 'good life' of neoliberal development, autism advocacy is called into
being as that which must generate more and more ways to neutralize the
non-normative threat of autism by acting now on individual bodies to
secure better (i.e., more normative) futures for all.

In examining and analyzing these enactments of advocacy, one of
the central observations I make is how autism is, almost monolithically,
represented by those individuals and organizations engaged in dominant forms of autism advocacy as an undesirable pathological condition
of the (social and individual) body, a condition that is conditional to
particular (unfortunate) individuals and their (equally unfortunate)
families, communities, and nations. Of course, the discursive tie connecting autism and autism advocacy goes both ways. The shape of autism
(accomplished, in part, by acts of advocacy), in turn, gives shape to
autism advocacy itself.

The final two chapters address more directly the very real, very material effects of autism discourse on the lives and bodies of people. Building on the notion of danger expressed in the red flag warning systems
analyzed in chapter 2 and the sense of urgency of the temporal environment depicted in chapter 3, chapter 4, "'We Have Your Son . . .': Frames
of Terror in Advocacy's War on Autism", examines the tactics and targets

of a culture at war with autism. Born of a culture ruled by normative versions of life, the figure of autism enters our dominant frames of recognition as a kind of cultural outlaw, always and already guilty of life-threatening crimes of terror. I connect this so-called war on autism with another and contemporaneous war—the global war on terror—so as to reveal the points where these war-time discourses converge into a shared neo/liberal, biopolitical frame. I suggest that such a frame conditions the possibility for very particular appearances of pathologically terrifying and terrorizing figures in need of militarized ally/advocate intervention: dangerous enemies to be combated and ultimately eradicated.

The final chapter of this book explores the necessary casualties of a culture at war with autism. Chapter 5, "Collateral Damage: Normalizing Violence and the Violence of Normalcy," demonstrates how covert and overt discourses of autism advocacy that narrate autism as some 'thing' that is 'in' and not 'of' some people function to shape life as conditional and cast autism as (one of) its condition(s). I tease out the danger of this everyday way of conceptualizing autism as a *some 'thing'* and not a *'someone'* through an examination and analysis of a series of newspaper articles reporting on three recent murders of autistic children. As autism is discursively and ideologically made and kept separate from the vital category of life itself, and as bodies and minds of living people are routinely and relentlessly split into vital and nonvital parts, individual and collective life 'with' (the condition of) autism becomes life that can be plotted along a vital spectrum anchored by oppositional poles of life and death. Such a spectrum inaugurates the possibility of new, graded categories of life and death—'almost living' lives as well as 'mostly dead' ones. By demonstrating how such an understanding of the conditionality of life is a necessary precondition for normative acts of violence—violence enacted in the name of securing the norm and violence that is normalized as necessary—I issue a call for all of us engaged in autism advocacy to attend to the powerful and power-laden stories we have and tell of autism and of advocacy and to tell these stories differently and otherwise.

CHAPTER ONE

Delivering Disorder

Historical Perspectives on the Emergence of Autism and Advocacy in the West

———— ꝏ ————

"How does one establish that a person suffers from autism? There is no single physical or behavioural sign which would uniquely secure the diagnosis. The whole history of the patient has to be considered from birth, the nature of the impairments, their severity, and their change over time."

    —Houston and Frith (2000), *Autism in History: The Case of Hugh Blair of Borgue*, p. 10

"We could write a history of limits—of those obscure gestures, necessarily forgotten as soon as they are accomplished, through which a culture rejects something which for it will be the Exterior; and throughout its history, this hollowed-out void, this white space by means of which it isolates itself, identifies it as clearly as its values. For those values are received, and maintained in the continuity of history; but in the region of which we would speak, it makes its essential choices, operating the division which gives a culture the face of its positivity: this is the originary thickness in which a culture takes shape."

    —Michel Foucault (2006 [1961]), *History of Madness*, p. xxix

Autism is widely understood, in contemporary times, as a disorder: a diagnostic category particular to the twentieth and twenty-first centuries. Vis-à-vis this 'disorderly' autism, contemporary autism advocacy is most commonly framed as that which must ensure autism's return to order (McGuire, 2012). Autism's purported disorder, together with the seemingly natural/neutral need for advocacy's orderly response to it, is, however, much less often contemplated as a social phenomenon that can teach us something about how contemporary social relations are ordered (for further discussions on the sociopolitical dimensions of autism and advocacy see, for example: Dawson, 2005; Broderick and Ne'eman, 2008; Ne'eman, 2010; Heikler and Yergeau, 2011; Baggs, 2012; Gross, 2012; Sequenzia, 2012c; McGuire, 2012; Murray, 2008; Douglas, 2013; Brown, 2011a). This chapter serves as an overview of the multiple historical underpinnings that provide the conditions of possibility for contemporary Western/izing conceptions of autism and for the emergence of contemporary versions of autism advocacy. By tracing an historical genealogy of autism and autism advocacy in the West, I reveal how the social significance of these related phenomena—the meanings we attribute to them and the understandings they provoke—is achieved against a contingent cultural backdrop. In this chapter, then, I not only introduce the historical context of autism and autism advocacy, I also introduce the discursive field that collects autism and autism advocacy as an historically contingent, socially mediated, political, and interactional space of power relations that contains and constrains.

Presenting Histories and Histories of the Present

As I give an historical account of autism's emergence as a diagnostic category of classification—as some 'thing' one could be found to 'have'—I am necessarily offering one perspective of the history of autism. In contradistinction to the dominant empirical demand for a singular, linear "whole history of autism," as is exemplified by Frith's statement in the opening epigraph, I do not attempt to provide a complete or exhaustive account of autism's historical underpinnings, nor do I think that this is possible. To write a history—whether it is an individual history or a collective one—is to write an abbreviation. Instead of attempting to write an historical totality, I seek to, following Foucault (1997), "blow the dust off certain things" (p. 2).

This chapter uses a Foucaultian genealogical approach to write a "history of the present" of autism and autism advocacy and to examine the subjectivities that (are permitted to) dwell within the discursive field that collects these two phenomena (Foucault, 1995, p. 31). Foucault characterizes a genealogy as a process, one that, he says, is "gray, meticulous, and patiently documentary" (Foucault, 1984, p. 76). Genealogy, he continues, "operates on a field of entangled and confused parchments, on documents that have been scratched over and recopied many times" (Foucault, 1984, p. 76). Distinct from empirical historical methodologies, a Foucaultian genealogy does not seek to trace out the singular or linear history of a given phenomenon, as if this phenomenon were somehow preconstituted, needing only to be unearthed and captured. In this chapter, I bring together a great many "entangled and confused parchments," diverse and sometimes conflicting historical fragments of autism culture—historical events, scientific and psychiatric documents, and personal observations and narrative, as well as alternative historical readings informed by feminist, race, queer, disability, and class studies. Resisting the seductive desire to make causal connections, a genealogy of autism, following Foucault, "opposes itself to the search for origins" (Foucault, 1984, p. 72). This chapter seeks to make familiar, everyday assumptions about autism and advocacy "strange" in order to underscore the contingency of our present day "evidences" and our commonsense understandings of how these phenomena interact (Foucault, 2001, p. 77).

A critical genealogy of autism is not so much focused on the question of what autism was or is, instead focusing on how the category, autism, has been constituted and negotiated over time. To borrow from Foucault's characterization of the task of writing a genealogy of the history of madness, a critical genealogy of autism does not ask "what in a given period is regarded as sanity or insanity, mental illness or normal behaviour," but rather asks "*how* these divisions are operated" (Foucault, 1991, as cited in Mills, 2003, p. 98, *original emphasis*). I will begin, then, by focusing on how tactics of power—such as processes of pathologization and normalization—are engaged in constraining the embodied categories of 'deviant' and 'normal,' 'autism' and 'non autism,' and are indeed shaping what gets counted as self-evident and necessary responses to autistic difference in contemporary times. In tracing the emergence of ways of knowing autism and autism advocacy and by following the trajectories and tactics of power operating within and on these categories, I provide a foundation for interrogating the cultural production of particular kinds of advocacy subjects: the subject of the advocate and that of the advocated for.

Contemporary understandings of autism emerged out of a psychiatric/biomedical history of identifying and diagnosing its 'disorder.' In her book *Constructing Autism: Unravelling the 'Truth' and Understanding the Social* (2005), Majia Holmer Nadesan argues that the fact that autism emerges as a diagnostic category in the twentieth century is neither happenstance nor coincidence, but is rather a condition of particular historical events and ideologies. "The historical matrix of events, knowledge, and professional identities that emerged out of the end of the nineteenth century," writes Nadesan, "set the stage for the creation and expansion of twentieth century child psychiatry, and ultimately provided the conditions of possibility for autism to emerge as a diagnostic category" (Nadesan, 2005, p. 53). As a way of examining the conditions of possibility that gave rise to the contemporary emergence of autism and its advocate, I begin by offering an overview of the historical underpinnings of autism as an articulated and articulable category.

Delivering Autism

The term 'autism' or autismus (derived from the Greek *autos*, meaning 'self') was first articulated in 1911 by Dr. Eugen Bleuler, a Swiss Freudian most noted for his research on schizophrenia (Feinstein, 2010; Kuhn, 2004; Nadesan, 2005; Shorter, 2005). According to Adam Feinstein's (2010) history of autism:

> Bleuler distinguished two modes of thinking: logical or realistic thinking and autistic thinking. For Bleuler, autistic thinking was not a pathology confined to a group of children [. . .] Bleuler considered autistic thinking a normal mode of thinking in both children and adults. It was evident, he said, in dreams, pretend play and reveries and in the delusions of the schizophrenic. (p. 6)

Bleuler's conceptualization of autism did not understand it as a disorder in and of itself. Autism was, for Bleuler, a mode of thinking. And while normal subjects may, from time to time, slip into reverie and 'think autistically,' Bleuler also connected this mode of thinking to psychiatric non-normativity. Autistic thinking was, according to Bleuler, an essential component of a disordered schizophrenia. Feinstein (2010) writes: "[Bleuler] originally included autism as one of what he called the 'four schizophrenias,'" a group that was in turn bound together by the so-called 'four A's,': associated disturbance, affective disturbance, ambivalence and autism (p. 6).

In the early 1900s, as today, schizophrenia was narrated by psychiatry as an undesirable and even dangerous pathological illness of the mind, a narrative that relies on simultaneous medical and moral schemas of classification (Rose, 1989; Szasz, 1995; Szasz, 2010). As it became understood as a sign pointing to schizophrenia's presumed pathology, autistic ways of thinking, too, became classified, along moral and medical lines, as outside of 'logical' and 'realistic' ways of thinking. But it was not until the late 1930s and the early 1940s that conceptualizations of autism as itself a distinct disorder were first articulated through the contemporaneous work of American child psychiatrist Dr. Leo Kanner and Austrian pediatrician Dr. Hans Asperger (Feinstein, 2010; Grinker, 2008; Nadesan, 2005).

The 'Fathers' of Autism: Kanner and Asperger

The term 'autism' was first articulated as a disorder (as opposed to as a symptom) by Kanner in his 1943 article, "Autistic Disturbances of Affective Contact" (Kanner, 1943). In this now famous study, Kanner conducted case study analyses of eleven children, who he observed to be exhibiting "a rare syndrome," which he most often articulated as "early infantile autism," and less often as "Kanner's syndrome" (Kanner, 1943, p. 242). In this article, Kanner writes of autism's "fundamental disorder," which was "[the autistic child's] inability to relate themselves in the ordinary way to people and situations from the beginning of life" (Kanner, 1943, p. 242). Kanner documented that the parents of the children in his study referred to their children as:

> having always been "self sufficient"; "like in a shell"; "happiest when left alone"; "acting as if people weren't there"; "perfectly oblivious to everything about him"; "giving the impression of silent wisdom"; "failing to develop the usual amount of social awareness"; "acting almost as if hypnotized." (Kanner, 1943, p. 242)

In contrast to Bleuler's earlier claim that autism is a symptom of schizophrenia that could be treated as a way of treating schizophrenia, Kanner claimed autism as a condition unto itself. He writes:

> [Autism] is not, as in schizophrenic children and adults, from an initially present relationship. It is not a 'withdrawal' from formerly existing participation. There is from the start an *extreme autistic aloneness* that, whenever possible, disregards, ignores, shuts out anything that

comes to the child from the outside. (Kanner, 1943, p. 242, *original emphasis*)

Elsewhere Kanner writes:

> We must, then, assume that these children have come into the world with innate inability to form the usual biologically provided affective contact with people, just as other children come into the world with innate physical or intellectual handicaps. (Kanner, 1943, p. 250)

Unlike Bleuler, who recognized autism as a symptom, Kanner recognized autism as an innate condition—a condition that was itself composed of many symptoms. Autism was thus reconceived by Kanner as itself the central pathology and threat to (mental) health. Kanner went on to simultaneously notice, describe, and pathologize a variety of non-normative movements and/or behaviors that are, to this day, widely considered to be 'classic' symptoms of autism, including obsessiveness, literalness, stereotypy, echolalia, insistence on sameness, aversion to eye contact, dislike of loud noises or unexpected/intrusive movements, and an "altogether different" relation to others[1] (Kanner, 1943, p. 250). Indeed, many of Kanner's initial observations appear as the diagnostic criteria for autism in the current iteration of the *Diagnostic and Statistical Manual of Mental Disorders* (DSM–5) (American Psychiatric Association, 2013).

Asperger, apparently unaware of the work being done by Kanner in the United States (Attwood, 2007), was also and at the same time documenting and articulating autism—what he referred to as "autistic psychopathology"—as a distinct disorder (Asperger, 1991; Grinker, 2007; Nadesan, 2006; Shorter, 2005). Asperger was working at the University Pediatric Clinic in Vienna and published an article in 1944 based on several case studies of children. Like Kanner's research, Asperger's work was engaged in the incessant observation and documentation of 'abnormal' signs and symptoms pointing to an innate, interior disorder. For Asperger, whose studies predominantly focused on so-called 'high-functioning' autistic children, signs of disorder revolved around perceived core social and communicational deficits.

Asperger identified autism's impairment as primarily caught up in social relations. He writes: "The nature of these children is revealed most clearly in their behaviour toward other people. Indeed, their behaviour in the social group is the clearest sign of their disorder" (Asperger, 1944, as cited in Attwood, 2008, p. 55). It is, I think, crucial to note that Asperger's work demonstrates the move from merely noticing and documenting signs of difference, to interpreting these as insights into the true nature of the children under study. Of course, as I will discuss in detail in chapter 3, acts of observing and processes of looking are highly organized. Dehli writes: "Child psychology's "way of seeing"—its gaze—brings a selection of events, expressions or emotions into view as significant incidents while rendering others as peripheral and unimportant" (Dehli, 1994b, p. 90). These 'ways of seeing' are caught up in the production of particular observations and, indeed, work to govern what is and can be seen (Dehli, 1994b; Foucault, 1975; Michalko, 1998; Rose, 1989).

The articulation and documentation of autism signs and symptoms have political and historical significance insofar as they have been and continue to be employed as bodily markers that work to pathologize, discredit, and even render vulnerable non-normative bodies and behaviors. This relentless surveillance, of course, also paves the way for the correction of the noted signs of difference. Indeed, it is significant to note that the birth of a disorder does not (cannot?) happen in the absence of a simultaneous call for order. As Kanner and Asperger recognized autism as a pathological disorder, they simultaneously moved to recognizing it as in need of improvement or correction—a disorder in need of order (Kanner, 1943; Nadesan, 2005).

A history of autism cannot proceed without coming to terms with the particular historical context in which Kanner and Asperger made their discoveries and conducted their research. The time period in which these two psychiatrists developed their theories of autism—theories that still very much influence the ways in which autism is dominantly conceived of today—also saw the proliferation and popularization of eugenics movements in Europe and North America; an historical juncture that saw the promotion of ideologies of racial hygiene and even the extermination/elimination of those bodies who did not fit this racist profile (disabled bodies, for example, poor bodies, bodies of color, and many other bodies classed as 'degenerate') (Gilman, 1985; Gleason, 1999; Snyder and Mitchell, 2006).

Eugenic notions of racial 'purity', 'fitness', and 'hygiene' provided the necessary social conditions for increased public and private surveillance of normal and abnormal behaviors. The heightened surveillance of embodied difference was framed as particularly necessary in childhood, a stage that was (and continues to be) most commonly understood as in need of paternalistic observation and intervention (Burman, 1994). The perceived need for clear lines separating normal and abnormal and the subsequent surveillance of such divisions sustained morally coded notions of right/fit and wrong/unfit ways of being in the world.

While such normal/abnormal, fit/unfit distinctions seemed to be rooted in (purported) individual pathologies and/or departures from the 'good' (white, heterosexual, middle class, nondisabled) human race, their significatory meaning stretched well beyond the individual. The fitness, health, or hygiene of the individual was understood as absolutely inseparable from that of the state as a whole.[2] Indeed, a fit, healthy (i.e., strong, virile, productive, and developed) state—the state with militaristic, economic, and colonial power—required, and so idealized, particular kinds of healthy, fit citizens (i.e., those bodies who displayed strength, virility, productivity, and, of course, good/normal human development) (Payne, 1995; Spackman, 1996). It therefore became possible to speak and think of culturally devalued forms of difference in terms of pathologies: embodied threats that weakened the health and strength of the state/nation. This is sharply exemplified if we think of the violence enacted against particular, pathologized subjects in Europe in the 1930s and 1940s and of how such violence was conceptualized in at once racist and ableist terms. The millions upon millions of racialized, disabled, queer, and politically/religiously persecuted people who were systematically murdered by the Nazi regime were figured first as pathologically deviant bodies threatening the health and virility of the nation and the race (Snyder and Mitchell, 2006). The Jewish body, for example, was often framed by the Nazi regime as a "cancer on the breast of Germany" (Davis, 2007; Gilman, 1993), an unhealthy malignancy that, of course, required particular kinds of (at once medicalized and militarized) responses, namely excision and eradication.

Both Kanner and Asperger, the so-called fathers of autism, shared a direct, personal connection with the eugenic/genocidal programs that were being implemented in Central and Eastern Europe under Nazi occupation. Kanner was an Austrian Jew, and his mother and three of his siblings were murdered in the Holocaust (Grinker, 2008). Asperger was a pediatrician working with disabled children at a hospital in Nazi occupied Austria (Attwood, 2008; Grinker, 2008). By noting Kanner's and Asperger's (no doubt, different) relationships to Nazi eugenics in Europe in the 1930s and 1940s, I am not suggesting a psychological or even a causal explanation for their interest in surveilling bodies, minds, and behaviors or in tracing the line separating normalcy from abnormalcy. However, it is nonetheless important to understand that Kanner and Asperger were living in and touched by a social context where diagnostic lines were often lines separating life and death.

Such divisions were and are extremely instructive; the incessant repetition of—and myriad scientific justifications for—the equation of abnormalcy with death becomes so ordinary, so commonplace as to be routinely interpreted as a rational, reasonable, or even natural equation. It is therefore not coincidental that an historical moment that gave us the possibility for mental/physical purity, fitness, and hygiene, as well as the belief that the healthy body/mind is reflective of a healthy society, also saw the proliferation and success of relatively new fields of study aimed at the surveillance of the earliest aspects of human development: child psychiatry and child study. Indeed, the so-called fathers of autism were embroiled at the center of these emergent fields. Kanner himself noted that historically specific cultural attitudes were absolutely central to the birth of child psychiatry. He writes:

> When the twentieth century made its appearance, there was not—and there could not be—anything that might in any sense be regarded as child psychiatry. It took a series of definite steps in the development of cultural attitudes to make possible the inclusion of children in the domain of psychiatry. (Kanner, 1935, p. 5)

A close examination of the early institutions of child psychiatry and child study further reveals the entanglements of the study of the mind and behaviors of the child and socio-biological notions of fitness and hygiene.

Consider, for example, the early days of the Yale Child Studies Center, founded by Arnold Gesell, a pioneer in child psychiatry and the director of Child Hygiene for the State of Connecticut (Fagan, 1987). In 1911, Gesell was appointed as faculty of Yale, where he went on to observe, document, and measure 'normal' and 'abnormal' child behaviors and develop a systematic approach to the study of childhood growth and development (Rose, 1989). Gesell's work flourished and his initially small clinic grew into a full-fledged center in the years to follow, gaining particular influence during the early decades of the twentieth century— the height of the eugenic period—when the need for clear and recognizable means of classifying 'healthy' and 'deviant' bodies was understood to be of utmost concern and importance for the project of perfecting the human race. Gesell's own personal commitment to a eugenic ideology was clear. His 1913 article "The Village of a Thousand Souls," originally published in *American Magazine*, draws a map of a small, unidentified town populated by growing numbers of 'feebleminded' people prone to alcoholism, prostitution, criminality, and social and economic failure. He writes:

> In many cases, the feeblemindedness is not recognized or understood. The family realize [sic] that the boy is 'slow' and wish that people would not tease him so much. 'But he will get along alright' the parents say; and this prediction is partially justified. In a village, particularly a rural village, where gardens, barns and domestic animals are common, the conditions of life are primitive. They may not be too severely complex, for even the feeble-minded boy, who learns how to tend stable, is happy in a simple routine of chores, and masters a simple occupation like sawing wood. [. . .] The trouble is, someday a 'harmless' fellow who has been sawing wood in the village goes into the country, marries and has children . . . about 80 percent of all cases of feeblemindedness are due to neuropathic heredity . . . and the feeble-minded have much larger families than normally prudent parents. (Gesell, 1922)

He concludes this scenario by underscoring the need to 'supervise' and 'segregate' the 'feebleminded' such that they are prevented from reproducing. He writes:

> Only the rankest pessimists and believers in noninterference will condone the increase of feeblemindedness and insanity which is occurring in the villages of the land. We need not wait for the perfection of the infant science of eugenics before proceeding upon a course of supervision and segregation, which will prevent the horrible renewal of this defective protoplasm that is contaminating the stream of village life. (Gesell, 1922)

There can be little doubt: Gesell's commitment to the supervision and segregation of the 'feebleminded' influenced his psychiatric research looking at 'normal' and 'abnormal' childhood development (Gesell, 1922). Though the historical underpinnings of the Yale Child Studies Center is but one example of many, it gestures nonetheless to the tangled history of child psychiatry/study and the premises and practices of eugenics. It demonstrates how eugenic practices and ideologies were both absolutely reliant upon and generated the need for more and more means of identifying deviance, more and more lines separating 'normalcy' from 'abnormalcy.'

Such historical entanglements, in which Kanner and Asperger were invariably caught, became the cradle for contemporary conceptions of autism. Born in and of the heyday of child psychiatry and child study in the 1930s and 1940s, contemporary versions of autism, as determined by Kanner and Asperger, were responses to an historically particular demand for clear ways of distinguishing and dividing abnormality from normality, pathology from health in the name of a scientifically perfectible human race.

With the end of World War II and the subsequent moral shift against a eugenics tainted by the atrocities of the Nazi death camps, a strictly biologically driven approach to autism fell out of favor (at least for a while). The late 1940s, 1950s, and 1960s witnessed a rise in the popularity and influence of psychoanalysis, an approach that placed less emphasis on an individual's innate nature or biology and instead favored tracing the origins of disorder to the psychosocial environment. Edward Dolnick observes that, in a post-WWII context, "to be pronuture was to be in favour of progress and open-mindedness, while to be pronature was to be backward looking and backward thinking . . . Nazism stood for 'nature,' thus psychoanalysis' identification with 'nurture' gave it invaluable moral stature" (Dolnick, 1998, p. 63). The relentless and nuanced documentation of autism symptoms by Kanner and Asperger quickly gave way to the search for their psychosocial origins.

*shift to
Psychosocial*

Bettelheim and the 'Mothers' of Autism

In its most traditional forms, psychoanalytic theory frames normal and abnormal development of the psyche, or the personality, as a function of early childhood experiences. More particularly, psychoanalysis takes up the role of the mother as a crucial arbiter in the psychosocial development of the child (Gleason, 1999; Hyvonen, 2004; Nadesan, 2005). In the 1950s and 1960s, various foundational precepts of psychoanalysis became popular—particularly in white, middle-class households—in relation to maternal practices of child-rearing (Hyvonen, 2004). While the mother was understood to be uniquely and even 'naturally' positioned as the rearer of children and as the prime nurturer of their psychosocial development, she was nonetheless always (and differentially, with respect to, say, the mother's social class, race, disability identification) framed to be at risk of mothering wrong and so always (and differentially) positioned as at risk of catalyzing 'poor' child development outcomes. Dehli writes that "it was, at one and the same time, "only natural" that women were the obvious rearers and teachers of children and an apparent fact that some women were less able than others to fulfill their "natural" potential. At the same time, it was evident that, even if they were imbued with "natural" potential for maternal virtue, all women, regardless of class or ethnicity, had to be trained in a method largely devised by men in order to rear and teach children correctly" (Dehli, 1994a, p. 202). Given the ostensible fragility of the psychosocial development of the child, Nadesan (2005) points out, that not only did "mothering [take] on new import," it "increasingly required the input of experts" (p. 70). "The development of the child" she continues, "could not be pre-supposed; rather it became an accomplishment in itself" (Nadesan, 2005, p. 70). The child was recast as an accomplishment: an accomplishment, no less, of the mother. The looming risk of 'poor' mothering and the threat of 'poor' child development that flowed as a natural consequence of this, recast the child as a kind of product and the mother as a kind of skilled worker. Motherhood required particular qualifications and skill sets to ensure (most ironically) the 'natural' development of the child. One's mothering skills, it seemed, could (and should)—with the help and guidance of child psychology experts—be worked on, practiced, evaluated, measured, and improved so as to make the mother better qualified to engage in the ever-important task of child-rearing.

Expert knowledge at this time held that good parenting must be nurturing, and good nurturing must be administered by the (naturally, though not flawlessly) nurturing mother and in the naturalized sphere of the typically white, bourgeois middle-class home (Arnup, 1994; Grinker, 2008). Nadesan argues that a variety of factors shaped a psychoanalytic emphasis on the role of the mother in this particular post-WWII historical moment, including but certainly not limited to: "the heightened import afforded childhood in relation to the larger project of social engineering [and] the push to remove women from the work force after World War II" (Nadesan, 2005, p. 83). Indeed, signs or symptoms of psychological disorder—including the disorder of autism—were routinely traced back to the working mother who 'abandoned' her mothering role and to her 'disorderly' home. Gleason writes that "wage-earning women and 'family disorganization' were closely associated [. . .] [and this] put added pressure on women to consider leaving behind the world of work after the war" (Gleason, 1999, p. 57). The educated, white, middle-class mother who worked—the mother who departed from the traditional sphere of the bourgeois middle-class home—was cast as the mother who was neglecting to work on her mothering qualifications by refining her skills as a nurturer. Such a system of governance, of course, presupposes a particular kind of gendered subject: a mother who *can* dwell in the sphere of the bourgeois middle-class home. As Dehli suggests in the passage above, working class mothers, racialized mothers—and here we might also add disabled mothers—were conceived of as, always and already, un/underqualified for the job of good nurturing and so, un/underqualified for the job of good mothering (I will address such exclusions shortly).

Not surprisingly, then, this particular post-WWII moment saw a wave of popular child development literature (e.g., advice columns, parent magazines and brochures, childrearing workshops, and so on) that were aimed specifically at the white, bourgeois middle-class mother (Arnup, 1994). Consider, for example, Dr. Spock's immensely popular child-rearing manual, *Baby and Child Care* (Spock, 1946, as cited by Hyvonen, 2004, p. 10). In relation to the autistic child, the role of the mother was put under constant scrutiny via psychoanalytic analysis and critique. In this way, the 'fathers' of autism were the expert surveillers, while the 'mothers' of autism became the subject of paternalistic surveillance. And so, even as autism at that time was understood to be a disorder unto itself, it still was, at least in certain ways, being read as a symptom pointing to a (as we shall see, particular kind of) deviant mother.

With respect to autism, the ties that connected mother and child also bound them together in pathology. The figuration of a cold, non-nurturing 'refrigerator' mother was inaugurated, at least in part, by Kanner's earlier observations of autistic children (Kanner, 1949, p.423). Indeed, the children observed by Kanner tended to have parents who were, in his words, "pre-occupied by abstractions of a scientific, literary or artistic nature" (Kanner, 1943, p. 42). From case studies examining fifty-five autistic children, Kanner observes:

> All but five of the mothers [. . .] have attended college. All but one have been active vocationally before, and some also after, marriage as scientists, laboratory technicians, nurses, physicians, librarians, or artists. One mother who was not a college graduate was a busy and well-known theatrical agent in New York City. One, who has a Ph.D. degree, collaborated in the publication of a Middle English diction-

ary. One stated: "I majored in zoology and could have majored in music. I play the organ, piano, and cello. I wanted to be a doctor but my family didn't have the stamina. I have often regretted it. I taught school for two years, then worked in an endocrinology laboratory." (Kanner, 1949, p. 420–21)

Kanner seemed to wonder whether such 'preoccupations' from the (bourgeois, middle-class) home were not, effectively, evidence of bad mothering. He went on to observe what he called a "genuine lack of maternal warmth" (Kanner, 1949, p. 422). While Kanner did seem to think that these observations were worthy of further inquiry, he ultimately did not understand them to be evidence of an originary cause of autism (recall, autism was, for Kanner, understood to be innate). His image of the cold, unfeeling 'refrigerator mother' was, however, famously rearticulated by Jewish-American psychoanalyst Dr. Bruno Bettleheim, as an origin of autism's disorder.

Like Kanner and Asperger, Bettelheim (1972) also described the autistic child as exhibiting an "altogether different" relation to others—as detached, existing in a "private world," and appearing as if locked in a "shell" (pp. 146, 327). However, Bettelheim made a crucial distinction from the conclusions of his predecessors: he rejected Kanner's and Asperger's postulations that autism was innate or 'inborn.' In his words: "My own belief . . . is that autism has essentially to do with everything that happens from birth on" (Bettelheim, 1972, p. 393). Bettelheim suggested that autism is not simply a disorder that one is born with, but is an acquired condition caused by early childhood experiences. Autism, for Bettelheim, was not simply an innate state of "profound aloneness" (as it was for Kanner and Asperger) but a *withdrawal*; Bettelheim described autism as an "empty fortress" (Bettelheim, 1972). Indeed, he went as far as to draw the comparison between the autistic child's perceived reclusion from humanity and the position of the Jews imprisoned in concentration camps under Nazi rule. Bettelheim—himself a survivor of Dachau and Buchenwald—writes: "Some victims of the concentration camps had lost their humanity in response to extreme situations. Autistic children withdraw from the world before their humanity ever really develops" (Bettelheim, 1972, p. 7). He continues: "what was external reality for the prisoners [of Nazi concentration camps] is for the autistic child his inner reality" (p. 65). As I explore in the later chapters of this book, Bettelheim's powerful image of autism as a shell or prison (or camp) that incarcerates an otherwise 'normal' or nonautistic self continues to this day to have profound, reverberating, and dangerous effects on the ways in which autism is conceived and autistic people are treated.

Like a good psychoanalyst, Bettelheim postulated that the origin of autistic people's 'self-incarceration' lay with the parents (particularly the mother). He writes: "I believe the initial cause of withdrawal is rather the child's correct interpretation of the negative emotions with which the most significant figures in his environment approach him" (Bettelheim, 1972, p. 66). He went on to describe the parents of autistic children as the perpetrators of grievous negligence akin to Nazi prison guards, postulating that only the "extreme of negative feelings in the parents can set the autistic process into motion" (Bettelheim, 1972, p. 127). These 'extreme' negative feelings are described by Bettelheim as behaviors and responses exhibited by parents who long for their child to have never been born, or to no longer exist (Bettleheim, 1972; Hyvonen, 2004).

Before I move on to explore some of the responses to this popular notion of the 'refrigerator mother,' it is important to first examine how discourses of race and class came to mingle with discourses of gender in the psychoanalytic production of autism and its maternal causes. As I have already demonstrated, not just any-body could come to occupy the subject position of good mother nurturer: bodies that (who) transgressed the normative contours and the moral constraints of the embodied figure of the nonworking, white, middle-class, bourgeois mother—bodies of color, for example, working-class bodies, disabled bodies, women's bodies that (who) worked too much outside of the home—were cast, albeit differentially, as bad mother nurturers in need of white paternal psychiatric supervision. While there were very limited ways in which one could perform the duties of a good mother nurturer, there were many ways to be a bad mother, and such subjugated positions came with their own productive constraints. As Dehli (2008) notes, a subject position is not always "equally available or can be temporarily or tenuously inhabited" (p. 47). In other words, not just any-body could come to embody the clearly delimited and highly pathologized subject position of the bad/cold mother of the autistic child and, by extension, neither could just any-body occupy the subject position of autistic.

Indeed, these subject positions were often only available to those parents who were perceived to be intelligent, educated, successful in the workplace, and so economically privileged. In this way, the organization of the subject position of parent of an autistic person—and by extension the subject position of autistic person—worked to exclude, for example, people of color from participation[3]. The very same social and historical contexts that gave birth to autism as a recognized and recognizable category also worked to constrain just who was able to be recognized as autistic. As one mother of an autistic person recalls in the documentary film *Refrigerator Mothers* (2003):

> According to my doctor, my son could not be autistic. I was not white, it was assumed that I was not educated and therefore he was labeled emotionally disturbed. Here your child has a disability that you recognize and they said, nah, you can't be that. You can't even be a refrigerator mother [laughs], the irony of it all.

Classist and racist systems of oppression and domination worked together to deliver the autistic subject as white and middle class, while sexist paternalistic structures organized the role of the mother as the regulator of the normal development of the child, and the subsequent healthy development of the state as a whole. In this way, the figure of the refrigerator mother is a product of comingling systems of racism, ableism, classism, and sexism that function together to pathologize autistic difference and blame the (middle-class white) mother, while working to exclude bodies of color from even participating in the social phenomenon of autism.

The Birth of Autism Advocacy

This political, social, and historical terrain not only provided the conditions of possibility for the emergence of autism as a recognized and recognizable disorder (a category, as we have seen, with its own particular constraints), it also provided for the emergence of a new (and equally constrained) response to autism: the response of advocacy. The first formal autism advocacy society was established by a group of parents in the United Kingdom in 1962 (Green Allison, 1997). This organization, which at the time was called the Autistic Children's Aid Society of North London, eventually was transformed into what is now known as the National Autistic Society (NAS).

In "Perspectives on a Puzzle Piece" (1997), founding member Heather Green Allison writes of the birth of the advocacy group:

On 23 January 1962, a group of desperate parents crowded into the living room of 71 Torrington Park, North London and from this meeting The National Autistic Society was born. This was the first group of parents of autistic children to meet with the specific aim of founding a Society to represent the interests of their children. (Green Allison, 1997, para. 1)

In her article, Green Allison discusses some of the challenges faced by the burgeoning organization, and in so doing she gestures toward the very particular social and historical context that surrounded the emergence of autism advocacy. She writes:

In 1962, the need for an independent society for our children was challenged on all sides [. . .] the founder members of our Society were facing not only the facts of their children's handicap, but also stresses deriving from the views held on it at the time. There was a widely-held view, based on a misinterpretation of Dr Leo Kanner's research, that the handicap was caused by 'cold, intellectual parents', in particular, 'refrigerator mothers'. The handicap was devastating to be accused of causing—it was tantamount to an accusation of child abuse. (Green Allison, 1997, para 3)

Green Allison's reflection bears witness to the relationship between what were commonly held biomedical beliefs of the time about the nature and origin of autism (i.e., autism was understood and accepted by bio-medicine to be caused by a working and, so, unnurturing mother) and the shape of autism advocacy. The medicalization and pathologization of autistic difference permitted and even required the emergence of very particular versions of advocacy. To go further, what these social and historical processes gave birth to was an advocacy dominated by parents (particularly mothers) that were required to rehabilitate themselves as nonpathological, and so as not blameworthy for the purported pathologies of their children. The solution of autism advocacy has—and continues to have—everything to do with the cultural meanings we ascribe to the problem of autism and vice versa. The shape and meaning of these two phenomena were—and continue to be—intimately bound up in one another.

Vis-à-vis social views of the time that held that being a mother of an autistic child was, according to Green Allison, equivalent to accusations of child abuse, the group formulated an advocacy response that sought to raise awareness about autism as its own disorder (i.e., a disorder unrelated to the actions of the mother) (Green Allison, 1997). The expressed aim of the National Autistic Society was to engage in fundraising initiatives and to lobby the state for the development of social structures and institutions that would treat and educate children with autism (Green Allison, 1997). In an effort to achieve this aim, those engaged in advocacy work employed the direct strategy of raising public awareness of autism—i.e., producing and circulating knowledge about autism throughout the public sphere (Green Allison, 1997, para. 2). The work or labor of autism advocacy, then, took the shape of (1) working on or treating autistic people and, more generally, (2) raising awareness or educating the public about autism as its own disorder (an awareness that, of course, also worked on rehabilitating the images of mothers cast as disorderly). As is evident throughout the chapters in this book, these twin aims continue to define formal and informal enactments of autism advocacy to this day.

The remainder of the 1960s and 1970s saw the proliferation of parent advocates and the establishment of many mainstream autism advocacy organizations led by nonautistic parents and autism professionals. A great many national autism advocacy organizations were founded during this time period, including the Autism Society of America (ASA) in 1965, the Autism Research Institute (ARI) in 1967, and the Autism Society of Canada (ASC) in 1976. Similar to the establishment of the NAS in the United Kingdom, these North American advocacy groups were founded by parents or family members of autistic people and articulate the twin goals of treating autistic people and raising awareness about autism. And as parent-led advocacy organizations fulfilled their mission to both rehabilitate the autistic subject and educate the public as to the nature of autism, they became, and remain to this day, deeply enmeshed in the contemporary social production of autism itself. Autism advocacy is therefore not simply a response to autism but a productive force that generates and governs what autism is and can be. Dominant enactments of autism advocacy have, for example, worked to solidify the awareness of autism as a pathological disorder-in-need-of-order and the related awareness of the autistic subject as nonagentive and thus as, essentially, malleable. Significantly, autistic self-advocacy and neurodiversity movements have worked to contest such damaging formulations of autism and autistic subjectivity and thus have been and continue to be deeply involved in reshaping meanings of autism. I explore these contestations and reformulations in greater detail later in this chapter.

With the growing presence and influence of autism advocacy, and the subsequent growing awareness of autism as a distinct category of classification, the 1970s and 1980s saw more and more people being diagnosed as autistic (Grinker, 2008). Along with the increase in autism diagnoses came a proliferation of responses to autism. And so emerged new scientific fields of study—behaviorism and the related fields of the cognitive and neuro psychologies—all ways of making sense of embodied difference that continue to structure the dominant contemporary paradigm. The work of researchers such as Marian DeMyer (1981) combined with the increased presence of and pressure from parent-run advocacy organizations effectively worked to loosen psychoanalysis' hold on autism, and ultimately the psychoanalytic approach was destabilized as the dominant way of orienting to and understanding autistic difference[4] (Grinker, 2008; Nadesan, 2005). Moving away from a psychoanalytic approach that focused on the mother as the origin of autism's (purported) pathology, new fields of study began to emerge that took the biological body (including the mind-as-body) as the primary target of inquiry. New fields in the biomedical psychologies began to turn their lenses of analysis toward the individual autistic body—toward behaviors, mental processes, and biology. Over the course of the past thirty years, the autistic body was thus transformed into both the site and origin of its own disorder.

'Bad' Bodies and 'Mis-wired' Brains

BEHAVIORISM

Perhaps the most notorious behaviorist with respect to discourses of autism is the clinical psychologist Dr. Ole Ivar Lovaas. In contemporary times, his behavior modification approach—termed the 'Lovaas technique' and widely recognized as Applied Behavioral Analysis (ABA) and Intensive Behavioral Intervention (IBI)—remains a so-called best practice in the treatment of the so-called disorder of autism (Rosenwasser and Axelrod, 2002; U.S. Department of Health and Human Services, 1999).

In 1987, Lovaas published a landmark study, "Behavioral Treatment and Normal Educational and Intellectual Functioning in Young Autistic Children," that described autism in terms of outward behavioral manifestations deemed pathological in nature (Lovaas, 1987). Returning to some of the original symptoms noted by Kanner, Lovaas described autism in terms of behavioral characteristics: "failure to develop relationships"; "problems with language"; "ritualistic and obsessional behaviours" (Lovaas, 1987, p. 3). Most significantly, Lovaas noted the fourth characteristic of autism—"potential for normal intelligence" (Lovaas, 1987, p. 3). Lovaas and his contemporaries gave shape to autism as not only a state of simple abnormality (as it was by, say, Kanner and Asperger) but as a set of abnormal (what Lovaas terms "inappropriate") behaviors understood to be correctable and therefore improvable. The 'abnormal' autistic body was encoded with the potential for a return to normalcy. In this way, Lovaas's work lay the foundation for a strategy (behavioral intervention) to treat (read: normalize) an autistic person's perceived abnormality and thus to release their presumed potential for normalcy. Lovaas's behavioral modification approach enforces normative behaviors through correction and repetition. Rewards and aversives (i.e., the "delivery of a loud 'no' or a slap on the thigh contingent upon the presence of the undesirable behavior") are often used as ways to "suppress pathological behaviour" (Lovaas, 1987, p. 8). Lovass notes that the ultimate goal of such interventions and modifications is to produce an autistic subject that is "indistinguishable from their normal friends" (Lovaas, 1987, p. 8).

It is perhaps tangential, but nonetheless elucidating, to briefly discuss the origins of the Lovaas technique and its early 'successes' at producing normal or 'indistinguishable' subjects through the suppression of behaviors deemed inappropriate/pathological. In the 1970s at UCLA, Lovaas (who not only played an influential role in the founding of the Autism Society but is now widely recognized within mainstream autism advocacy communities as a kind of hero for his research on autism treatments) was a principal investigator on the now-infamous *Feminine Boy Project* (Burke, 1997; Dawson, 2008).

The project—which received at least $1.5 million in federal funding at the time—was aimed at young boys who were observed (by parents or by medical 'experts') to be displaying behaviors deemed 'feminine' (Burke, 1997). In much the same way as he later observed, documented, and described deviant autistic behaviors, Lovaas's earlier research described the deviant behaviors of the 'feminine' boy (Burke, 1997; Dawson, 2008). Ostensibly deviant behaviors included:

(a) plays with girls,
(b) plays with female dolls,
(c) feminine gestures, including limp wrist, swishy hand, arm or torso movements, sway of hips, etc., and

(d) female role play, including impersonating or pretending to be a female (like actress, mother, female teacher) when playing games (like house, school, etc.). (Burke, 1997, p. 39)

The primary goal of this project was to target such 'inappropriate' behaviors and treat them by using techniques such as the repetition of normal (i.e., socially determined 'masculine') behaviors and the use of aversives and rewards (Burke, 1997, p. 39). The funding for the *Feminine Boy Project* was withdrawn in 1976, and over the course of the next several decades Lovaas distanced himself from the research that was conducted under the umbrella of this project. However, Lovass continued his behavioral modification work up until his death in the summer of 2010 in the UCLA Department of Psychology with a focus on the treatment of autistic children through behavioral intervention.

Perhaps in part due to Lovaas's close ties with the major US national advocacy organizations, behaviorism continues to be influential in shaping and shifting advocacy work and autism awareness. The same historical moment that gave rise to a behaviorist ideology that told the story of autism as a disordered but improvable body also witnessed a shift in advocacy's awareness of autism. For example, Dr. Bernard Rimland—founder of both the Autism Society and the Autism Research Institute and personal associate of Lovaas—began to formally advocate that autism was a "biological disorder that could be treated—or at least ameliorated—with biomedical and behavioural therapies" (Venables, 2006). This embrace of biomedical/behaviorist perspectives as the best way to know and respond to autism—an embrace that is reflected in the vast majority of advocacy platforms to this day—gestures toward the contingent social, political, and historical dimensions organizing and governing autism advocacy. While behavioral modification is still considered a best practice in Western/ized countries when it comes to treating autism's perceived deviance, one dominant way of knowing, understanding, and becoming aware of autism's behavioural deviance is by way of such fields as cognitive psychology, cognitive neuropsychology and the neurosciences.

COGNITIVE PSYCHOLOGY AND THE NEUROSCIENCES

The rise of the cognitive paradigm in the 1970s and 1980s provided still another highly influential response to autism and it continues to be utilized and developed as a dominant way of, first, recognizing and, then, knowing autistic difference. For cognitivists, the assumed pathological nature of autistic behavior is not an end in and of itself but is, rather, an *indication* of an underlying difference in the mind and/or brain. Cognitivism is distinguishable from its antecedents—psychoanalysis and behaviorism—in a number of critical ways. Unlike behaviorism, which holds observable behaviors as its focal point, cognitive psychology is primarily focused on internal mental states (beliefs, desires, intentions, and so on) (Baron-Cohen, 1997; Frith and Frith, 1999). While behavioral observations are one critical component of cognitive psychology, a subject's behavior is conceived of not as an end in and of itself but as a clue or a sign pointing to a subject's inner mental state and/or brain function. While the field of cognitive psychology shares with psychoanalysis an interest in so-called inner mental states, it rejects a psychoanalytic reliance on subjective perceptions and reflection in favor of a scientific research method—premised on empiricism and objectivity—as a way of studying the cognitive processes of the mind.

A popular area of inquiry in the field of cognitive psychology, particularly with respect to autism, is the study of human Theory of Mind (ToM). Theory of Mind is a concept that is used to signal a person's ability to "attribute mental states (such as beliefs, desires, intentions, etc.) to [the self] and other people, as a way of making sense of and predicting behaviour" (Tager-Flusberg, Baron-Cohen, and Cohen, 1993, p. 3). Theory of Mind hypothesizes that the ability to quickly and effortlessly attribute mental states (empathy) is the natural ability of the normal human. In fact, as I have written about elsewhere with Michalko (McGuire &and Michalko, 2011), Theory of Mind is often articulated in cognitivist research as *the* defining ability of the human; the marker of what constitutes humanness (see also: Yergeau, 2013). "A theory of mind," writes Baron -Cohen (2001), "remains one of the quintessential abilities that makes us human" (p. 174). Similarly, cognitive psychologist Michael Tomasello (et al.) writes in a 2005 article published in *Behavioral and Brain Sciences*: "We propose that human beings, and only human beings, are biologically adapted for participating in collaborative activities involving shared goals and socially coordinated action plans (joint intentions)" (Tomasello et al., 2005, p. 676). Vis-à-vis this question of the human, the field of cognitive psychology has developed a barrage of empirical tests (e.g., false belief tests) that are drawn upon to determine whether or not an individual possesses an underlying capacity for Theory of Mind. Based upon test results that measure external behaviours and responses, cognitive psychologists have concluded that autistic people have an internal deficit of the mind: "children and adults with the biological condition of autism suffer, to varying degrees, from "mindblindness" [. . .] they fail to develop the capacity to mindread in the normal way" (Baron-Cohen, 1995, p. 5). As Yergeau (2013) points out, the logic, here, is as simple as it is dangerous: "Humans are human because they possess a theory of mind, and autistics are inhuman because they do not" (n.p.). Tomasello's 2005 article provides us with a clear example of this disturbing logic in action. After establishing ToM as the marker of humanity, the authors go on to locate "some children with autism" (along with great apes) outside of the very category of the human (Tomasello et al., 2005, p. 675; for a fuller discussion of this interpretive move, see: McGuire and Michalko, 2011). Framed as lacking the normal/natural cognitive skills of the human (i.e., ToM), the autistic subject has been cast by cognitivists as less than or not fully human, a move which in turn has made possible all kinds of dehumanizing (violent) acts against autistic people (see Yergeau, 2013).

As we have seen over and again throughout this chapter, the production of a disorderly autism is thoroughly cultural, its meaning shaped and re-shaped by the world in which it appears (Yergeau, 2013; Heilker and Yergeau, 2011; Broderick and Ne'eman, 2011; Murray, 2008; Nadesan, 2005). At the same time that cognitive psychology was emerging as a new and viable way of understanding and classifying the mind with a priori forms and structures, the global/izing West was in the midst of another considerably influential cultural phenomenon—a veritable boom in computers, science, and technology (Nadesan, 2005). The 1970s and 1980s saw expeditions to space, the Cold War and the race to develop better, 'smarter' arms technology, the development of the circuit, and a plethora of research focusing on creating various forms of artificial intelligence. Most significantly, however, it was the so-called computer age in the West, an historical juncture that introduced the pocket calculator and witnessed the popularization of the personal computer (PC). Ironically, even with cognitive psychology's focus on 'natural' a priori aspects of the human mind, it relied heavily on technology metaphors (Nadesan, 2005; Neisser, 1976). The form and structure of the mind was articulated as 'hard-wired'; mental processes were thought of in terms of synaptic 'connections'; cognition was described in terms of 'computational processes'; the mind was understood as working via 'information processing'; and so on.

Ulric Neisser (1976), who was first to coin the term 'cognitive psychology', argued that it was this so-called computer age that enabled the
cognitive paradigm to emerge as a dominant mode of understanding the
mind. The computer age did not simply provide the conditions of possibility for the emergence and mainstreaming of the cognitive psychology
paradigm. As Nadesan writes: "the cognitive paradigm takes an 'information processing' approach to studying the mind" (Nadesan, 2005, p.
104). The computer metaphor, in other words, was not simply a useful
way of describing (normal/abnormal) mental processes. Rather, understandings of computers and artificial intelligence influenced the way the
embodied mind was and continues to be interpreted and measured.

Cognitivism, along with its technologically inspired way of both knowing and understanding the mind, provided a story about the mind that
was, and continues to be, immensely appealing to a variety of established
fields of thought, and some of its central tenets were, and continue to
be, adopted by other fields of psychology such as, for example, behaviorism. It has also spawned new and related (nonpsychological) biomedical fields of study such as, for example, cognitive neuropsychology and
cognitive neuroscience. By conflating cognitive states of mind and physi-
ological brain states, these sibling neuro fields make even more explicit
the proposition that there are empirically knowable—biological—origins
of normalcy and abnormalcy (e.g., where cognitive psychologists might
empirically measure one's possession of Theory of Mind by a false belief
test, cognitive neuropsychologists might study abnormal neural connec-
tivity using brain imaging techniques). These new ways of thinking of
the mind and brain—or perhaps the mind-as-brain—have had profound
and reverberating effects on the ways autism is monitored, measured,
and treated.

Consider, for example, the far-reaching biomedical industry that is,
what Nadesan (2006) terms, "autism brain science," which endeavors to
isolate and visualize biological and anatomical 'anomalies' of the autistic mind/brain (p. 148). While neuroimaging technologies (e.g., MRIs,
fMRIs, EEGs, PET and CAT scans, and so on) seem to allow scientists
to glimpse at how the living autistic brain is 'functioning' and 'malfunctioning' (Nadesan, 2005), clinical studies supported by the Autism Tissue Program, for example, examine pathological brain samples from
deceased autistic people in order to "unravel the mysteries of [autism]
and related neurological conditions" (Autism Speaks, 2011a, para. 2).
Remarkably, contemporary biomedical practices of measuring and map-

ping the 'disordered' autistic brain are detached and divided out from (ongoing) ableist, racist, sexist, and heterosexist histories that draw on comparative anatomy and notions of biological determinism as a means of structuring an empirical hierarchy of embodied life. As I explore in the later chapters of this book, this divide is both artificial and dangerous.

As cognitivism and the related neurosciences have become dominant ways of understanding the mind/brain, cultural understandings of normal and abnormal have shifted once again. The cognitive paradigm described above provides a model of a human mind/brain that is not only fluid, changing, unfixed, but is even, much like behaviorist conceptions of human behavior, *improvable*. The neurosciences have introduced, for example, the concept of neuroplasticity, which proposes that the brain (and so as these concepts are utterly tangled, the mind) is not simply 'hard-wired' once and for all but is *plastic*—it can change over time (Nadesan, 2005). In this way, the mind/brain cannot only be charted, it can be 'engineered' and even—where there is 'mis-wiring'—can be 'rewired' or 'repaired.' Returning to the example of Theory of Mind research, while autistic people are clearly and in no uncertain terms framed by cognitive psychologists as lacking the capacity to mindread, many therapeutic approaches nonetheless endeavor to 'teach empathy' (and thus teach humanness) through, for example, social skills training programs. With this in mind, the crucial distinction that marks the uniqueness of this particular historical moment is that neurological normalcy is constructed not as something one has or does not have but as an ongoing embodied *practice*. The normal mind/brain has become an object that can be tinkered with, worked on—whether by the self and/ or by medical experts, observant parents, or by intervening advocates. The normal mind/brain is framed as something that can be eventually achieved. Achieved, or perhaps more accurately, approximated.

The Autism Spectrum and the Improvable Body

The meaning of autism changed, at least diagnostically speaking, in the mid-1990s with the release of the fourth edition of the *Diagnostic and Statistical Manual* (DSM-IV). Based on the work of Lorna Wing and Judith Gould in their 1979 Camberwell study, autism was reborne as a so-called *spectrum disorder*. Autism was, in other words, reconceived of, not as a single disorder with fixed deficits, but as a conglomeration of several disorders and syndromes with many deficits ranging from 'mild' to 'severe.' Despite the seeming openness and fluidity of the spectrum metaphor, this spectral conceptualization of autism nonetheless functions as a way to further classify, and so further pathologize, the minutia of autistic difference. In the DSM-IV, autism is comprised of Asperger's syndrome, Childhood Disintegrative Disorder, Rett syndrome, and the catch-all Pervasive Developmental Disorder—Not Otherwise Specified (PDD-NOS) (Attwood, 2008; Grinker, 2008). Interestingly, in the most recent version of the *Diagnostic and Statistical Manual*—the newly released DSM-5—these separate diagnostic labels have been collapsed under a singular designation of Autism Spectrum Disorder. Autism is now explicitly measured in terms of gradations of severity. Rejecting a strict categorical diagnosis (i.e., either one meets criteria or not) and moving toward a dimensional one (i.e, to what degree does one meet criteria), the DSM-5 version of autism is not so much a coherent group of pathological signs and symptoms but is rather understood as a spectral range of pathological referents anchored by oppositional poles of severity. This understanding of autism as not merely one treatable disorder but as a spectrum of many treatable symptoms, whose manifestations range from 'mild' to 'severe,' conceptually gels so easily with neuroscientific notions of plasticity and behaviorist notions of improvability. The concept of autism as a graded spectrum of impairment severities has become crucial to dominantly held contemporary understandings of the autistic body that narrate it as some 'thing' to be worked on, modified, and improved, as well as to understandings of the role of the advocate as the worker, the improver, the modifier.

As is evident in the discussions throughout this chapter, disorder is no longer conceived of as something that can only be intuited on a psychiatrist's couch; new ideological and technological developments have spawned new fields of inquiry such as the cognitive and neurosciences and, as seen above, these fields have opened up new ways of seeing—and so new ways of knowing—autism's apparent disorder. The dominant contemporary belief that autism dwells, not between people, but *in* individual bodies has fueled a prodigious and multifaceted biomedical (gold[5]) rush to find its origin story. The branches of contemporary biomedical research focused on the etiologies of autism are as numerous as they are diverse, their objects of study ranging from 'flawed' genes to toxic childhood vaccines, from 'bad' brain anatomy to acid rain. In the next section, I briefly overview what is widely considered to be the most accepted way of seeing autism's biological origins: the study of genetics.

'Flawed Genes'

The past number of decades have seen the emergence of whole subfields of scientific research focused on the genetics of autism. These studies seek to reveal underlying neurobiological pathways connecting genetic mutations ('flawed genes') to the behavioral signs and symptoms that are understood as characteristic of autism. As Nadesan (2005) writes: "observable 'autistic' behaviours and cognitive deficits are thus believed to be epiphenomena of the underlying organic disorder(s)" (p. 149). It is widely accepted by geneticists that autism has some genetic component and this understanding has generated multimillion dollar research initiatives, such as the Autism Genome Project (AGP), that attempts to map autism susceptibility genes and identify genetic markers (Autism Genome Project, 2011), and the Autism Genetic Resource Exchange (AGRE), which is the "largest private, open-access repository of clinical and genetic information dedicated to help autism research" (Autism Speaks, 2011b, para. 1). While significant amounts of time and money have been invested in coming to know autism's genetic origins, the search has generated more complexities and revealed few clear answers. Concluding his overview of contemporary genetic autism research and referencing Hacking's reflections on autism, Michael Fitzpatrick (2009) writes:

> 'So what do we know about autism?' asks philosopher Ian Hacking, 'Not much' is his laconic reply (Hacking, 2006). This, of course, is true: there appear to be a relatively large number of genes, in a wide range of locations, interacting in complex and undetermined ways, and acting through neurophysiological pathways that are little understood. (p. 80)

However uncertain autism's genetic origins are, it is nonetheless important to consider what fuels these particular approaches to knowing autism. The motivating desire—and the presumed need—for more and more genetic discoveries grows from the desire/need for the development of methods of screening for (and so screening out) autism. The AGRE, for example, states that its ultimate aim is "more effective treatments, prevention, and possibly a cure for autism" (Autism Speaks, 2011b, para. 1). Such medical/moral desires, of course, take for granted an underlying (and highly contested) truth that a good autism research outcome is no autism at all.

With this in mind, I am not so quick to agree with the conclusions drawn by Hacking and Fitzpatrick above. If we consider the intricate network of underlying assumptions orienting the drive for more genetic research—beginning with the assumption that the sum-total of *what autism is*, is (and can be) determined by a careful examination of biology and ending with the assumption that autism is not a valuable (viable?) part of collective life—it then would seem we, collectively, know quite a bit about autism already. Namely, Western/izing culture seems to proceed with great certainty that autism is merely some naturally occurring unnatural pathology located in individual bodies, some 'thing' we, collectively, do not want to have around. The lack of conclusive answers coming out of the field of genetics is almost never taken up as a provocation to think deeply about the inherent uncertainties of the human body, our own and the bodies of others.

But "could genetics," to borrow Rosalyn Diprose's (1995) question, "make sense in another sense?" (p. 168). Rather than treating the lack of certainty with respect to autism's origins as a call for more efficient searching and re-searching, we might instead examine, for example, how the search for autism origins is embedded within a contemporary (neoliberal) historical moment that, as we shall see in chapter 3, is significantly defined by a regime of global capitalism (Rose, 2007). In this—our—historical context, biomedical practices of searching and re-searching represent the investment in and circulation of more and more capital. This is perhaps a commitment to the interminable mystification of autism. Not unlike the DNA it takes as its object of study, current genetic research divides, mutates, and replicates—generating, supporting, and/or invigorating multimillion dollar biomedical research industries. Given these somewhat dramatic shifts in the ways in which autism is dominantly imagined in contemporary times, I turn my focus now to an examination of how these shifts have shaped (and are shaped by) mainstream autism advocacy.

Becoming Aware of Autism as Biological Pathology

Not unlike the child rearing campaigns of the 1940s, a renewed drive to educate parents (again, particularly white, middle-class mothers) reentered public life in the 1980s and this drive continues into contemporary times. There are, however, several particularities that distinguish the series of parent campaigns that took hold in the 1980s

and 1990s from earlier ones. Most significantly, the way in which the
normal/abnormal child is studied is now motivated by new biomedical paradigms of understanding the body and mind such as the ones
described above—cognitivism, neuroscience, genetics, and so forth. As
psychoanalysis was the primary way of understanding the normal and
abnormal development of the child in the 1940s, the parent campaigns,
at that time, scrutinized parents (mothers) themselves. As we explored,
the 1940s campaigns saw an increase in the surveillance of the mother
and her mothering practices—the disorder of the child was merely a
reflection of the disorder of the mother and her home. By contrast, in
the 1980s, 1990s, and beyond the disorder of autism itself—conceived as
some (pathological) 'thing' that happens to some people—has become
the target of these campaigns. Surveillance, then, is focused on the individual body of the child, a body that might be harboring within it—in its
genes, its mind, or its brain—a biologically pathological autism.

As we have seen, autism meets the certainty of contemporary biomedical paradigms with no small amount of uncertainty and this is reflected in the parent campaigns from the 1980s, 1990s, and beyond. While
autism's embodied pathology is understood to be certain, its etiological
origins remain unknown. Because of this unknown origin, all bodies are
understood as *potentially* disordered. The mother, who was not so long
ago under surveillance and scrutiny, must now adopt the paternalistic
position of surveiller—she must watch her children and look for bodily
manifestations or signs of disorder and seek biomedical intervention.
This, of course, does not free the mother completely from being herself
an object of scrutiny. However, what has changed is what is being scrutinized. In the 1940s, motherhood was governed in terms of a mother's
ability to nurture her children, to bond properly with her children, and
thus help them develop a normal character and personality. In the 1980s,
1990s, and beyond, the mother now must watch herself as she watches
her children's development; the role of the mother has transformed into
that of a pseudo-biomedical expert poised to identify potential signs of
pathology in her child. Consider, for example, the best-selling pregnancy
book of the 1980s and 1990s, *What to Expect When You're Expecting* (1981),
where good mothering is synonymous with being aware of the signs of
the normal child . . . of what to expect. It is this particular, contemporary
moment that has given us such organizational devices as early warning
signs and red flags—devices that are often promoted and propagated by
advocacy organizations as they seek to raise awareness about autism (see
chapter 2 for a more in-depth unpacking of this contemporary drive

to 'flag' non-normative bodies and behaviors). Motherhood is governed by the mother's ability to notice these childhood 'warning signs,' stage 'early interventions,' and seek biomedical therapies such as Lovaas's normalizing Applied Behavioral Analysis.

Shifts in understandings of parenting are, of course, intimately connected to shifts in the shape and scope of advocacy work, particularly as parents and family members of autistic people are often found at the center of formal and informal enactments of advocacy (Klar-Wolfund, 2008). It is ironic and interesting to note that autism advocacy, a phenomenon that was born out of a vehement rejection of the surveillance of the mother, readily embraces, endorses, and promotes this new and more covert form of surveillance. Still, the reintroduction of biological—particularly genetic—determinants of autism does tread dangerously close to the mother blaming of yore and this proximity has diverted forms of advocacy (and so ways of knowing autism) in new directions. I turn now to an examination of what is often referred to in advocacy discourse as the 'autism epidemic' and advocacy's subsequent 'war on autism.'

The Era of Autism Epidemic and Advocacy's War on Autism

The past two decades have witnessed a steep rise in the number of people being identified and diagnosed as autistic. In a 2004 white paper, the Autism Society of Canada stated that "autism, once considered a 'rare' disorder, has increased dramatically from a prevalence of 4-5 in 10,000 (1 in 2,000 to 2,500) 15 years ago to at least 1 in 500 in 2001" (Autism Society of Canada, 2004, p. 4). A decade later, in 2014, the Centers for Disease Control and Prevention (CDC) reported that the prevalence of autism had reached '1 in 110'[6] (Centers for Disease Control and Prevention, 2010, p. 27). The CDC declared, moreover, that this increase in autism prevalence was "an urgent public health concern" (Centers for Disease Control and Prevention, 2010, p. 22). Many social theorists have compellingly demonstrated that the increase in autism diagnoses has much to do with the shifting social, political, economic, and historical contexts in which autism appears (Gernsbacher, Dawson, and Goldsmith, 2005; Grinker, 2008; Nadesan, 2005; Timimi, Gardner, and McCabe, 2010). Despite this work, autism is often narrated in contemporary times, particularly by those engaged in autism advocacy, as an 'epidemic' (Gernsbacher, Dawson, and Goldsmith, 2005) (for a more detailed discussion of autism statistics, see chapter 4).

The word 'epidemic' has powerful connotations and demands particular kinds of responses. Epidemic implies a sudden widespread occurrence of an infectious disease. Epidemic evokes fear—something undesirable, often life-threatening, is spreading through a helpless population. Grinker writes that the term 'epidemic' "[calls] up associations with plagues that sweep through the streets, something contagious in the air you breath, or in the food you eat, threatening the ones you love" (Grinker, 2008, p. 3). This notion of epidemic has been shaped by and has, in turn, shaped the landscape of science. It has also sparked the emergence of a great many nonscientifically supported studies and related treatment protocols. The past decade has seen innumerable studies, both scientific and pseudoscientific, examining and evaluating a wide range of environmental causes of autism. Perusing my collection of newspaper clippings, journal articles, and other pieces of data collected over the past decade, autism is, reportedly, caused by such environmental factors as exposure to acid rain, ultrasounds, lead, gluten and/or yeast in the diet, antibiotics, pollution, electromagnetic radiation, decomposing iPod batteries, circumcisions, pesticides, excessive hygiene practices, and so on and so forth, ad infinitum. Surely the most notorious of the environmental causes postulated over the last decade has been the link made between autism and childhood vaccines. While some researchers have argued that autism is caused by the use of thimerosal mercury in vaccines (Geier and Geier, 2003), others have suggested that autism is caused by the measles, mumps, and rubella vaccination, which Wakefield (1998) famously—and falsely—claimed damaged children's immune systems (see "Retraction—Ileal-Lymphoid-Nodular Hyperplasia," 2010 for the *Lancet*'s retraction of the Wakefield article). In short, the sciences and (especially) the pseudosciences of today tell us in both covert and overt ways: *the pathology of autism could come from anywhere.* It may be caused by the rain or by toxins in our food. It may be in the genes or in the brain. It may even be in the soul.[7] Insidiously, it has infiltrated those measures we take to secure our children from harm or sickness. Hygiene practices. Vaccines. Ultrasounds.

This culturally and historically specific 'epidemicization' of autism and the anxiety and fear it invariably elicits has shaped advocacy once again. The past two decades have seen the establishment of thousands of autism advocacy organizations (an 'advocacy epidemic,' if you will) around the globe and the vast majority of these are oriented to autism as a biological problem requiring biomedical intervention—a disease in need of prevention or cure. Some of the larger North American organizations include: Families for Early Autism Treatment (FEAT), founded in 1993; the National Alliance for Autism Research (NAAR), founded in 1994; Cure Autism Now (CAN), founded in 1995; Safe Minds, founded in 2000; the Autism Canada Foundation, founded in 2002; the National Autism Association founded in 2003; and Generation Rescue, founded in 2005. And in a 2005 corporate-style takeover headed by Bob Wright, the former CEO of NBC, vice-chairman of General Electric, and grandfather of an autistic child, a number of these organizations—NAAR, for example, and CAN among several others—were merged to form Autism Speaks. Based originally in the United States, Autism Speaks has since gone global, setting up branch offices in Canada, the United Kingdom, and the Middle East. Autism Speaks is, without a doubt, the largest, the richest, and thus the most influential autism advocacy organization in operation today and it is leading the way in propagating notions of autism as a terrifying epidemic that needs to be stopped by a wide variety of preventative and rehabilitative biomedical interventions.

As is evident in the chapters that follow, contemporary advocacy work performed and supported by organizations, together with informal acts of advocacy performed by independent advocates (parents, teachers, social workers, and others who may not be affiliated with a formal organization but who engage, nonetheless, in performances of advocacy), remains focused on treating autistic people and raising awareness about autism. Yet the shape of these twin aims of advocacy has been altered in accordance with the dominant views of our times. In dominant contemporary discourses of advocacy, to be aware of autism is to be aware of it as a disease of epidemic proportions and to treat autism is to seek to 'cure' it (i.e., to eliminate or lessen the characteristics of autism). As autism comes to be understood as a spreading epidemic afflicting otherwise normal people, the work of autism advocacy becomes the work of ensuring, securing, and/or recovering the normal (read: nonautistic) body and mind. The work of contemporary autism advocacy is, for example, the work of securing funding for (biomedical) forms of research looking to cure autism and/or eliminate autistic ways of being (e.g., the Autism Tissue Project and the Autism Genetic Resource Exchange are both private, Autism Speaks-funded programs, and Autism Speaks also provides significant funding for the Autism Genome Project); the work of hypothesizing how autism might be avoided (e.g., Generation Rescue's campaign against MMR vaccination); the work of raising awareness of autism as a biological problem in need of immediate intervention (e.g., the launching of red flag awareness campaigns aimed to help identify signs and symptoms of developmental difference); and even the work of attempting to recover the normative body of nonautism (e.g., the implementation of and/or facilitation of access to speech therapies, drug therapies, dietary therapies, behavioral therapies that attempt to diminish or even eliminate the signs of autism).

As it represents and thus conceives of autism as a threat to the normative individual and social body, contemporary advocacy work issues an effective and powerful 'call to arms' against autism. The orientation of contemporary advocacy is clear: to be a 'good' autism advocate is to be positioned 'against' autism, to 'fight' it, 'combat' it, 'defeat' it, and so on. Having emerged out of a World War II moment, autism makes an appearance in this moment in the midst of another war—a war with fresh targets and new tactics. It is this war on autism that I take as my focus for the remainder of this book. I do this so as to interrogate how a militarized autism advocacy is systemically producing and sustaining a social environment that is hostile to autistic difference—an environment that, as we shall see, structures and supports possibilities for violence against those who embody autistic difference.

Thus far, this chapter has been focused on tracing a history of dominant discourses of autism and autism advocacy. Throughout this history, I hope to have demonstrated how relational and hierarchical power structures are governing our collective, cultural conceptualizations of autism and advocacy, conceptualizations that are, in turn, shaping the meaning of people. I conclude this chapter by gesturing toward emergent *autistic* histories of autism and advocacy. The following section attends to the ongoing ways autistic and neurodiverse people and their allies have been contesting received meanings of autism and, indeed, are cultivating and sustaining non-normative advocacy communities. Vis-à-vis a long history where autism has been framed as a pathological problem and where advocacy has emerged as one possible solution to this problem, neurodiversity communities are demonstrating alternative narrative frameworks for conceptualizing the meaning of autism, advocacy, and the relationship between these.

The Politics of Neurodiversity

As Foucault (1980) notes, wherever there is power there is also resistance. In the face of the widespread pathologization of autism and the powerful cultural desire for its elimination, autistic scholars and activists have been instrumental in organizing various and diverse self-advocacy movements that are bound together by notions of neurodiversity. As a concept, neurodiversity references the assumption that human neurology is neither static nor singular. Nick Walker (2012) writes about neurodiversity as a paradigm—a way of rethinking medicalized understandings of human brains and minds that unsettles the understanding that "there is only one 'right,' 'normal' or 'healthy' way for human brains and human minds to be configured and to function" (p. x). In this paradigm, non-neurotypicality (e.g., autism) becomes one of many natural forms of human variation. Autism, of course, is just one of many examples of "neurodivergence" here (Sibley, 2015). Notions of neurodiversity have come to include a wide array of neurological or neurodevelopmental differences including attention deficit disorder, Tourette's syndrome, dyslexia, bipolar disorder, dyspraxia, and epilepsy (Jarsma and Welin, 2012). In addition to providing a narrative framework for neurological diversity, the term also represents, as noted by McGee (2012), an act of "political naming" (p. 12). Neurodiversity references a distinct political and cultural orientation that has emerged as response to the inequality and oppression faced by neurodiverse people. It is this latter aspect of neurodiversity—neurodiversity as political phenomenon—that I take as the primary object of focus for the remainder of this chapter.

As with other more dominant understandings of autism, understandings of neurodiversity are inseparable from the cultural context in which they appear. The notion of neurodiversity was first articulated in the late 1990s by Australian sociologist and autist Judy Singer. Notions of neurodiversity were precipitated by the rise of spectrum thinking in the 1980s and 1990s. As noted by Singer (1999), "the key significance of the 'Autistic Spectrum' lies in its call for and anticipation of a politics of Neurological Diversity, or what I want to call 'Neurodiversity'" (p. 64). For Singer, neurodiversity was also a direct response to dominant cultural articulations that define autism as a state of biological 'wrongness' and moral inferiority. Reflecting on the term in a 2008 *New York Magazine* article, Singer states: "I was interested in the liberatory, activist aspects of it—to do for neurologically different people what feminism and gay rights had done for their constituencies" (Solomon, 2008). Given the political origin of the term, it is, of course, no coincidence that the concept was first articulated in the midst of the 'advocacy epidemic' of the 1990s. Recall that, at this historical moment, countless professional/parent-led advocacy organizations were emerging and there was a proliferation of discourses of autism as an undesirable disorder/disease in need of management and/or cure. Vis-à-vis such overwhelmingly dominant cultural understandings of autism, notions of neurodiversity offer a creative, alternative, and liberatory narrative. They reclaim autism from the vice-grip of pathology and reassert the autistic subject as autonomous, agentive, and uniquely invested participant in the work of social advocacy. Thus, the neurodiversity paradigm has and continues to ground the autistic self-advocacy movement.

The Rise of Self-Advocacy

Robertson and Ne'eman (2008) suggest that the autistic self-advocacy movement must be figured against the broader historical backdrop of the disability rights movement. "The history of the disability rights movement," they write, "contains many legendary stories of empowered people with disabilities taking control of their political, social, and legal representations from people without disabilities who sought to speak for them" (n.p.). Indeed, the politics of autistic self-advocacy has been, and continues to be, cultivated and nourished under a banner of disability politics and the long history of disabled people's struggles for civil liberties and social justice. Drawing on the cornerstone refrain of disabled people's movements for the past two decades, the autistic self-advocacy movement strongly asserts: "nothing about us without us" (Charlton, 2000; Robertson and Ne'eman, 2008).

In his chapter in the edited collection *Loud Hands: Autistic People Speaking* (2012), Jim Sinclair recounts the history of the formation of the first autistic-led social advocacy group. Founded in 1992, Autism Network International (ANI) was born of a friendship and collaboration between three autistic people: Jim Sinclair, Donna Williams, and Kathy Lissner Grant (Sinclair, 2012; Williams, 1995). The three met via a pen pal list maintained by a parent-run organization (Sinclair, 2012). While some autistic members on the list did attempt to gather at autism conferences put on by parent-run organizations, Sinclair describes this environment as inaccessible and thus inhospitable to autistic organizing—"hostile from both a sensory and emotional standpoint" (p. 18). Sinclair writes of the conferences:

> There's simply too much going on—too many people, too much movement, too much noise, often fluorescent lights, and above all,

the overwhelming onslaught of speakers and articles and exhibits all stressing that there's something terribly *wrong* with us, that we're a horribly defective type of human, and that our very existence is a source of never-ending grief for our families. (p. 18)

In response to the hostility of normative spaces of advocacy, Sinclair, Williams, and Grant arranged a face-to-face meeting in the winter of 1992, at Grant's house in St. Louis, Missouri (Sinclair, 2012; Williams, 1995). "We talked a lot during those two days," writes Sinclair, "and laughed a lot, and played around with each other's fixations, and sat on the floor stimming a lot" (p. 19). Both Sinclair and Williams describe the claiming of this non-normative (autistic) space of encounter as a kind of homecoming. Sinclair writes:

We spent two or three days together, in a place where *everyone* was autistic, and where there were only three of us instead of a large crowd. [. . .] It was an amazing and powerful experience to be able to communicate with someone in my own language. I had sometimes been able to establish meaningful communication with people before, but it always involved my having to learn the other person's language and do constant laborious translating. (Sinclair, 1988) Here, with people who shared my language, meaning flowed freely and easily. (p. 19)

Likewise, Williams writes: "Despite thousands of miles, our 'our world' concepts, strategies, and experiences even came down to having created the same made-up words to describe them. Together we felt like a lost tribe" (p. 18). Sinclair emphasizes the necessary connection between non-normative community/cultural formations and the emergence of non-normative forms of social advocacy. Indeed, being together in what Sinclair describes as "autistic space," Sinclair, Williams, and Grant were better positioned to "glimpse the possibilities of autistic peer support" (p. 19). Autistic Network International *(ANI)* was officially born later that year, producing their first printed newsletter written by and for autistic people in November 1992.

ANI continues to maintain a variety online forums and a large listserv (ANI-L). In 1996, ANI organized their first autistic-led retreat/conference, called Autreat, which is now hosted on an annual basis. Recalling the meeting in Missouri in the winter of 1992, Autreat reasserts that importance of non-normative space to autistic advocacy. According the its website, "autreat is an opportunity for autistic people and those with related developmental differences, our friends, and supporters to come together, discover and explore autistic connections, and develop advocacy skills, all in an autistic-friendly environment." (For more on Autreat and the kinds of ways this conference establishes autistic space, see the group's website, http://www.autreat.com/autreat.html.) Since the establishment of ANI, the last two decades have seen the rise of a wide array of autistic-run groups and self-advocacy organizations with differing (and sometimes conflicting) platforms—for example, The Autism Women's Network (AWN), the Global and Regional Asperger Syndrome Partnership (GRASP), and Aspies for Freedom (AFF) and the Autistic Self Advocacy Network (ASAN). The rapid growth and expansion of these groups cannot be separated from another social and historical context discussed earlier—the steep rise in the number of people receiving an autism diagnosis in the 1990s (and beyond) has meant that more and more people identify (or are identified) as autistic. Relatedly, the dominance of parent-led advocacy has conditioned the very possibility of and need for an autistic self-advocacy movement.

The popularization of the Internet has also been a key technological development in the history of autistic self-advocacy. Insofar as it can be accessible to autistics who communicate solely via computer and to those who find sustained social stimulation stressful and/or impossible, the Internet represents a unique discursive space of autistic resistance. A wide variety of online autistic communities have flourished over the past two decades via social media sites (e.g., Facebook, Twitter), video sharing sites (YouTube), virtual worlds (e.g., Second Life), as well as various forums and listservs. These virtual communities are, in turn, opening up a whole range of new possibilities for autistic interaction, locally and worldwide. The World Wide Web has also provided a platform for a great many autistic bloggers and online writers who are creating new meanings of autism and autistic identity. The online work of such activists, artists, self-advocates, and academics as Michelle Dawson, Phil Schwartz, Jim Sinclair, Joel Smith, Kathleen Seidel, Laura Tisoncik, Ari Ne'eman, Mel Baggs, Bev Harp, Amy Sequenzia, Melanie Yergeau, Julia Bascom, Nick Walker, Ibby Grace, Lydia Brown, Zach Richter, Kassiane Sibley, and Paula Durbin-Westby (and so many others) is composing a rich archive of autistic narratives, art, and political and cultural critique. Of course, the question of who can access these online communities (and thus who can claim the 'voice' of resistance in online settings) is determined by access to certain kinds of technology. Autistics who are incarcerated, institutionalized, homeless, those who live in a geographical context without regular access to the Internet or who do not have financial access to the necessary computer technology are underrepresented in online neurodiversity and self-advocacy communities. The balance of power in these communities is thus invariably mapped along class, race, and gender lines.

In the midst of proliferating online communities, and in many ways because of these, the West has seen the growing presence of autistic organizations that operate in nonvirtual or 'real' environments (Robertson and Ne'eman, 2008). Established in 2006 by self-advocates Ari Ne'eman and Scott Michael Robertson, the Autistic Self Advocacy Network (ASAN) emerged in direct response to a lack of autistic representation on the national autism advocacy scene (http://autisticadvocacy.org/about-asan/our-history). Ne'eman describes a glaring underrepresentation of autistic people in social advocacy: "as the national conversation about autism has increased in tone and fervor, we who are the targets of this discussion have not been consulted" (Ne'eman, 2010). "ASAN was created," according to the organization's website:

> to serve as a national grassroots disability rights organization for the Autistic community, and does so by advocating for systems change and ensuring that the voices of Autistic people are heard in policy debates and the halls of power while working to educate communities and improve public perceptions of autism. (ASAN website)

In less than a decade, the organization has grown rapidly, now with a head office in Washington, DC, chapters across the United States, and a full staff comprised of both volunteers and paid employees. In contrast to the professional/parent-run advocacy groups described in earlier sections (which, as we have seen, typically focus on raising awareness about autism as pathology and advocating for the elimination of autism through treatment, rehabilitation, and/or cure), ASAN focuses on group rights, social justice, and systemic change. Some recent initiatives have included:

- **Contesting oppressive and/or inaccurate representations of autism**. In 2007, for example, the organization was successful at pressuring New York University to withdraw its Ransom Notes Campaign (see chapter 4 for more on this campaign and the self-advocate response to it);

- **Tracking and protesting instances of violence against autistic people**. In 2012, ASAN organized the first Disability Community Day of Mourning.
- **Lobbying government for inclusive policy and law reform.** ASAN has been a vocal opponent, for example, of policies and laws condoning seclusion, restraint, and the use of aversives on disabled people. More recently, ASAN launched a twitter campaign *#stopcombattingme* aimed at pressuring the federal government to align the goals of the Combatting Autism Act with the needs of the autistic community.
- **Working toward increasing the participation of autistic people in public policy development, research, service provision, and media representation.** ASAN cofounder Ari Ne'eman was appointed as a member of the IACC, the governing body for the national (US) autism research agenda.

Let us return, for a moment, to the relationship between *autism* advocacy (typically led by nonautistic parents/family members of autistic people and/or autism professionals) and *autistic* self-advocacy (led by people who identify as autistic) and to the question of power that invariably structures this relationship. In his written account of the development of ANI, Sinclair describes encountering opposition from established autism advocates (Sinclair, 2012, see also Brown, 2011b). As the emergent self-advocacy network began to grow, Sinclair describes being shut out by the Autism Society of America and having his own autistic status openly questioned by mainstream advocates (Sinclair, 2012). He writes:

> It seems that one autistic person at a time—and preferably a passive one—might be welcomed as an interesting novelty or an amusing diversion or possibly even a valuable source of information and insight. But autistic people organizing together, autistic people pursuing our own interests rather than furthering the interests of parents and professionals—suddenly we were perceived as a threat (p. 24).

Though in his chapter, Sinclair initially describes the "hostility" of mainstream advocates as "surprising," he goes on to demonstrate that it perhaps should not be. He reminds us that "any attempt by a group of disempowered people to challenge the status quo—to dispute the presumption of their incompetence, to redefine themselves as equals of the empowered class, to assert independence and self-determination—has been met by remarkably similar efforts to discredit them" (Sinclair, 2012). The premises and practices of autistic advocacy—that non-normative ways of being are valid and valuable, for example, that autistic people are agentive subjects with demands and desires—do indeed threaten: they disrupt the normative orientations of mainstream autism advocacy and of our culture more generally (Brown, 2011b).

While the self-advocacy movement came into being as a critical response to the monolith of professional/parent-led advocacy organizations, and while the central paradigms of autism versus autistic advocacy often remain at odds, some cross-organization coalitions are currently being built (e.g., recent collaborations between the ASA and ASAN; see chapter 4 for further discussion of these collaborations). Such coalition work seems to recognize what the remainder of this book seeks to affirm: in the midst of a culture in which it has become normal to advocate 'against' autism, we need the alterity of non-normative (autistic) kinds of advocacy.

Toward a Non-normative Advocacy

In her chapter "The Meaning of Self-Advocacy," Amanda (Mel) Baggs (2012) warns us that we should not limit our understanding of self-advocacy to the work that goes on in organized movements or formally recognized groups. "These are all valid kinds of self-advocacy," writes Baggs, "but they set people up to believe that only certain kinds of people could ever become self-advocates" (p.223). For Baggs, the transformative power of self-advocacy lies not in the particular form it takes but in the ways it resists normativity. Baggs goes on to discuss self-advocacy as an unfixed set of strategies—formal and informal interruptions to normative spaces and the violence of normativity. She writes:

> Whether it is going through the legal system to close an institution, fighting back physically against intolerable surroundings, talking back to staff, sabotaging the power of staff over the lives of disabled people, being listened to when we communicate in non-standard ways, learning that it's okay to have a voice and make decisions, or passively resisting the dominance of others over our lives, real self-advocacy will always upset the status quo in some way (p.226).

Autistic self-advocacy call us all—autistic and nonautistic—to critically engage with the normative foundations of everyday acts of advocacy and examine the shape of the normal advocacy subject. In the following three chapters, I hope to heed this invitation by analyzing the cultural production of normative versions of autism and advocacy and interrogate the constrained subjectivities of the advocate and the advocated for.

Raising the Red Flags of Autism

Advocacy's Call to Arms

———— ❧ ————

"The old world writhed in convulsions of rage at the sight of the
Red Flag."
   —Karl Marx (1933), *The Civil War in France*, p. 45

". . . raise the scarlet standard high/within its shade we'll live
and die . . ."
   —Jim Connell (2007 [1889]), "Song of the Red Flag," para. 2

In this chapter, I will further explore how the phenomenon of autism is
being structured by autism advocacy work in the contemporary moment
by performing an analysis of the social significance and productive
effects of advocacy campaigns that draw on biomedical knowledges—
particularly the disciplinary discourse of human development—as a way
to raise awareness about the signs of autism, it's so-called red flags. In
so doing, I demonstrate how this version of advocacy—a dominant and
almost monolithic one in contemporary times—is giving new meaning
to the phenomenon of autism, as well as to the work of autism advocacy
itself. Lastly, I show how discourses of the normally or 'naturally' developing human are involved in constraining (and so producing) particular and novel subject positions within the field of contemporary autism
advocacy, most notably the subject positions of the advocate and the
advocated for.

To perform the work of advocacy is often to advocate *for something* (e.g., one might advocate *for* better health care). Sometimes the work of advocacy is to advocate *for someone* (e.g., one might advocate, by contrast, *for* people's access to better health care). Other times the work of advocacy is conceptualized as *self-advocacy* (e.g., a process that may mean advocating *for* one's individual self or on behalf of other people in similar situations or contexts) (Baggs, 2012; Durbin-Westby, 2012). While these versions of advocacy are diverse and are shaped by different kinds of power relations, they do share a common thread: to advocate is, very often, to advocate *for*. Yet contrary to what the term 'autism advocacy' might seem to indicate, dominant, contemporary performances of autism advocacy are not generally concerned with advocating *for* autism (Broderick and Ne'eman, 2008; Ne'eman, 2010; Heilker and Yergeau, 2011; Yergeau, 2010; Kras, 2010; McGuire, 2012; Baggs, 2012; Gross, 2012; Sequenzia, 2012c). Rather, as I will explore in the pages to follow, the role of the contemporary autism advocate is limited; the 'good' advocate must first 'take a stand' *against* autism and, next, actively work in the development of nonautism (normalcy). As subjectivities are always implicated in the relational constitution of other subjectivities, the delimitation of the subject of the autism advocate as one that is 'against' autism invariably places strict restrictions on what or who the subject of the advocated for can be.[1] Within contemporary autism advocacy discourse, the subject of the advocated for—the autistic subject—is narrated as a pathologically underdeveloped way of being to be against and, thus, as a way of being that is always in need of development.

One of the first moves in any advocacy movement is to raise awareness about that which is being advocated for. Our awareness of autism is always oriented; it is directed by and inseparable from other kinds of awareness. Our awareness of autism is, for example, directed by and inseparable from the prevailing and problematic awareness of autism as a puzzle in need of a solution (for a demonstration of the damaging effects of the puzzle metaphor, see Harp, 2012). Or the awareness of autism as a biomedical (developmental) deviance that can strike any-body—an abnormalcy that can appear anywhere, at anytime, and therefore a problem that, as a matter of commonsense, requires collective attention and heightened vigilance. In contemporary times, autism awareness is, most often, normalcy's awareness of autism's abnormalcy; its deviance and therefore its danger. Autism awareness becomes awareness of the embodied signs that announce autism's abnormalcy—warning signs, red flags.

Tanya Titchkosky (2007) writes of the critical importance of attending to the multiple, complex, and often conflicting ways that bodies get constituted in and through textuality, in and through discourse. Bodies, in other words, come into being via the multiple, discursive con-texts that give them shape and structure and that allow them to appear as they do. The discourse of normal human development is one such context that works to shape the bodies of autism advocates and the bodies of those who are advocated for and give them meaning. Vis-à-vis a world of text, Titchkosky issues a critical call to "watch our watching, read our readings" so as to "uncover a few of the ways we identify differences" (Titchkosky, 2007, p. 4). It is in this spirit that I will begin to examine *how* textual discourses of normal human development are being employed by autism advocacy as a way to identify autistic difference.

Before I move to an interpretive analysis of particular appearances of the red flag metaphor and consider how the perceived need for heightened vigilance is producing and constraining the field of possible conducts for both the advocate and the advocated for, I will begin by exploring that power-laden discourse so crucial to any contemporary notion of embodied abnormalcy: the discourse of normal human development.

Discourse, Power, Subject

"Discourse," following Foucault (1972), is the "general domain of all statements, sometimes as an individualizable group of statements, and sometimes as a regulated practice that accounts for a number of statements" (p. 80). Discourse, then, at least in a Foucaultian sense, is an organized group of statements, practices, utterances, and knowledges that work to shape how a particular phenomenon appears at a given historical moment and within precise geographical spaces. Within a network of power relations, particular phenomena are thus produced by way of highly organized sets of rules that constrain and restrict what is and, indeed, can be said, done, and often, what can even be imagined. These regulatory sets of rules and structures—that is to say, commonsense shared understandings and assumptions about a particular phenomenon—are often unwritten, commonly unspoken, and yet actively work to *produce* this phenomenon by delimiting the field of possible awareness of and responses to it. A given discursive regime works to produce (via a creative kind of constraint) particular subjectivities—subjects who possess the necessary qualifications to dwell within the discourse's frameworks of meaning and within the parameters of its methods of recognition. Autism is one such phenomenon that has, as I have outlined in the previous chapter, been shaped over the course of the last century by a variety of discourses. A dominant discourse involved in the production of autism, and one that is often drawn on—and particularly embraced—by contemporary autism advocacy work, is the biomedical discourse of human development.

In *The Order of Things* (1970), Foucault describes his interest in the formation of cohesive and discrete scientific discourses in the following way:

> I tried to explore scientific discourse not from the point of view of the individuals who are speaking, nor from the point of view of the formal structures of what they are saying, but from the point of view of the rules that come into play in the very existence of such discourse: What conditions did [the so-called 'father' of taxonomy] Linneas (or Petty or Arnauld) have to fulfill not to make his discourse coherent and true in general, but to give it, at the time when it was written and accepted, value and practical application as scientific discourse. (pp. xiv-xv)

With respect to scientific knowledges, what is of interest to Foucault is not what is said, whether it is empirically accurate or inaccurate or even who is saying it, but what rules structure the knowledge, what techniques secure it, and what assumptions must already be in place for scientific knowledge to appear as valuable or even as sensical in a particular historical moment and geopolitical space. What is also of interest for Foucault, is the work accomplished by such knowledge and its generative effects.

Foucault's work implicitly asks: how are highly organized rules of discourse structuring and, indeed, delimiting the field of the possible (the range of possible articulations, actions, responses, behaviors, questions, choices, and so on) and what are the effects of this? How does discourse actively work to both constrain and enable what we perceive, how we understand, how we react, what we do, and even who we are and can be? These constraints work to produce particular phenomena *as though* these phenomena belonged simply to the realm of the 'natural,' the 'real,' or the 'true.' Rather, Foucault argues that commonsense understandings of nature, reality, or what he terms "regimes of truth" are not self-evident, but are inaugurated and sustained by institutions (e.g., governments, universities, practices and institutions of medicine, and so on) by way of networks of power relations (Foucault, 1980; Foucault, 2003; Mills, 2003).

Indeed, modern scientific and medical knowledges, or what Foucault refers to as the "biomedical knowledges," are, perhaps above all other kinds of knowledge or ways of knowing, almost unilaterally treated in contemporary times as a set of practices derived from and working to first see (i.e., perceive) and then relay the (objective) story of 'natural,' 'true,' and 'real' phenomena (Foucault, 1980; Foucault, 2003). As is evident in the previous chapter, the 'gaze' of medicine looks at the body and, in the look, it comes to know the body (Foucault, 2003, p. 109). Biomedical knowledges—and the positivistic sets of procedures and practices generated by these knowledges—so often tell us how things are, what things are, and who we are. It is much less often imagined, however, that a reflection on the premises and practices of biomedical knowledges might tell us something about the culture in which we live— about our cultural aspirations and worries, about what we legitimize, recognize, value, and who.

Foucault's work (and those who have taken up his work) demonstrates how biomedical knowledges, far from being simply objective accounts of the nature of phenomena, are powerful and shifting discursive spaces (Canguilhem, 1991; Foucault, 1975; Foucault, 2001; Kuhn, 1962; McClintock, 1995; Rose, 1989; Walkerdine, 1998; Tremain, 2006; Tremain, 2008). For example, Foucault's work has demonstrated how biomedical discourses have actively shaped material divisions that work to reify and, indeed, inaugurate discrete categories of madness and sanity (Foucault, 2001). In the previous chapter, I explored how biomedical discourses have been equally influential in constraining, and thus producing, material categories of abnormalcy and normalcy, autism and nonautism. These examples demonstrate how biomedical knowledges and procedures play a critical role in the production of the very phenomena under scrutiny. As with any discursive formation, biomedicine is revealed as a set of social practices, of highly organized rules, procedures, and articulations governed by historically and geopolitically specific relations of power.

It is important to emphasize that power, for Foucault, is not an object or 'thing' that can be possessed by a given individual or institution; it cannot be imposed on or wielded over another individual or institution. Rather, power, in Foucault's terms, "must be analyzed as something which circulates" (Foucault, 1980, p. 98). Foucault conceptualizes power not as a noun but as a verb—it is not something one has, but rather, it is something one does (Mills, 2003, p. 35). Power, rather than hovering above at the level of suprastructure, is *exercised*; it is "invested directly in the distribution and play of forces" (Foucault, 2003, p. 52). It is thus crucial to note that Foucault conceives of power not as repressive—but rather as essentially productive. As Foucault notes, power "needs to be considered as a productive network which runs through the entire social body, much more than a negative instance whose function is oppression" (Foucault, 1980, p. 119). He writes of "a power that is not conservative but inventive, a power that possesses within itself the principles of transformation and innovation" (Foucault, 2003, p. 52). Somewhat paradoxically, then, constraint, for Foucault, *is* productive; the tensions and contractions of power relations, in turn, give form and structure to discursive knowledges that are both the effect and condition of power (Foucault, 2003, p. 52).

Foucault's analysis of biomedical regimes of truth and his conceptualization of the essential productivity of power guide me throughout this chapter, as I explore the ways discourses of development are producing the novel subjectivities of 'advocate' and 'advocated for' and how this production is accomplished via powerful discursive constraints. I interrogate, in other words, how these autism/advocacy subjectivities are being governed by limited (permissible) rules of conduct, ways of knowing and frames of recognition. I do this, of course, with the keen awareness that the productive constraints of discourse are always applied, translated onto the bodies of actual people. Discursive categories and subjectivities govern the bodies and minds of people—they function to limit the ways people can (are permitted to) move, think, act, and exist in the world. Moreover, they function dangerously to produce those people who do not, cannot, or choose not to fit into received subject positions as incoherent: nonsensical, irrational, or even as threatening. I proceed, then, with the assumption that discourse is and always must be material.

In *Discipline and Punish*, Foucault writes of the power-laden disciplinary processes inherent in the formation of embodied subjectivities. "Discipline," Foucault states, "makes individuals" (Foucault, 1979, p. 170). What Foucault refers to as discipline, of course, is not necessarily an overt, external force—an instrument of domination—but is often a subtle discipline, a covert coercion of the docile body of the individual. Subjecthood, then, is not, strictly speaking, a pre-given from elsewhere— from the state or the sovereign—but rather is revealed to be a process of becoming that begins at the level of the individual. While, following Butler (1993), "there is no body prior to its marking" (p. 98)—we always and only exist, in other words, in relation to others who shape us and give us meaning—we do engage in the process of making ourselves into subjects

(Foucault, 1980). Within discourse, the individual must perform, condition, supervise, and know the self according to the (contingent, power-laden, normalizing) rules of the given discursive regime and always in relation to others. Foucault speaks of these confessional "technologies of the self" as central to how we, as individuals, come to occupy the mediated subject positions that are invariably tied to a given discursive regime, as well as to other subjectivities that are permitted within a given regime (Foucault, 1988). Within discourse, the individual must adopt those comportments—embodied qualifications—that comply with the rules of discourse. The individual must perform her subjecthood in particular ways so as to be permitted to dwell within the discourse's parameters of recognition and so as to secure a status of coherency.

The emphasis on the self-making individual should not be confused with a radical free will. Any notion of radical freedom disappears with the recognition that there are limited subject positions available for habitation in a given discursive regime. Coming to inhabit a set subject position is necessary insofar as it, in Butler's words, "qualifies a body for life within the domain of cultural intelligibility" (Butler, 1993, p. 16). Through confessional technologies of the self, individuals thus become tied to the subject positions made available to them in a given discourse, subjectivities that qualify them with the privilege of cultural coherence and intelligibility. In this way, the discursive regime of human development that structures contemporary autism advocacy work gives birth to various historically and geopolitically defined subjectivities: the subject of the autism advocate as well as the subject in need of advocacy. In an effort to tease apart the particular constraints operating on the subject positions of (autism) 'advocate' and 'advocated for,' it becomes necessary to further examine the historical and geopolitical dimensions of the disciplinary discourses of developmentalism and to trace out the ways power is operating in and through these discourses.

Disciplining Development

The workings of power relations are heavily inscribed in the field of developmental psychology and in the material practices of intervention that are informed and authorized by it (education and special education; rehabilitation therapies; behavioral intervention; social work; and so on) (Burman, 2008; Dehli, 1994; Gilman, 1985; Goodley, 2010; Morss, 1990; Rose, 1989; Walkerdine, 1998). Insofar as it is imbued with the dominant (power-laden) empirical authority of biomedicine, the discourse of human development works creatively, following Foucault, via constraint or limitation, to produce particular phenomena. Human development is understood to be a descriptive account of developmental norms: naturally given normative benchmarks that are meant to represent, simply, how things are . . . how bodies ought to be at a given age. The result of what Haraway has termed a "god trick," the dominant story of human development is so often told *as if* it is the only possible one (Haraway, 1991, p. 584; Titchkosky, 2007).

Still, we might change our orientation to this thing called human development and look at it not as merely a given truth per se but rather as a "regime of truth" (Foucault, 1980). In other words, we might attend to human development as a discourse that is made in and by culture, as something that exists only insofar as it is always and inevitably organized by discrete, historically/geographically specific techniques and procedures that give it shape and meaning, bestow upon it particular value(s), and provide its very conditions of possibility. Orienting to human development not as a truth but as a regime of truth offers us new possibilities for thinking and theorizing the body as it appears among and in relation to other bodies (culture). With this orientation, the stages of human development can no longer be conceived of, strictly speaking, as either accurate or inaccurate objective descriptions of how bodies are at a given age. Rather, human development, taken as a regime of truth, can be theorized as one of many ways of talking about and understanding the body and its comportment: a story that is tied to and thus inseparable from our social relations and systems of power and knowledge.

I turn now to a deeper consideration of the ways power-knowledge relations are at work within the discursive field of human development. In this section, I draw on key critical development texts by Rose (1989), Walkerdine (1998), Gilman (1995), and McClintock (1995). Read together, their influential work shows how the discourse of development has been, and continues to be, thoroughly governed by the politics of class, sexuality, race, and gender, as well as by political systems and ideologies such as imperialism, colonization, nationalism and citizenship. Of course, a careful analysis of development discourse also requires a consideration of the ways this discourse is dependent upon constructs of disability. In the section that follows, I demonstrate some of the ways notions of disability coalesce with ideologies of race, class, gender, and sexuality in the cultural production of normal human development.

In *Governing the Soul*, Rose (1989) analyzes how relations of power underpin the emergence of developmental psychology as a category of inquiry and the positivistic accounts of normal and abnormal human development that developmental psychology relies upon. "A developmental norm," he writes, is

> a standard based upon the average abilities or performances of children of a certain age on a particular task or a specified activity. It, thus, not only present[s] a picture of what [is] normal for children of such an age, but also enable[s] the normality of any child to be assessed by comparison with this norm. (Rose, 1989, p. 145)

Developmental standards—paradoxically—both absolutely require and generate the need for acts of comparison between a given body and the empirically derived normal or 'standard' body. These acts of comparison, moreover, occur for a given body, not merely in relation to another 'standard' body, but rather the comparison is made between a given body and a ghostly myth—a conceptual assemblage of isolated aspects of normalcy along a temporal axis of age. It is only by way of comparison to this mythic average that individual children can be determined to be either normal for their age or not.

In *Governing the Soul*, Rose lays out a number of illustrations and photographs that document how the child became the focal center of psychiatry's normalizing gaze in the twentieth century. Rose argues that the scales, charts, photographs, arrays, and drawings depicting human development made the human visible and legible in new ways. According to Rose:

> Behavioural items that were characteristic and distinctive of different age levels were defined and organized into scales with specifications of the ages at which a given proportion of children could achieve the different levels on each scale. Non-intellectual behaviour was thus rendered into thought, disciplined, normalized, and made legible, inscribable, calculable. Norms of posture and locomotion; of vocabulary, comprehension, and conversation; of personal habits, initiative, independence, and play could now be deployed in evaluation and diagnosis. The discourse of development established a system of perception that was capable of grasping any feature of life that could be construed as changing over time. It grasped life in a form that could

be effected through a few simple operations: advanced or retarded? By how many months? In the table, life comes pre-digested, pre-calibrated, pre-normalized. (Rose, 1989, pp. 152–53)

In this way, the norm, via simultaneous processes of medicalization and moralization, was inaugurated and celebrated as the ideal. And, more than this, the norm was made natural.

Rose's work points to the inextricable connection between the emergence of notions of childhood development at the turn of the twentieth century and the contemporaneous emergence of notions of evolution: "Observations of young children could, it appeared, cast light upon the nature of human evolution and the characteristics distinguishing man from animals" (Rose, 1989, p. 145). The child, it was noted, grew and changed from infancy to adolescence in such a way that seemed to mimic the evolution of humans from a 'primitive' state to one of 'civility' (Francis Galton's claim that 'phylogeny recapitulates ontogeny') (Burman, 2008). Notions of natural evolutionary development (Darwin's 'survival of the fittest'), together with ideas about linear chronology and progress, combined to produce morally coded understandings of a developing human body that was either 'fit' or 'unfit,' 'advanced' or 'retarded,' 'savage' or 'civilized,' 'normal' or 'abnormal.' Inherent in developmental psychology's claim that children develop in a series of coherent, progressive, and naturally unfolding stages, which culminate in the attainment of that faculty reflective of ultimate human civilization—reason—is the inauguration of a deviant, un-natural, un-civilized, or, more succinctly, a degenerate subjectivity. The word 'degenerate'—from the Latin *degenus*—emphasizes an essential departure from 'good,' 'proper' and 'natural' biological/racial origins. As I explore in the remainder of this section, the subject position of the social degenerate—upon which any conceptualization of normal human development relies and, indeed, is premised—binds particular socially undesirable bodies together as problem bodies in need of remedial response. It also underscores the existence and persistence of power within the field of developmental psychology.

In her chapter "Developmental Psychology and the Child Centered Pedagogy," Valerie Walkerdine (1998) examines how systems of power/knowledge have provided the conditions of possibility that have given way to developmental psychology as a legitimized field of inquiry as well as a recognized scientific pedagogy. Walkerdine traces the history of the emergence of schooling as a kind of intervention, one possible solution to particular problem bodies, most notably in the 1800s, the degenerate bodies of the pauper and criminal (Walkerdine, 1998, p. 165). Critically, Walkerdine points out that both crime and pauperism were understood in terms of deteriorated or *underdeveloped* moral character, 'bad habits' that could be corrected by proper instruction/intervention (Dehli, 1994; Walkerdine, 1998). She writes: "It was this understanding of bad habits as the cause of crime and pauperism which led to the possibility of seeing popular education as the answer to the nation's ills, that is by the inculcation of good habits" (Walkerdine, 1998, p. 165). In this way, the development of civilized reason—a primary mandate of schooling—was put forward as the solution to various social problems (problem populations). The intervention of schooling, itself a civilizing project, enabled problem students to 'realize their potential,' to release, in other words, the possibility of their becoming 'good,' rational human beings. As the moralization of social problems (bodies with bad habits, immoral bodies) quickly blended with a medicalization of these same problem populations (underdeveloped bodies or pathologized bodies), the means of targeting these populations changed. Hence, argues Walkerdine, the psychologization of education (Walkerdine, 1998, p. 169).

Walkerdine traces this marriage of developmental psychology and pedagogy back to Darwin and the idea that developmental progress requires both the biomedical concern of suitable stock (heredity, for example, or contemporarily, genetics) and the moral preoccupation of ideal environmental conditions—nature and nurture. She writes:

> The movement which produces the individual as an object of science defined in terms of the twin poles of heredity and environment produces simultaneously the need for the development of scientific and empirical apparatuses and techniques of detection and some form of institutional provision which help produce and normalize such individuals. (Walkerdine, 1998, p. 170)

Normal human development, informed by the blending of moral and medical understandings of the body and conceived of, ironically, as 'natural,' became something to be facilitated or taught (Dehli, 1994). Humanness was made teachable, and necessarily so. The historical emergence of an understanding of 'well developed' or 'good' humanness as something that can and should be taught, holds great significance when held in tension with contemporary developmentalist discourses, discourses that pervade autism advocacy work and contemporary Western/

ized culture more generally. I unpack this significance later in the chapter, as I explore the generative effects of the common stipulation within discourses of autism advocacy that the ('good') advocate subject must engage in the task of working on (developing) the inherently under- (or 'badly') developed autistic subject.

The work of Rose (1989), Walkerdine (1998), McClintock (1995), Gilman (1985), and Burman (2008) demonstrates that what (and who) is considered a social problem is related to social, political, geographical, and historical contexts and thus changes with changing historical tensions and shifting power relations. Consider, for example, how development discourse emerged in the midst of European industrialization and colonialism (Burman, 2008). Walkerdine states that in the 1900s, the "concern with degeneracy finds expression in the necessity of building an 'imperial race' and the consequent concern for national efficiency, that is the building of an efficient workforce suitable to the development of the empire" (Walkerdine, 1998, p. 173). This understanding evokes multiple implications. The emphasis on strength and efficiency within the ranks of the imperial race require the (white, northern, European) citizenry of the metropole to, quite literally, 'measure up' to developmental expectations of the normative/natural human subject. The so-called degenerate white populations of the metropole (those who did not measure up to the standard—women, criminals, the 'insane' the 'feebleminded,' the 'crippled,' the 'poor,' 'prostitutes,' 'alcoholics,' 'homosexuals' and so on) were framed as necessitating early disciplinary intervention (be it psychological, pedagogical, and/or judiciary), aimed to facilitate normal human development and produce the respectable bourgeois body. "Degeneracy," in Walkerdine's words, "could be nipped in the bud, by regulating the development of children in order to ensure their fitness as adults" (Walkerdine, 1998, p. 170). Or at least in theory. Of course, this civilizing project was not without its failures; not all bodies are equally amenable to a pedagogical rehabilitation. In terms of their ability to pass as the respectable norm, bodies were differentially and hierarchically positioned. The body of an able-bodied, white, working-class child, for example, was better suited for (i.e., more compliant to) a normalizing pedagogy of development than the physically impaired body of a white, working-class child. In other words, some degenerate bodies were understood to be incapable of the norm; this is evident, for example, both in colonial conceptualizations of non-white Europeans and non-European people of color living in the colonies.

Anne McClintock (1995) describes how, in colonial times, bodies of color and indigenous bodies were—and insofar as colonization is an ongoing process, continue to be—conceptually imagined as anachronistic, residing in a "permanently anterior time within the geographic space of the modern empire as anachronistic humans, atavistic, irrational, bereft of human agency—the living embodiment of the archaic 'primitive'" (McClintock, 1995, p. 30). Of course, we need not look to the eighteenth century for examples of this kind of colonial logic that delivers the colonized body as a developmental anachrony. Consider, for example, the ubiquity and dominance of contemporary representations that depict indigenous people as always and already spectral, an antiquated remnant of more primitive times (Bergland, 2000).

The developmental perspective dominated (and continues to dominate) colonial rule, particularly through ideologies spawned by evolutionism (Foucault, 1997, p. 257). Colonial dominance was/is maintained through the surveillance and policing of all bodies, the sharpening of the boundaries separating normal from abnormal development and the recognition that departures and deviations from 'normal' (and, thus, always and already white, male, able-bodied, heterosexual, and middle-classed) development represented somatic *pathologies* (Gilman, 1985). Under colonial logic, people of color and indigenous people, queer, disabled and poor people, people classed as 'feebleminded,' 'insane,' 'crippled,' 'alcoholic,' 'prostitute' became conceptually linked through their purported pathological deviance from the esteemed status of 'fully' developed human (Gilman, 1985). The biomedical gaze that watches for and recognizes difference as pathology simultaneously inaugurates the necessity for biomedical/pedagogical interventions that aim to restore not simply health and but also civility.

When considering the interlocking nature of multiple oppressions, it is important to note that pathologize/d subjectivities (e.g., as we have seen, racialized bodies, gendered bodies, classed bodies, disabled bodies, and so on) are not equivalent or even comparable in any straightforward way. However, each process of oppression is implicated in the other, following Walkerdine, each "mak[es] and re-mak[es] the other possible, intertwining to produce a discursive and political nexus" (Walkerdine, 1998, p. 173). Understandings of the racialized body as a degenerate body, for example, are absolutely reliant on and, so, inseparable from simultaneous understandings of the (developmentally) disabled body. McClintock gestures toward the entangled nature of these subjectivities under colonial rule:

In the metropolis the idea of racial deviance was evoked to police the 'degenerate' classes—the militant working class, the Irish, Jews, feminists, gays and lesbians, prostitutes, criminals, alcoholics, and the insane—who were collectively figured as racial deviants, atavistic throwbacks to a primitive moment in human pre-history, surviving, ominously in the heart of the imperial metropolis. In the colonies, black people were figured, among other things, as gender deviants, the embodiments of prehistoric promiscuity and excess, their evolutionary belatedness evidenced by their 'feminine' lack of history, reason and proper domestic arrangements. (McClintock, 1995, pp. 43-44)

The work of Rose, Walkerdine, Gilman, McClintock, and others demonstrates, historically, how biomedical formulations of normal human development produce and reproduce colonial power relations of race, disability, class, gender, and sexuality.

As I explore in the next chapter, these relations continue to be embedded, albeit differently, in contemporary biomedical formulations of development work. This is evidenced, for example, in the global(ized) exportation of health and mental health standards (particularly to so-called 'underdeveloped' countries) by the World Health Organization (WHO) as a part of an ongoing 'development' process (Titchkosky and Aubrecht, 2009). As we shall see, the resonances between contemporary development work, histories of scientific racism, ableism, sexism and heterosexism, and ever-present and authoritative biomedical notions of progressive and normal human development cannot be separated, if for no other reason than the shared nomenclature of 'development' that can be found at the center of each of these projects and the ghostly myth of the (white, able-bodied, male, heterosexual, middle-classed) norm that is, inevitably, evoked and sustained by this nomenclature.

I begin my critical consideration of the use of developmentalism in autism advocacy by situating this discourse within these historical proximities not only to underscore the power-laden terrains that invariably structure any evocation of notions of development but also to begin to attend to the multiple ways that stories we have and tell about bodies (our own and those of others) are caught up in the very constitution of the category of the human. Any enterprise that draws upon and utilizes notions of human development—and mainstream autism advocacy is one such enterprise—must critically and ethically attend to the field's historical and present involvement in the production of such opposi-

tional categories as normalcy/abnormalcy, health/pathology, and to the conceptual associations that tie these categories to notions of progress/antiquity, reason/irrationality, civility/primitiveness, and so on. Moreover, in light of the multiple power relations that circulate through the discourse of developmental psychology, it becomes necessary to reflect on how this discourse is involved in the production of various medicalized/moralized subjectivities. I will now turn to two autism advocacy 'red flag' awareness posters—which I read as disciplinary mechanisms that draw on the disciplinary categories propagated by developmental psychology—and will consider how such dominant enactments of advocacy are implicated in regulatory processes that bear down, simultaneously, on both the individual under observation (the body of the potentially autistic) and the individual doing the observation (the body of the potential advocate).[2]

Raising the Red Flag

The metaphor of the red flag is commonly employed within advocacy discourse as a way of raising awareness about autism. Consider the following two different, and yet distinctly related, autism awareness posters, produced and circulated by two Western autism advocacy organizations. Both posters are exemplary of a whole genre of advocacy campaigns that I will refer to as red flag awareness campaigns.

I have chosen these two examples in particular—a poster from a prominent Canadian advocacy organization and one from the United Kingdom—not only to attend to their common message but also to demonstrate the pervasive, border-crossing nature of the message. Indeed, the notion that autism is simply a series of 'bad' (abnormal, pathological, underdeveloped, and so primitive) ways of behaving, acting, and interacting that require immediate corrective intervention, and the imperative that 'good' advocacy must intervene and correct autism's perceived abnormalcy are the two cornerstone assumptions of almost every autism advocacy organization operating in the Western/ized world today.

The first example is a poster, released in 2007 by the Canadian advocacy organization Autism Ontario (fig. 2). At the top of the poster there is a wide band, deep red in color, that stretches across the width of the poster and provides a background for the bolded header: "Red Flags for Autism." Just below this band of text are the words, "Parents should ask their child's family doctor for referral to a developmental pediatri-

Red Flags for Autism

Parents should ask their child's family doctor for referral to a developmental pediatrician if there are concerns with <u>any</u> of the following:

Communication Red Flags

- No babbling by 11 months of age
- No simple gestures by 12 months (e.g., waving bye-bye)
- No single words by 16 months
- No 2-word phrases by 24 months (noun + verb – e.g., "baby sleeping")
- No response when name is called, causing concern about hearing
- Loss of any language or social skills at any age

Behavioural Red Flags

- Odd or repetitive ways of moving fingers or hands
- Oversensitive to certain textures, sounds or lights
- Lack of interest in toys, or plays with them in an unusual way (e.g., lining up, spinning, opening/closing parts rather than using the toy as a whole)
- Compulsions or rituals (has to perform activities in a special way or certain sequence; is prone to tantrums if rituals are interrupted)
- Preoccupations with unusual interests, such as light switches, doors, fans, wheels
- Unusual fears

Social Red Flags

- Rarely makes eye contact when interacting with people
- Does not play peek-a-boo
- Doesn't point to show things he/she is interested in
- Rarely smiles socially
- More interested in looking at objects than at people's faces
- Prefers to play alone
- Doesn't make attempts to get parent's attention; doesn't follow/look when someone is pointing at something
- Seems to be "in his/her own world"
- Doesn't respond to parent's attempts to play, even if relaxed
- Avoids or ignores other children when they approach

To help your child succeed, help them to communicate.

- Autism is treatable and early intervention is critical.
- Enabling communication is an essential component of an intervention program.
- DynaVox Technologies offers a wide range of speech-output solutions that can help your child make meaningful connections with the world.

DynaVox
TECHNOLOGIES
Technology for human expression.

Contact your local DynaVox representative at 416-568-3342 or email danielle.franklin@dynavoxtech.com for more information. **Website:** www.dynavoxtech.com

Autism is treatable. Early intervention is critical.
Know the warning signs of autism in young children. Act early.

FOR MORE INFORMATION:
AutismONTARIO - Durham Region
Toll-free Phone/Fax: 1-866-495-4680
Email: durham@autismontario.com
Office: 21980 Highway 12, Sunderland, ON L0C 1H0
Website: www.autismontario.com/durham

AutismONTARIO
Durham Region

Fig. 2 Autism Ontario (2007) "Red Flags for Autism" poster. Poster originally published on Autism Ontario (Durham) website, 2007. Poster reproduced with permission from Autism Ontario.

cian if there are concerns with any of the following . . ." The poster, then, is divided into three subsections, three categories of red flags: "Communication Red Flags," "Behavioral Red Flags," and "Social Red Flags." Each of these subsections, like the title, appears against a deep red background.

Under each of the subheadings are bulleted lists describing the so-called red flags for autism: means of communicating, behaviors, and ways of socially interacting that, we can assume, signal autism's presence. For example, the bullets read, "no babbling by 11 months of age"; "no simple gestures by 12 months (e.g., waving bye-bye)"; "no 2-word phrases by 24 months (noun + verb—e.g., 'baby sleeping')"; "Odd or repetitive ways of moving fingers or hands"; "Lack of interest in toys, or plays with them in an unusual way (e.g., lining up, spinning, opening/closing parts rather than playing with the toy as a whole)"; "Does not play peek-a-boo"; "prefers to play alone"; and so on. In addition to the bulleted lists of various red flags, each subsection displays a different graphic depicting smiling children engaged in activities that appear in stark contrast to the red flag behaviors—the children depicted are playing together, making gestures to one another, playing with toys in conventional ways. One graphic shows a boy grinning as he holds up a frog to a grimacing girl. Another graphic shows a young smiling boy building a tower with his blocks. A third and final graphic shows two children happily playing together on a seesaw. Below the red flags and the graphics that accompany them appears a bright green band that highlights the statement: "To help your child succeed, help them to communicate." At the foot of the poster, there is a commercial advertisement for communication software[3] and several prescriptive statements, including: "Autism is treatable, early intervention is critical. Know the warning signs of autism in young children. Act early." The poster then directs you to the Autism Ontario website for more information.

Figure 3 represents yet another example of a red flag advocacy poster produced by the United Kingdom's National Autistic Society (NAS) (2008) (fig. 3). The NAS poster displays the bolded title: "Autism is . . ." Beneath this title, the text states that autism is

a lifelong developmental disability that affects how a person communicates with, and relates to, other people, and how they make sense of the world around them. It is a spectrum condition, which means that, while all people with autism share certain difficulties, their condition will affect them in different ways. Over 500,000 people in the UK have autism—that's one in a hundred. (NAS, 2010)

The poster features fourteen illustrated vignettes that depict stick figures engaged in various activities. Some stick figures appear alone, while others appear in the company of other stick figures or in the company of inanimate objects. The vignettes illustrating "some" of the possible "ways in which autism is displayed" (NAS, 2010) show, for example:

- A stick person sitting in a chair with a thought bubble and a speech bubble both containing the image of a train—the text narrates: "Talks incessantly about only one topic";
- A stick figure, on its knees, building a tower of teacups: "Lack of creative, pretend play";
- A stick figure flapping its arms: "bizarre behaviour";
- A smaller stick figure turning away from a taller one: "no eye contact."

Beneath the vignettes appears the statement: "Early diagnosis is essential if people with autism are to achieve their full potential. It is only when their disability is understood that they can be helped to maximize skills and minimize problems" (NAS, 2010). The small print at the bottom of the poster tells the viewer that it is an adaptation from an original from the University of Queensland in Australia, which further underscores the border-crossing nature of the poster's message (see also fig. 4 for a selection of examples of near identical posters written in Urdu, Hindi, Spanish, French, and English from organizations in Pakistan, Argentina, India, Belgium, and the United States). Finally, the poster's viewer can find the organization's contact information and their slogan, "accept difference, not indifference."

Peppered with prescriptions, rules of conduct, and bullet shaped flags, the posters lay out the field of possibility—the range of possible actions, choices, and responses—for both the advocate and the advocated for. At the same time, the posters support and sustain a hierarchy of power that positions the subjectivity of the nonautistic advocate over and against that of the autistic advocated for. The posters direct the eye of the potential advocate—the posters' imagined audience, namely the nonautistic parent, the teacher, the social worker, anybody who interacts regularly with children. They orient her stance, train her gaze, educate her in the rules of normalcy, always via its deviant double: abnormalcy.

Fig. 3 National Autistic Society (2008) poster "Autism is . . ." Poster available for sale on the National Autistic Society website, 2008. Please note that the poster is no longer representative of the organization's views on autism. The NAS has made many significant changes in how they are raising awareness about autism. For the most up-to-date awareness materials, please see the NAS website: www.autism.org.uk. Poster reproduced with permission from the National Autistic Society.

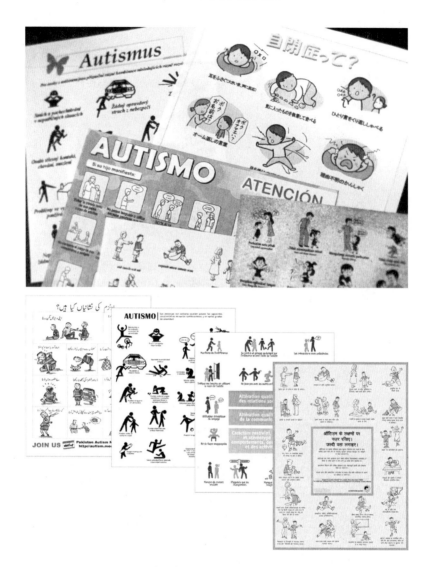

Fig. 4 International autism awareness posters. Photograph by Eduardo Trejos, 2011. Reprinted with artist's permission.

The posters simultaneously call up a very particular body of the advocated for, the autistic body, the body to be watched for—the body to which the flags point and of which the flags warn.

I have chosen to group both posters within the genre of red flag autism advocacy campaigns. The Autism Ontario poster (fig. 2) is an example of one of many advocacy campaigns that explicitly draws upon the metaphor of the red flag. While the red flag terminology is not explicitly mentioned in the NAS poster (fig. 3), as we shall see, the latter poster is functionally the same as the former, as it 'flags' possible developmental signs of autism and orients the viewer to recognize these signs as signs of developmental deviance, as signs to beware. "Images," writes Stuart Hall (2007), "do not carry meaning, or 'signify' on their own. They accumulate meanings, against one another, across a variety of texts and medias" (p. 232). The meaning of such autism posters is gained as they are "read in context, against and in connection with one another" (Hall, 2007, p. 232). The poster that lists signs of autism offers the viewer cues that belong to a visual culture where any *sign* of autism is implicitly narrated as a *warning sign*. In this way, the NAS poster need not overtly state that these signs are red flags; the viewer sees the signs of autism and, inevitably, sees red.

Patterns, Regularities (handwritten margin note)

Seeing the Signs

The autism red flag is raised by and branded with the immutable authority of the institution of biomedicine. While the potential advocate (i.e., the posters' intended audience) is perhaps not yet immediately familiar with the signs of autism being disseminated, they nonetheless immediately recognize the kind of textual document that is before them. The bulleted lists, the embodied warning signs, implicitly call up and reference that instrument of measurement so familiar in this historical moment and geopolitical space: the human developmental continuum.

While an explicit reference to the normal developmental continuum does not appear on the Autism Ontario poster—the poster does not say, for example, that the average infant waves 'bye-bye' at twelve months—this kind of explicit reference is not necessary for the poster's audience. The potential advocate is, inevitably, very familiar with its point of reference: what it is saying and the authority it holds. As Rose (1989) points out, developmental scales have been widely available and extensively disseminated since the 1920s and 1930s, found in psychology textbooks, parent books, teacher resources, and so on. In a contemporary digital age, the scales of development have gone viral. This rapid spread of information is, of course, due in large part to the inexhaustible resources of the World Wide Web. A Google search for "stages of normal childhood development," for example, yields over a hundred million hits in 0.4 seconds. Popular parent websites such as babycenter.com offer email listserves that send update messages to parents describing the 'normal' child's week-by-week developmental progress with email subject headings like "Is your baby walking?" or "Toddler developments: 10 red flags." The popularization of the digital camera and social networking sites have opened up new possibilities for parents to show, tell, and compare their child's developmental achievements[4] as well as new ways of documenting developmental concerns.

Companies are widely using notions of healthy development and developmental fitness to market their commercial products, particularly targeting the lucrative niche of anxious middle-class parents seeking to 'engineer' their children for 'excellence' (see Nadesan, 2002). Proper human development, in other words, has become a hot commodity. Take Juicy Juice, for example, a Nestle variety of fruit juice branded by the slogan "growing up healthy at every stage." Offering a range of juice products, including "Juicy Juice for Brain Development," the brand claims to help parents raise 'healthy' (i.e., neurologically/developmentally well developed) kids (*Juicy Juice*, 2010). In addition to purchasing 'brain juice,' parents can log on to the company's website and read up on the normal child development milestones, take a quiz about healthy childhood brain development, access expert advice from pediatricians, or print out high-contrast flashcards meant to stimulate their infant's brain development. Moving from the World Wide Web to the local shopping mall, children's books sold at major bookstore chains are arranged and shelved not according to similar themes or genres but according to the age-specific developmental skills that they might cultivate. Similarly, children's books and toys are now often sold with instructions for parents as to how to use the toy or book in such a way that best stimulates (ensures) normal child development. Of course, the success of these development products and marketing strategies rely on a consumer base that is already somewhat educated as to the scales and stakes of human development.

Rose underscores that this popularization and wide dissemination of the normal developmental continuum changes how we orient to the bodies of children, how we see and read them and therefore how we treat them. He writes: "All who dealt with children in their professional or personal life could now have their mind instructed through the education of their gaze" (Rose, 1989, p. 153). Developmental reference points—tables, charts, pictures, illustrations, and information—found anywhere from parent magazines to curriculum documents to juice cartons, educate us. Our gaze has been well trained. The cultural emphasis on the normal developmental continuum renders the body—and by the body I most certainly mean to include the mind!—visible in particular ways. The viewer of the red flag poster (the potential advocate) is directed to see and thus read the viewed (the potentially autistic) through a singular lens of biomedicine, the lens of developmental psychology. The essential dynamism of the body/mind—its uncertainty and mystery, its fluidity and unpredictability—is neutralized, tamed into an observable, knowable object-body. Some 'thing' that is and can be clearly seen and straightforwardly identified and managed.

The potential advocate, then, must learn to substitute her individual, subjective gaze with the all-seeing objective gaze of medicine. This gaze, as Foucault reminds us, is one "that [is] not bound by the narrow grid of structure (form, arrangement, number, size), but that could and should grasp colours, variations, tiny anomalies, always receptive to the deviant" (Foucault, 1975, p. 89). The potential advocate (e.g., the always nonautistic parent, the teacher, the social worker) must learn and take on the role of the medical expert in those spaces out of the reach of the doctor's gaze, those spaces outside the limits of the clinic; the 'good' advocate, then, becomes the doctor (i.e., the biomedical expert) of the home, the school, the office. Developmental psychology, and its central tool of observation and measurement, the continuum of normal human development, produces normative divisions among individuals whereby individuals (both the advocate and the advocated for) must either fall within the borders of the normal or are excluded from these borders. Divisions sprung from the effects of what Foucault terms "discipline-normalization" produce particular bodies not only as either normal or abnormal but, correspondingly, as 'right' or 'wrong,' 'good' or 'bad' (Foucault, 2003, p. 52).

"In discipline," writes Foucault, "punishment is only one element of a double system: gratification-punishment" (Foucault, 1979, p. 180). Moreover, these two poles are situated at the nexus of political and moral constraints and, so, take on hierarchical meaning in relation to one another: 'good' becomes aligned with dominant normative acts and expectations and 'bad' with deviation from this norm. Under disciplinary power, Foucault reminds us, proximity to the norm is invariably rewarded, valorized (and therefore constructed as permissible, moral, desirable, and even natural) while deviation from the norm is punished, marginalized (and constructed as immoral, undesirable, unnatural, and even criminal). Graham and Slee (2008) remind us, "normalization is a man made grid of intelligibility that attributes value to culturally specific performances, and in doing so, privileges particular ways of being" (p. 86). In the context of the red flag poster, both the advocate and the advocated for are bound up in the effects of discipline-normalization.

The advocate who performs or approximates a normalized and normalizing version of advocacy is inscribed/recognized as a 'good' advocate. However, the advocate who does not or cannot approximate the normative demands of advocacy—namely the advocate with non-normative aims, beliefs, values, or the advocate with a non-normative body or mind—is discursively cast out of the frames of advocacy altogether, inscribed as a 'bad' advocate or is not recognized as engaging in advocacy work at all. In the blog post "The De-legitimization of Autistic Voices" on autistichoya.com, Lydia Brown writes: "de-legitimization is the name for what happens when people, usually but not always non-Autistics, attempt to remove any legitimacy from the words or opinions of the Autistic person, so that that voice is rendered silent and unheard, so that that voice is not lent credence or granted validity" (Brown, 2012). Indeed, notions of 'bad' or 'improper' advocacy have long worked to de-legitimize the advocacy work of autistic self-advocates and activists (Brown, 2012; Yergeau, 2013; Ne'eman, 2010). As is exemplified by the red flag poster campaigns, mainstream autism advocacy often promotes the idea that the true or authentic autistic is trapped within him/herself, unable to effectively socially interact or communicate. As many autistic self-advocates and activists have described, autistics who do challenge dominant discourses of advocacy are often denied their authenticity as 'true' autistics and therefore are not considered to be in an authoritative position to do the work of autism advocacy (Sinclair, 2012; Baggs, 2012; Brown, 2012; Yergeau, 2010). As Zisk poignantly puts it in her poem "I Hid": "I know I'll be 'too autistic' to understand, until 'I'm not autistic enough'" (Zisk, 2012).

The effects of discipline-normalization also bear down on the subject of the advocated for. The autistic subject that is successful at performing or approximating the normative signs of human development is rewarded with the insecure and ever-precarious status of the good or near 'fully' developed human. By contrast, the autistic subject who does not, cannot, or chooses not to approximate these norms—the subject who betrays 'red flag' behaviours, responses, movements—is punished and framed as a bad or 'under' developed human. I want to be careful, however, to not set up a straightforward binary here. As I discuss in greater detail throughout the latter half of this book, the space between the human and the nonhuman is, at once, porous and slippery: an insecure space of incremental advances and recessions. Whether the autistic subject is inscribed as 'nearly' developed or 'under' developed, developmental discourses always situate the autistic subject as partially developed, and thus as not fully human. As Yergeau's (2013) work on Theory of Mind so clearly demonstrates, rhetorically speaking, the category of autism is framed by developmentalism as a state of nonhumanness. The question, in other words, is never 'is this autistic subject fully developed?' but rather, 'to what degree is the subject developed?' and 'how quickly are they advancing along normative developmental timelines?' While autistic approximations of developmental typicality are no doubt socially and materially rewarded, and normative deviations punished, both extremes are, in different ways, precarious. Developmentalist discourses frame the autistic subject in need of advocacy as a kind of development project, the autistic body becomes understood as 'develop-able.' The autistic is, in other words, framed as one who needs to be taught humanness (or normative, developmental versions of humanness). As we saw in the historical examples from earlier in this chapter and as I demonstrate in the chapters to come, to be cast as someone who needs to be taught humanness, as someone who remains tenuously tethered to that vital category, is always to be at risk of losing human status altogether.

Recalling Foucault, disciplinary power is transformative—it alters individuals, it propels us in the making of our selves. Through discipline, the individual's conduct is made knowable by both the self and other in relation to a distribution of possible conducts anchored by oppositional and hierarchical poles of 'good' or 'bad'. As a way to highlight the insidiousness of disciplinary power and its technologies of the self, Foucault draws on Bentham's panoptic prison—the architectural structure that makes it possible for the observer (the warden, the doctor, the teacher, the supervisor) to observe and scrutinize inmates (prisoners, patients, school children, workers) at all times, all the while making it impossible for inmates to know whether/when they are actually being monitored. In the panopticon, following Foucault (1979), "visibility is a trap" (p. 196). In the central tower, the prison guard watches out over a surrounding ring of single-celled inmates: "the panoptic mechanism arranges spatial unities that make it possible to see constantly and to recognize immediately" (Foucault, 1979, p. 196). From his central vantage point, the prison guard is all-seeing but also unseen. The inmate, unable to see the prison guard, only sees himself through the gaze of his observer. Foucault writes: "the panopticon is a machine for dissociating the see/being seen dyad: in the peripheric ring, one is totally seen, without ever seeing; in the central tower, one sees everything without ever being seen" (Foucault, 1979, p. 196). Foucault proposes that, under presumed scrutiny, the inmates become hyper-aware of their every movement, action, gesture and eventually begin to come to know, surveil, and ultimately police their own behaviors. Observable signs of deviance are, first, monitored and then gradually controlled and corrected by the self. Foucault writes: "The perpetual penalty that traverses all points and supervises every instant in the disciplinary institutions compares, differentiates, hierarchizes, homogenizes, excludes. In short, *normalizes*" (Foucault, 1979, p. 183).

Processes of normalization are enacted via the 'trap of visibility' in several different ways in the red flag poster. The poster is, indeed, the site where multiple gazes converge. First, there is the gaze of the potential advocate, the imagined viewer of the poster. The red flag poster directs and instructs the gaze of the potential advocate to *look at* the behaviors, actions, and interactions of all children, but most importantly to *look for* a particular set of non-normative behaviors, actions, interactions that may require further intervention, that is to say, more looking. This 'more looking' reveals yet another gaze that is present at the scene of the poster: the gaze of the doctor, the developmental specialist, the medical expert. As the poster says: "parents should ask their child's family doctor for a referral to a developmental pediatrician if they are concerned with any of the following . . ." (fig.2). While the intimacy of the potential advocate's (i.e., the parent, the teacher, the social worker) particular vantage point (i.e., the home, the school, those spaces outside of the clinic) is crucial to the process of seeing abnormal development, her gaze is not sufficient.

Expanding on Foucault's metaphor of the panopticon, the child-object exists in the ultimate peripheric ring: the child's every behavior, action, and interaction is seen by the advocate, but the child remains unseeing. As I discussed earlier, the autistic subject here is conceptually forbidden from autism observation. The panoptic space of the red flag poster, however, adds another peripheric ring to its disciplinary mechanism, as the advocate watches the child, she too is watched from the central tower of biomedicine: the advocate sees the unseeing child, but she must also see herself, for biomedicine sees all—the advocate watcher, the watched child—and is always unseen. The asymmetrical flow of visibility secures the biomedical gaze as a way of seeing that is not required to see itself (Michalko, 1998). For the remainder of this chapter, I focus my analytic sights against this grain of panoptic visibility. I will look not

[handwritten marginal note: Biomedical gaze]

at the bodies being looked at but rather at the (normative) processes of looking: the gaze of biomedicine and the gaze of advocacy that are always, following Foucault, "receptive to the deviant" (Foucault, 1975, p.89). Such gazes come into focus at the scene of the red flag poster and are caught up, as we shall see, in the very constitution of the human.

Be Aware

There can be little doubt that instruction is a significant intent, function, and effect of the red flag poster. The poster, in other words, acts as a pedagogical tool; it gives the viewer an education that is at once medical (i.e., the poster provides a list of clinical signs and symptoms of developmental disorder) and moral (i.e., it frames particular comportments as threatening/dangerous). One thing the poster teaches its viewer is to become visually literate in the understanding that bodies are readable, and thus knowable, by attentive observation to the signs they emit. The red flag poster teaches the potential advocate to be aware of autism's red flags and, in so doing, it teaches the potential advocate how to look. In the Autism Ontario poster (fig. 2), red bands of color stretch across the top of the poster highlighting, for the potential advocate, where to look. 'Stop,' the red bands on the Autism Ontario poster tell the advocate.[5] 'Look here,' direct the iconic stick figures in the NAS poster (fig. 3). 'Look closely,' for as the Autism Speaks' First Signs website reminds us, the signs of autism "can be subtle or, to the untrained eye, easy to miss" (First Signs Inc., 2010, para. 2). Arrest your gaze on the bodies of children. Will their gaze return yours? When their bare feet make contact with the rough texture of freshly cut grass, see if their toes recoil or relish. Focus on how people move, how they act, how they interact, how they fear. Observe them as they are at play:[6] Are they interacting enough with other people? Are they interacting too much with (the wrong kinds of) objects?

'Watch,' the posters tell the potential advocate, but only if you embody normalcy. For it is normalcy, the posters point out, that is endowed with the power of the qualification to see. Abnormalcy is unseeing—deviance can and must only be seen—it does not possess the qualification to dwell within the limits of the space of the see-er. Autism is not qualified to see itself. The Autism Ontario poster depicts the faces of normative children conforming to the (already, we can note, gendered, raced, classed, sexed, disabled) stages of normal childhood development. A grimacing girl makes a gender normative gesture of distaste to a grinning boy with a toad: she is, we are to assume, 'grossed out' by 'boy stuff.' A smiling white boy exercises the power that comes with the capacity for coherent and recognized acts of creativity as he builds a tower, in a developmentally suitable way, with blocks (and not with teacups, as in fig. 3). A light-skinned boy and a dark-skinned girl play together on a seesaw, laughing and gesturing to each other, ever maintaining the neatness of a contemporary normative demand for a multicultural diversity of representations and the equally normative requirement that diversity can be included only if it affirms and supports the image of normalcy. Of course, an image of a girl child, a brown child, (and/or perhaps even a disabled child) can appear as images of normalcy, so long as these images conform to and uphold the ideal of white, male, heterosexual, middle-class, able-bodied normalcy.

The smiling faces of normativity in the Autism Ontario poster provide a striking contrast, when juxtaposed with the absent faces of deviance. The normative children in the Autism Ontario poster face the viewer, while abnormalcy is represented only with faceless bullets, textual descriptions of deviance. In the NAS poster, too, the faces of abnormalcy are missing, obscured, shaded—they do not and cannot face the potential advocate. The faceless bodies depicted in the NAS poster cannot look back at their viewer, as their abnormal bodies are presented only to be seen. Autism does not possess the qualification to see itself for it does not have the qualification of normalcy. In this way, the red flag poster requires that the looker—the potential advocate—must embody normalcy. One significant implication here is that this field of advocacy, peppered by red flags, leaves little room for autistic self-advocates. As we have seen, the posters provide a landscape of what the potential advocate must see when she looks at children. However, the posters also provide a legend so that the potential advocate may orient herself in this new landscape of autism. The posters not only instruct the advocate where s/he must look, but *how* to look, not only how to see, *but how to read* (Titchkosky, 2007). The posters not only tell the viewer that they must be aware, but also that they must *be wary*.

Be Wary

While all bodily signs must be *watched* for potential pathology (a medical imperative), so-called signs or red flags of autism must be *watched out* for (a moral imperative). In this way, the red flag poster gives birth to a very particular (and necessarily watchable) medically/morally deviant subjectivity in need of advocacy: the subject of the autistic. The Autism Ontario poster, for example, provides the key to decode the meanings of various ways of communicating, of behaving, of socially interacting. The poster shows potential advocates how to 'read' autism—its shape, its landmarks—as nothing more than primitive and pathological deviance, a state of pathological *under*development. The fluttering of fingers can no longer be a way of moving, of experiencing space, of interacting, of expressing anxiety, or of showing excitement. Preferring to play alone is no longer a viable option. In the presence of the red flag poster, the excited, angry, upset, or calm choreography of fingers fluttering is simultaneously medicalized and moralized: re-encoded as "[an] odd or repetitive way of moving fingers." The quiet play of a lone child in a busy playground is now seen as a pathological sign pointing not to personal choice or preference or even to social exclusion but to (medical/moral) deviance.

Consider yet another example of this process of transforming difference into deviance. In the two posters exemplified in this chapter, the autistic subject is encoded as, simultaneously, excess and lack. James I. Porter (1997) writes:

> Viewed in itself . . . a disabled body seems somehow too much a body, too real, too corporeal, it is a body that, so to speak, stands in its own way. From another angle which is no less reductive, a disabled body appears to lack something essential, something that would make it identifiable and something to identify with; it seems too little a body: a body that is deficiently itself, not quite a body in the full sense of the word, not real enough. (p. xiii)

The red flags point to autism, following Porter, as both 'too much' and 'not enough.' Autism is seen as either empty presences (a body that is somehow more than a normal body—a body abnormal in its excess: "*inappropriate* giggling"; "*over*sensitive to certain textures"; "talks *incessantly*"), or excess absences ("*no* babble," "*no* gestures," "*no* eye contact," "*no* response"; "*lack* of creative play" and so on). Of course, the absent (and yet in its absence very present) referent inherent in these observational moral qualifications of too much/not enough is the body of normalcy that is, we must presume, 'just right.' In this way, the red flag poster overtly points to 'bad' deviations from the developmental norm (too much/not enough), and thus invariably reenforces the 'good' requirements for normalcy (just right).

Let us finally note how the poster is also, perhaps more covertly, engaged in enforcing the boundaries of what can be recognized as a good advocate. The normal or good viewer of the red flag poster—the good parent or teacher, the respectable autism advocate—must, as we have seen, direct her gaze in chorus with the demands of the poster, and so the demands of the biomedical institution of developmental psychology. Under the powerful guidance of biomedicine, the good autism advocate must watch and worry about her watching, as she watches and worries about her children. In the midst of watching (being aware) and worrying about (being wary) normal/abnormal development, the potential advocate is, finally, positioned by the red flag poster to see autism as something that inherently signals danger, something to be feared, something against which we must be warned—some 'thing' to *beware*.

Beware

The red flag metaphor is a well-established one in the contemporary West; its symbolic meanings are widely accessible as a matter of common sense. We are very literate as to the cultural significance of the red flag, aware of its demands. The evocation of the red flag references a variety of meaningful scenarios and, in so doing, weaves together several different, yet related, meanings. Faced with the metaphor of the red flag, we might be put in mind of the red cloth waved by a matador inciting the bull to charge or the red banner raised by the revolutionary as a call to revolt, insurrection. The red flag metaphor evokes the image of the socialist raising the flag, rallying the working class, or the sailor hoisting the red pennant, as a warning of rough waters ahead. We are reminded of the crimson standard raised by the soldier in a cry of battle. At once, the evocation of the red flag incites, provokes, defies, decries, and warns. And in the midst of all of these demands . . . autism.

Although the NAS poster makes no explicit use of the red flag metaphor to orient and instruct the viewer in the ways of looking, it succeeds in accomplishing the same effect through its use of the icon of the stick figure. The stick figures that appear on this poster are quite familiar; these figures are ubiquitous in everyday life. We often see the stick figure crossing the street, slipping on wet floors, falling off ladders, minding the gap, and, if the figure appears using a wheelchair, perpetually pointing to a more accessible space (Titchkosky, 2011). Indeed, the stick figure used in this poster is perhaps most famous for his appearances on directional/instructional signage, traffic signs, and caution/warnings signs.

The stick figure represents the universal figure. It is meant to be gender-less, race-less, class-less, age-less (although, admittedly, the figure does sometimes appear wearing a particular accessory—a skirt, a hard-hat, a wheelchair—depending on the regulatory function of the sign). Due to this absence of identificatory features, the default figure serves to 'stand' for the neutral 'any-body.' Any-body can cross this street. Any-body must mind the gap. Any-body can use this washroom. Any-body can do any of these things, that is, so long as these any-bodies conform to the regulatory stipulations of the spaces that the sign marks (i.e., we intuitively know that not just any-body can use the nonaccessible women's washroom, for example). And so we know a few things about the appearance of an any-body. We know, for example, that its appearance is almost always an instance of regulation. Typically, the any-body appears on caution signs (e.g., the icon of the figure slipping on 'wet floor' signs) or directional signs (e.g., the standing, skirted washroom icon indicating where to access the woman's washroom). In both these examples, however, when this figure makes its appearance it is in order to issue a warning to its viewer, a red flag. The any-body slipping on the wet floor issues an overt warning: 'Attention! Be careful! Proceed with caution! You may be in danger!' The standing, skirted washroom icon issues the perhaps more subtle warning that only particular types of bodies are welcome, or more correctly, permitted within. To be permitted entrance into those spaces marked by the regulatory any-body of the standing, skirted washroom icon, we know we must possess certain qualifications.

Let us return now to the any-bodies marking the NAS poster. Recall, for example, the any-body, looking away from another any-body ("no eye contact"). Or the any-body flapping its arms ("bizarre behavior"). As these figures appear in a context of a whole genre of stick figures whose task is to warn, the poster's viewer is already—upon first look—oriented to see the stick figures and the (autistic) behaviors they denote as red flag warnings. Far from embarking on a project of "accept[ing] difference," as per the NAS slogan, the organization's poster issues a warning against certain unwelcome behaviors, actions, and interactions. In so doing, the poster reinforces which types of people are welcome or indeed are qualified to exist within the normative space of the social. As designer Eric Lewallen points out in "A History of the Stick Figure": "That little, iconic, round-headed fellow on signs [. . .] makes us think twice before taking the wrong door, or helps us so we don't really need to think at all" (Lewallen, 2008, para. 2). The stick figure helps us think twice, or not at all. Indeed, the same can be said of any warning sign. Or insofar as the function of the warning sign is to issue an alert that can be quickly and universally understood and promptly acted upon, the warning sign *makes us think twice until we don't have to think at all*. Forms of knowledge and ways of knowing here merge with the object of knowledge (Rose, 1989, p. 150). The red flag poster, the poster that functions to raise awareness, asks its viewer to notice—to think twice about—behaviors, actions, interactions. However, once the potential advocate's awareness is raised, once, to borrow from Paul Gilroy (2000), her "sensorium" has been "educated," the mere appearance of the red flag behavior is enough to 'naturally' change the behaviors, actions, and interactions of the advocate: the 'good' advocate sees the signs of autism and, without having to think at all, she is poised to act against it (p. 42).

As we learn to beware of certain bodies, certain actions, certain gestures, we also learn something about what these bodies, actions, gestures represent and it is here where we might glean just how the red flag advocacy poster is engaged in producing and constraining the limits of the compulsory human. Warnings are never issued for something we value, a condition that we would like to have in our collective life. Weather warnings are not issued for pleasant, sunny days with gentle breezes. Warnings, we know, warn against something undesirable: flood warnings, terror warnings, pandemic warnings, and so on. It is in this intertextual space of danger and warning that autism is made to appear. In the discursive field of the red flag poster, autistic development is not conceived of as good development, and therefore is framed up as incomplete (human) development.

Seeing Red

As Marx reminds us in the opening epigraph, comportment is altered at the sight of the red flag. The "old world writhed in convulsions of rage," he says, at the mere glimpse of a waving piece of crimson cloth. We see the flag and our comportment changes. As vigilance is performed and as the signs of developmental deviance are noticed, the potential advocate slides into the position of good advocate. The subject of the good advocate, then, made in the moment of seeing difference/deviance, is poised to act in a particular and constrained way: see flags, see autism. See autism, see danger. See autism, see red.

In their analysis of the visual rhetorics of the color red and its persistent representational association with autism, Diehl et al. write:

> At a physiological level, the perception of red initiates a high galvanic skin response, and is thought to elicit anxiety (Jacobs & Seuss, 1975; Weller & Livingston, 1988; Wilson, 1966). Red is often used as a warning of danger, as in stop signs, traffic lights, or most recently the U.S. Department of Homeland Security's recently abandoned color-coded system for conveying terrorist threat level. Further negative connotations to red can be observed in diverse phrases, such as *in the red, seeing red, red tape, red herring, red faced, code red, red flag,* and *red-handed* (e.g., Elliot & Maier, 2007; Elliot et al., 2007; Pryke, Andersson, Lawes, & Piper, 2001; Setchell & Wickings, 2005). (Diehl et al., 2011, n.p.)

If the color red alone denotes warning and danger, the autism red flag mingles this danger with a sense of urgency. The red flag is a call to action or even a call to arms. In the shadow of the red flags that point to autism as pathological underdevelopment, the advocate is positioned to 'see red' and, in seeing red, to stand on guard, as if a sailor warned of rough waters ahead; to charge forward as if a bull barreling toward the matador's flag; and to fight as if a soldier being called to battle. *The viewer sees the flag and their comportment changes. See the flag. Sense the danger. Act now.*

Red flag posters affect a call to action that targets the very object under scrutiny: autism or autistic ways of being. Within the discursive space of red flag advocacy, the advocate subject's only intelligible choice is to swiftly and surely strike out against autism, to seek out medical doctors to treat its signs, to seek out interventions to diminish or eliminate all traces of autism's embodied difference, to ensure normalcy. See a developmental pediatrician, the poster tells the potential advocate, arrange intervention, eliminate conspicuous or even flagrant behaviors. The visual rhetoric of the red band of color in the Autism Ontario poster tells the potential advocate that danger is ahead, while below, a green band of color underscores the need for swift and immediate action: "Autism is treatable. Early intervention is critical." Similarly, the stick figures in the NAS poster function to flag danger, while the text at the bottom of the poster directs action. "Early diagnosis is essential," says the NAS poster, "*if* people with autism are to achieve their full potential. It is only when their disability is understood that they can be helped to maximize skills and minimize problems" (NAS, 2010, my emphasis). This is the rhetoric of early intervention and prevention and it runs deep in Western culture. Early intervention logic is fairly straightforward and sounds a lot like the turn of the century imperative to "nip degeneracy in the bud" (Walkerdine, 1998, p. 170). It goes something like this: when faced with disorder or its potential, however remote, we as individuals and as a society must take preventative/remedial action now—the earlier, the better!—so as to minimize the disordered element and ensure a better, more healthy future for all. Face to face with an imminent danger gestured toward by the appearance of the stick figure, the potential advocate is directed to seek an early diagnosis of autism for their child so as to ensure equally early interventions are attained to help, to borrow the language of the poster, "maximize" so-called developmentally appropriate or neurotypical skills and "minimize" red flag/autistic "problems" so as to, ultimately, allow the child to reach his or her "full potential."

I want to take a moment to highlight this rhetoric of 'potentiality' raised by both posters. The NAS poster makes very clear the common social understanding that human development is human potential. In the absence of early intervention and normative developmental progression, the autistic subject is thus framed as, inherently, without potential. Still, even as the poster re/presents autism as a naturally and inevitably unsuccessful human embodiment—a lack of potential—it simultaneously *promises* that potentiality is possible. While the red flags cry out: 'here goes the not-yet (developed) human,' the rhetoric of early diagnosis and intervention does the work of saying: 'maybe one day.' Not unlike the civilizing project of schooling from the nineteenth century, contemporary notions of early intervention are infused with the promise that humanness, if not born, can at least be developed . . . taught. Contemporary advocacy discourses offer the hope that with the proper (read: individualized, biomedical) intervention (ranging, for example, from doctor approved food products to biomedically endorsed therapies[7]) any body's potential for (full) human development can be released. Indeed, modern medicine and its therapeutic offshoots tell us that any body can meet or even exceed the norm (Nadesan, 2002). The notion of the changing and changeable, *improvable*, developing body as something to be watched, measured, and, should the body fail to measure up, corrected or enhanced, *seems* to open up possibility, but does it really?

The Developing Human and the Human Developer

Judith Butler writes critically about how certain lives are—through mediated frames of recognition and interpretation—made to fall outside of the limitations of a normative notion of what the human must be . . . lives that, by way of various discursive strategies and within multiple systems of oppression, are not regarded as human life, or are fashioned even as nonhuman life (Butler, 2004a; Butler, 2009). Of course, to be recognized as a human life that is 'not-quite-a-life' is to be placed in a precarious position indeed, and I will explore this further in the chapters to follow (Butler, 2004a, p. 34). While the red flag poster is clearly engaged in narrating the autistic life as 'not-quite-a-human-life,' the posters, and developmental discourses more broadly, are doing something other than setting up a straightforward distinction between human life and nonhuman life. The body to which the flags point and of which the flags warn is not a body that has simply fallen outside of human development and therefore outside of that space in which human life is and can be recognized. Rather, as we have seen, amidst red flags the autistic body is targeted as failing to develop *fully*. It is narrated, variously, as a *nearly* or *under*-developed body, unsuccessful (to a greater or lesser extent) at following the progressive, rigid stages of human development. The not-quite-a life of autism is delivered by the red flag campaign, then, not so much as a nonhuman subjectivity but as the intermediary subjectivity of the 'not-yet' human. Via simultaneous processes of medicalization and moralization, the poster implicitly promises that (normal or 'good') humanness, while not implicit, can be helped along, developed. Or, at least, this is the promise.

A qualification like any other, developmental normalcy, the posters promise, can be earned, or to borrow the language from the NAS poster, "*achieved*," but always and only within certain normative parameters. 'Full' humanity can only emerge, the poster reminds us, as autism is made to disappear completely. And so here we have the birth of a subject that must never be left alone until it fulfills the impossible promise of being "indistinguishable from [its] normal friends," to quote Dr. Ole Lovaas, whose Applied Behavioral Therapy is widely considered best practice for treating autism. With the promise of a develop-able human life, the subject position of the good advocate is framed as both the vigilant surveiller of human deviance ('look for warning signs') and a human developer whose vital aim is to 'act early' with the aim of facilitating normal human development. To teach humanness, as it were.

Throughout this chapter, we have seen that in order to secure the status of good/recognizable advocate—and therefore in order for it to be possible to do advocacy and be an advocate—the advocate must subscribe to and enact a normal and normalizing version of advocacy. Already possessing (and, always, always performing) the prerequisite qualification of normalcy, the good/recognizable advocate must learn to see autistic nonnormativity, to worry about it, to read it as danger. The contemporary autism advocate is always and already poised to act as a defender of normalcy, and so she is always and already poised to fight that which threatens normalcy: autism.

Autism's possibility is tangled up in the possibility of autism advocacy. Under the rule of normal human development, the only possible way for the autistic subject to be read as a good or at least nearly developed human is to learn, approximate, and perform normalcy. However, let us return once again to Sinclair's (1993) crucial intervention. "Autism is not an appendage," he reminds us, and thus cannot merely be removed from an autistic person (Sinclair, 1993, np). Autism is "pervasive," says Sinclair, a way of being in and moving through the world (Sinclair, 1993, np). Without autism there is no autistic person. Without autism there is no person. The promise of early interventions and developmental understandings of autism more broadly orients us toward a normative or nonautistic horizon of potentiality, a horizon that, for an *autistic person,* can never fully be reached. In this way, the autistic subject is configured within autism advocacy discourse and via notions of normal or natural human development, always, as the *not-yet (never-yet?)* human (Yergeau, 2013).

A body—whether it be the body of the advocate or the body of the advocated for—that does not, cannot, or chooses not to perform normalcy is a body that finds itself a kind of outlaw, cast outside the limits of possibility and potentiality. While related, of course, the material consequences of this "casting out" (Razack, 2008) differ as we move from advocate subjectivity to autistic subjectivity. While the advocate who moves outside advocacy's normative frames of recognition is at risk of being delegitimized and/or excluded from participation in recognized works of advocacy, the autistic body that (who) does not, cannot, or chooses not to perform or approximate normal human development risks being cast out from the ever exclusionary space of the human. Such an exclusion, as I will explore in the chapters to come, is also and necessarily a matter of life and death.

CHAPTER THREE

Act NOW

The S/pace of Advocacy in a Temporality of Urgency

———⌒⌒———

"This week is the week America will fully wake up to the autism crisis. If three million children in America one day went
missing—what would we as a country do? If three million
children in America one morning fell gravely ill—what would
we as a country do? We would call out the Army, Navy, Air Force
and Marines. We'd call up every member of the National Guard.
We'd use every piece of equipment ever made. We'd leave no
stone unturned [. . .] This is a national emergency."
   —Suzanne Wright (2013), "Autism Speaks to Washington—A
   Call for Action"

"The voluntary creation of a permanent state of emergency has
become one of the essential practices of the contemporary state."
   —Giorgio Agamben (2005), *State of Exception*, p. 2

"There's no time to think . . . ."
   —Bob Dylan, (1978), "There's No Time to Think"

In the summer of 2007, one of the many places where one could learn
about autism and autism advocacy was on the side of a special series of
paper Starbucks coffee cups. The over five million cups that were put
into circulation across North America displayed a statement from Bob
Wright, the founder of the self-proclaimed world's largest autism advocacy organization, *Autism Speaks*. Wright's statement read as follows:

> Every 20 minutes—less time than it will take you to drink your coffee—
> another child is diagnosed with autism. It's much more common than
> people think, with one out of every 150 children diagnosed. Learn
> the early warning signs of autism, and if you're concerned about your
> child's development, talk to your doctor. Early intervention could
> make a big difference in your child's future. (Autism Speaks, 2007)

What meaning might we make of knowledge expressed on the sides of
cardboard coffee cups? 'Every 20 minutes.' 'Early intervention.' '1 in
150.' A venti latte, no foam, two warnings, and a prescription. How do
these words, these numbers, come to matter? How do they make matter the bodies they grasp as well as the bodies that, quite literally, grasp
them? While these particular Starbucks cups tell us a great many things,
one thing is certain: they tell us that a striking relationship exists between
autism, advocacy, time, and consumption.

In his Starbucks cup statement, Wright characterizes autism in terms
of 'warning signs' and 'concerning' development—a state of being off-
tempo with the normative meter of human development. Late development. Missed milestones. And just as autism is narrated as a state of
being stuck in the infantile past, its meaning, simultaneously, becomes
enmeshed in notions of futurity: autism's developmental anachrony,
Wright informs us, is concerning precisely because it threatens all the
possibilities the future holds. What is more, instances of autism's 'too
slow' development, the statement tells us, are happening too fast. "Every
20 minutes," Wright reminds us, "*another* child is diagnosed" (*my emphasis*). The speed at which autism is happening is underscored by numerical measurements of its prevalence: "it's much more common than people think," the coffee cup reminds us, "with 1 out of every 150 children
diagnosed."

The ticking time clock that counts down appearances of autism delivers autism advocacy, too, as a function of time. Wright's statement addresses the potential autism advocate in the imperative. It says: "Learn the
early warning signs of autism, and if you're concerned about your child's
development, talk to your doctor." Now is the time for immediate action,
the coffee cup suggests. Act now for the earlier autism's warning signs
are noticed and identified, the faster (biomedical) help can be enlisted
to remediate autism's developmental untimeliness: "early intervention
could make a big difference in your child's future." Evoking understandings of lingering pasts and eclipsed futures, 'too fast' appearances of 'too
slow' bodies, late milestones and early interventions, Wright's Starbucks

cup statement demonstrates how the meaning of autism and advocacy get tied together by the ticking of the second hand.

This chapter attempts to look to—or 'get with'—our times by performing a reading of several cultural artifacts, ranging from the mundane—a disposable coffee cup—to the spectacular—an international resolution and a presidential pronouncement. I demonstrate how such artifacts function as prolific, productive, and powerful sites of meaning-making that have much to teach about the cultural meanings we ascribe to specific embodied subjectivities, particularly the subjects of the 'advocate' and the 'advocated for' within neoliberal discourses of autism. To frame neoliberalism as a time is to consider it as, at once, a particular historical moment—an economic system of governance of the late twentieth and early twenty-first centuries with characteristic emphasis on privatization, individual responsibility, and the unrestricted flow of capital—and as a tempo—a political rationality that manages the movement of bodies in time. Engaging recent discussions of materiality and temporality in the fields of disability studies, cultural studies, child studies, and queer theory, I ask: how do the particularities of our times—our particular historical and political time and contemporary understandings of the normative meter of time itself—provide the conditions of possibility for the appearance of dominant versions of autism and autism advocacy today? How do temporal representations of autism and autism advocacy shape our experience of the passing of time (i.e., as either 'too slow' or 'too fast') and our understandings of bodies in time (i.e., as being either 'on time' or 'late,' 'timely' or 'untimely')? Lastly, I ask, how is the urgent space and pace of advocacy working to constitute the relational subjectivities of both the advocate and the advocated for? I begin this endeavor, then, by taking a (quick!) look at the broader context of contemporary neoliberal times.

Getting with Our (Coffee) Times

As the Starbucks cup reminds us, we no doubt live in fast and furious times. The 'fast food' orientation of Starbucks, the disposable 'to go' character of the paper coffee cup, together with its 'every 20 minutes' factual refrain, certainly attest to this. Indeed, in a contemporary neoliberal context where 'timing is everything,' there is, as we often say, 'never enough time' and we are, it seems, perpetually 'running late.' In the neoliberal milieu, time is often treated as some 'thing' we, collectively, want more of and of which we can never have enough. In contemporary times, then, time is often treated as a desired and desirable commodity. It is common, for example, to hear talk of the desire or need to 'keep,' 'buy,' 'spend,' and 'save' time. We are regularly and routinely informed by magazines, television talk shows, and friends and family that we just need to 'make' or 'take' 'more time for ourselves,' and to this end we are offered a barrage of 'time saving tips' and a variety of products that will help us to better 'manage' and 'budget' our time. If time is a commodity—if it has become a kind of thing that can be and is bought, sold, and circulated—it is, perhaps, the quintessential commodity insofar as without it no other commodity is within reach. And so, under neoliberalism, we might read time as a kind of capital; ways of 'saving' and 'spending' time capital are deeply morally coded and so are associated with a spectrum of rewards and punishments. We encourage and privilege some ways of spending time as 'time wise,' while we discourage and even stigmatize others as 'wastes of time.' Time, today, is implicitly understood as something useful (and therefore by extension something that can be misused).

Commonsense understandings of the importance of grasping and keeping hold of time, the collective awareness that time is always running out as well as the moral organization of how we use our time deliver us into the heart of a very particular culture; a culture, as many theorists have noted, that is in the grip of a near constant and seemingly limitless state of acceleration (Harvey, 2007; Castells, 2009; Hassan, 2009; Virillio, 1986). It seems that in speeding up (our movements, our desires, our responses, or tasks, our pace of living)—in other words, in being 'time efficient'—we might somehow secure more time. Or, at least, so the logic goes. This notion of time efficiency has, of course, taken on very particular meaning in the contemporary moment. Gone are the days of rigid industrialist efficiency. In an always moving, border-hopping, forward-thinking, globalized and globalizing neoliberalism, efficiency requires flexibility (Kvande, 2009). Indeed, to be efficient one must be flexible. For Robert Hassan (2009), efficiency requires us "to be physically, cognitively, psychologically, and metaphorically able to 'move fast' when the time comes" (p. 19). Neoliberal time may, for example, permit or even compel us to move slowly from time to time (e.g., to 'take time' or to be made to wait) but always with the ultimate aim of moving forward, and fast. Adapt quicker, our culture demands, think faster, understand immediately, innovate continuously, develop earlier, learn younger, look further, work more, produce more, consume more. And do it now.

"Time binds a socius," observes Elizabeth Freeman (2010). Bodies and minds are made meaningful in and through the regulatory flows of time (p. 3). In his book *Empires of Speed: Time and the Acceleration of Politics and Society*, Hassan (2009) describes this regulatory process as one that is mediated by the cultural signs and symbols of our time:

> This is a life where one's whole subjectivity blends into a flow of blurring and accelerated tasks. Obligations, incursions, commitments and projects are constantly juggled and foreshadowed toward a short-term horizon. In the 24/7 chronoscopic world that surrounds us, its signs and symbols, signifiers and referents restlessly flicker and buzz to impress their urgency on our daily existence, compelling us to synchronize our lives to the increasing tempo of the overarching economy of speed. (pp. 23–24)

Hassan provides us with a snapshot of an (our) "economy of speed," which is in his words "borne of the interactions of globalization, neoliberalism and information technologies" (p. 23). Indeed, as a great many theorists have noted, so much of Western modernity's cultural acceleration—this so-called economy of speed—has precisely to do with the infiltration of market rationalities into the social order of the everyday; as Hassan remarks: "the 'need for speed' is tied to the basic need for the capitalist to derive profit" (Hassan, 2009, p. 56). 'Time is money', as they say. The fast-paced 'produce more, consume more, live more' ideology of the market seeps into our lives and propels us along at great speed, thus orienting our consciousness of time as well as governing our actions and reactions in time. For Hassan, contemporary subjectivities are swept up—are shaped by and 'blended' with—the restless buzzing and flickering of mediated 'signs of the time' (e.g., red flags, Starbucks coffee cup statistics) that "[impress] their urgency on our daily existence." Ticking Starbucks coffee cups bind us to life as a question of time, they help us to find this way of life sensible and even necessary. And while paper coffee cups are surely mundane cultural artifacts of the first order, following Puar (2007), "the trivial must be attended to precisely because marking it as such may mask or obfuscate its deeper cultural relevance" (p. 67). The disposable autism awareness coffee cup regulates us as subjects by altering the rhythms of our bodies as well as our understandings of ourselves and others.

The disposable Starbucks coffee cup—a 'sign of the times' to be sure—orients, explicitly, to time. As Tucker (2011) notes, coffee has long been "infused" with "social and symbolic meanings" (p.6). In the neoliberal West, there are a great many normative understandings of 'coffee time.' Coffee is, for example, often understood in everyday life as that which eases the transition between the stasis, and so the nonproductivity, of sleep and the movement and productivity of the work or school day. 'Don't talk to me before I have my morning coffee,' 'I need to have my caffeine fix before I get to work,' are common refrains of daily life. Coffee—a stimulant—wakes us up, speeds us up, helps us to 'get going.' The disposable character of the 'to go' coffee cup anticipates and even encourages this as it permits the consumer to consume the beverage on the go. 'Move on,' the cup hints, 'be on your way.' Now is the time for hurried movements down crowded streets with paper coffee cups in hand. Drink 'on the go' to ensure that you are 'on time' for the neoliberal demands of more production and more consumption. Buying a coffee-to-go might even 'buy you some time' for other things. Be flexible, the paper cup directs, multitask. In these times of so little time, don't waste time *only* drinking coffee. Consume while you move, while you work, while you socialize, while you read. And as we consume our coffee on the go, we also become available to consume other things. We might also consume a fact or two about autism, for example. Thus, the paper coffee cup not only orients us to drink on the go, 'the medium of the Starbucks cup is the message,' to take liberties with McLuhan (1967), it also permits and even encourages us to learn about autism while we drink, and so to learn about autism 'on the go.'

This fast-paced temporality is not conducive to high maintenance reusable coffee cups or leisurely coffee breaks. And neither is it conducive to the significant time necessary for thinking through the complex ways we imagine ourselves and others or how we relate to and across difference. Now is not the time for slow encounters with autism's meaning or for deep consideration of the difference autism makes in our culture and in our lives.[1] In their Marxist analysis of autism as commodity fetish, Rebecca Mallett and Katherine Runswick-Cole observe: "labourers, and thereby consumers, perceive products like autism to be beyond human making or changing and, as such the commodity is perceived as a fixed, static and ahistorical 'thing'" (Mallett and Runswick-Cole, 2012, p. 44). On the side of the Starbucks cup, autism's multiple meanings— individual meanings we endow it with, cultural meanings we ascribe to it, and so on—are streamlined, simplified, made easily accessible and quickly transferable. Autism is distilled down to a series of 'bad' signs and 'good' responses, 'too fast' rates and 'too slow' bodies, punctuated statistical odds—highly consumable facts that can rapidly be exchanged, bought, sold, and circulated in and through a fast-paced consumer culture that is always seeking to increase the speed of capital exchange and circulation in the name of efficiency and, of course, profit. Drawing on the work of Bruno Latour, Briggs and Hallin (2007) note that "[the movement of 'health information'] seems contingent on the status of biomedical 'facts' as 'immutable mobiles,' information that can go anywhere, jumping between genres, places, people, and scales without changing meaning" (p. 58). They go on to demonstrate how the flexible mobility of these facts works to constitute and define subjectivities; subjectivities that are, they write, "defined not by possessing knowledge per se but in participating in its movement: as producer, translator, disseminator, or receptor" (Briggs and Hallin, 2007, p. 58). Insofar as they are crucial components of the machinery of capitalism, such hybrid bodies must possess the flexible efficiency to move in time with the ever-quickening pace of economic processes of production and consumption (Latour, 1993).

It is therefore hardly insignificant that a message informing us of autism's developmental deviancy and the need for advocacy to assure autism's more timely development through swift and early intervention is delivered to us on the side of a paper coffee cup. The disposable cup, together with its message, functions chrononormatively, disciplining bodies and minds "toward maximum productivity" (Freeman, 2010, p. 3). In so doing, the cup works to delimit the normative contours of the good advocate as one who moves through the world in a 'timely' way. The Starbucks cup anticipates a good contemporary advocate subject who uses the commodity of time well—a flexibly efficient body that arrives on time (or even early) to its work and to its milestones. If time is understood as that quintessential commodity that puts us in touch with all other commodities, then to be on time is to assume a position where we might consume more, produce more. The good advocate, then, is the timely subject of the *now*, ready and willing to act, and so ready and willing to participate in—and even enjoy—the processes of consumption and production.[2]

Market Timing

On December 17, 2007, the United Nations General Assembly adopted resolution 63/139, which declared April 2 to be "World Autism Aware-

General Assembly

Distr.: General
21 January 2008

Sixty-second session
Agenda item 66 (*a*)

Resolution adopted by the General Assembly

[*on the report of the Third Committee (A/62/435)*]

62/139. World Autism Awareness Day

The General Assembly,

Recalling the 2005 World Summit Outcome[1] and the United Nations Millennium Declaration,[2] as well as the outcomes of the major United Nations conferences and summits in the economic, social and related fields,

Recalling also the Convention on the Rights of the Child[3] and the Convention on the Rights of Persons with Disabilities,[4] according to which children with disabilities should enjoy a full and decent life, in conditions which ensure dignity, promote self-reliance and facilitate the child's active participation in the community, as well as the full enjoyment of all human rights and fundamental freedoms on an equal basis with other children,

Affirming that ensuring and promoting the full realization of all human rights and fundamental freedoms for all persons with disabilities is critical to achieving internationally agreed development goals,

Aware that autism is a lifelong developmental disability that manifests itself during the first three years of life and results from a neurological disorder that affects the functioning of the brain, mostly affecting children in many countries irrespective of gender, race or socio-economic status, and characterized by impairments in social interaction, problems with verbal and non-verbal communication and restricted, repetitive behaviour, interests and activities,[5]

Deeply concerned by the prevalence and high rate of autism in children in all regions of the world and the consequent development challenges to long-term health care, education, training and intervention programmes undertaken by Governments, non-governmental organizations and the private sector, as well as its tremendous impact on children, their families, communities and societies,

Recalling that early diagnosis and appropriate research and interventions are vital to the growth and development of the individual,

1. *Decides* to designate 2 April as World Autism Awareness Day, to be observed every year beginning in 2008;

2. *Invites* all Member States, relevant organizations of the United Nations system and other international organizations, as well as civil society, including non-governmental organizations and the private sector, to observe World Autism Awareness Day in an appropriate manner, in order to raise public awareness of autism;

3. *Encourages* Member States to take measures to raise awareness throughout society, including at the family level, regarding children with autism;

4. *Requests* the Secretary-General to bring the present resolution to the attention of all Member States and United Nations organizations.

76th plenary meeting
18 December 2007

[1] See resolution 60/1.
[2] See resolution 55/2.
[3] United Nations, *Treaty Series*, vol. 1577, No. 27531.
[4] Resolution 61/106, annex I.
[5] See *International Statistical Classification of Diseases and Related Health Problems*, tenth revision (subcategories F84.0 and F84.1), endorsed by the forty-third World Health Assembly in May 1990.

07-47211

Fig. 5 United Nations Resolution 62/139 "World Autism Awareness Day" adopted at the UN General Assembly 76 Plenary Meeting, December 18, 2007.

ness Day" "in perpetuity" (Autism Speaks, 2011c, para. 1).[3] As I will demonstrate, the resolution (fig. 5) makes it clear that raising public awareness about autism is tantamount to raising public awareness about it as a biomedical problem in need of biomedical solutions. The resolution also hints at how a neoliberal ideology—an ideology grounded in the logic of the market—underpins discourses of autism advocacy and governs the formation of the subjects permitted to dwell within these discourses.

As I argued in the previous chapter, awareness of autism is always oriented; it is inseparable from our other, prior awarenesses. Awareness is always and inevitably shaped, in other words, by the social, political, historic, and economic particularities of a culture, as well as by our individual experiences in/of this culture. According to the resolution, the impetus for the creation of a designated day for autism awareness is premised on three other awarenesses. The first of these awarenesses is the

> Aware[ness] that autism is a lifelong developmental disability that manifests itself during the first three years of life and results from a neurological disorder that affects the functioning of the brain, mostly affecting children in many countries irrespective of gender, race or socio-economic status, and characterized by impairments in social interaction, problems with verbal and non-verbal communication and restricted, repetitive behaviour, interests and activities. (United Nations General Assembly 76 Plenary Meeting, 2008, para. 4)

The document quickly, concisely, and in no uncertain terms states that we might recognize the need for increased autism awareness only once we become aware that autism is a lifelong biomedical problem. It is recognized as a problem that is located in the (any) body of children (i.e., the document narrates an autism that freely transgresses borderlines of race, class, and gender), attributable to biological blunder (i.e., it states that autism is caused by a malfunctioning brain), and that manifests itself through a series of developmental deficits or delays (i.e., autism is narrated as the sum total of its developmental signs—impaired social interaction, restricted interests, problems with communication, and so on). Once again, as in earlier chapters, we are confronted with the awareness of autism as a state of pathological underdevelopment. The autistic body is framed by the resolution as (1) an 'inflexible' body, biologically ill-equipped to perform efficiently in neoliberal time regimes (i.e, a neurologically dis-ordered body with impaired communication and social skills and rigid, restricted behaviors, interests, and activities) and, because of this, as (2) a quintessentially 'late' body (i.e., a body that does not arrive 'on time' to the normative milestones of social, emotional, and behavioral development).

Next, the UN resolution makes us aware that a second impetus for the creation of a world autism awareness day is the awareness of the

> Deeply concern[ing] . . . prevalence and high rate of autism in children in all regions of the world and the consequent development challenges to long-term health care, education, training and intervention programmes undertaken by Governments, non-governmental organizations and the private sector, as well as its tremendous impact on children, their families, communities and societies. (United Nations General Assembly 76 Plenary Meeting, 2008, para. 5)

The UN resolution moves from narrating autism as merely(!) an individual problem to expressing it as a problematic (developmentally 'too slow'/inflexible) *group of bodies*. The need for more autism awareness is seen to be premised on the prior awareness of a 'deeply concerning,' 'prevalent' population trend, a trend that is occurring too quickly (at a 'high rate'), transgressing state borders and thus threatening to slow down social and economic development in regions all over the world. Autism, the resolution indicates, challenges the fast-paced and forward moving work of social and economic development and modernization by negatively impacting its foundational institutional building blocks (families, communities, societies). Awareness of autism, the resolution hints, is awareness of autism as a too-costly population, and so as a threat to neoliberal modernity.

The UN resolution thus demonstrates the dominant understanding that more autism awareness is needed only insofar as autism is understood as both a biomedical (neurological) problem that threatens the (good/timely) development of the body and as a prevalent problem population trend that threatens the (good/timely) development of the state. What is more, the resolution tells us that the solution to both the social and individual problem of autism—the third and perhaps the ultimate impetus for autism awareness—is to target and alter the body of the individual autistic person through 'early' diagnosis and 'appropriate' (read: biomedical) interventions. Interventions, we must presume, aimed at catalyzing a normative, timely development. The resolution states:

early diagnosis and appropriate research and interventions are vital
to the growth and development of the individual. (United Nations
General Assembly 76 Plenary Meeting, 2008, para. 6)

Yet what follows from the resolution, and what it fails to address, is how
the move to develop (speed up/make flexible) autism's purportedly
untimely state of underdevelopment, through biomedical therapies, for
example, also and most significantly works to develop private and public
economic interests in a number of interrelated ways. As I explore later in
this chapter, in neoliberal times there are considerable vested interests
underpinning the desire for fast and flexible subjects (Lane, 2007; Rose,
1999; McRuer, 2012). The relationship between the development of the
individual body and that of the state was all too evident, just over three
months after the General Assembly passed its resolution, on the first ever
World Autism Awareness Day.

Investing in Good Stock

On April 2, 2008, the inaugural World Autism Awareness Day (WAAD)
was observed in cities across the globe as a day to, according to the offi-
cial WAAD website, "[shine] a bright light on autism as a growing global
health crisis" (Autism Speaks, 2008b). In New York City, Autism Speaks
took this imperative quite literally when organization volunteers and
supporters rang the opening bell of the New York Stock Exchange and,
amidst a multitude of flashing and scrolling lights, ushered in another
trading day (fig. 6). That the world's largest autism advocacy organization
spent the very first moments of the very first World Autism Awareness Day
on the New York Stock Exchange trading floor—perhaps the nexus of
speed and consumption *par excellence*—holds both material and symbolic
significance. This is so insofar as the stock exchange represents: (1) a
substantial amount of private and public funds invested in, for example,
biomedical research, treatment, and intervention programs, and (2)
the potential economic productivity of autistic people, the desired 'end-
products' of the latest in biomedical research and its early intervention
programs. Finally, the stock market also represents (3) the cultivation
of the speed-driven temporality of urgency where capital—biomedical
capital (i.e., research and intervention therapies) and biological capital
(i.e., the bodies produced by research and intervention)—is produced
and circulated within increasingly narrow time margins. Autism Speaks'

ringing of the stock market bell in New York—now an annual event, which beginning in 2010 chimed in chorus with opening and closing trading bells around the globe[4]—gestures toward an undeniable blending of dominant contemporary versions of autism advocacy with increasingly global economic imperatives and neoliberal market rationalities (New York Stock Exchange, 2010). To better understand the material and symbolic implications of this blending of market rationalities with advocacy work, I turn to a consideration of three key market principles—investment, risk, and security—principles that are commonly evoked and employed, and so work to govern the field of autism advocacy today.

In contemporary times, autism is commonly brought into conceptual association with notions of social and/or economic investment where 'investment' is conventionally understood as the provision of resources (e.g., time, energy, money, and so on) with the expectation of future return or profit. And as the association between autism and investment is made and remade, autism itself gets (re)invested, as we shall see, with very particular cultural meanings and values. Returning to the UN World Autism Awareness Day resolution, we can note how its appeal for greater public awareness of autism is rhetorically framed in terms of an appeal for investment in our collective (global) future. Recall how the UN's declaration of the need for greater awareness of autism is premised on several other awarenesses, namely the awareness of autism as an individual problem body, the awareness of autism as a problem population that effects the social body, and the awareness of the need for biomedical solutions that target the individual body but work to secure a better future for both the individual and the social body. With this in mind, the document issues its resolution in four parts:

The General Assembly,

1. *Decides* to designate 2 April as World Autism Awareness Day, to be observed every year beginning in 2008;
2. *Invites* all Member States, relevant organizations of the United Nations system and other international organizations, as well as civil society, including non-governmental organizations and the private sector, to observe World Autism Awareness Day in an appropriate manner, in order to raise public awareness of autism;
3. *Encourages* Member States to take measures to raise awareness throughout society, including at the family level, regarding children with autism;

4. *Requests* the Secretary-General to bring the present resolution to the attention of all Member States and United Nations organizations. (United Nations General Assembly 76 Plenary Meeting, 2008, para. 7–10).

Using enticing and coaxing verbs that seem to bestow upon the addressee the freedom to choose (e.g., the General Assembly 'invites,' 'encourages,' 'requests,' and so on)—and so mirroring the principles of freedom, liberty, and choice that are so central to the logic and the functioning of the free market—the WAAD resolution calls on global nations, government and nongovernmental organizations, and indeed the whole of civil society to ('appropriately') observe World Autism Awareness Day and to do this in the name of more timely individual and social development outcomes. While the resolution makes no explicit mention of investment per se, it functions nonetheless as an appeal for both ideological and monetary investment in the diminishment of 'problem' (autistic) people and populations by promising 'better' (i.e., more profitable) nonautistic future returns. I will further elaborate on the relationship between problem people/populations and notions of global investment in a moment, but first I will examine how the good advocate is being here produced as a kind of investor.

The WAAD resolution makes an appeal for greater awareness and advocacy and, in so doing, is involved in the production of the good advocate subject. The good, aware advocate subject is delimited as s/he who must invest in the ideological presupposition that autism is a problem in need of a solution. Invest time, it hints, in becoming more aware of the problem of autism and its many solutions. Invest energy in raising others awareness about autism through the dissemination of informational facts about untimely arrivals to milestones, inflexible comportments, and 'too slow' rates of development. What is more, the presumably 'appropriate' ways of observing World Autism Awareness Day—exemplified around the world by the appearance of various autism organizations at global stock exchanges and by the lighting up of numerous iconic (and many corporate) buildings[5] in autism's 'trademark' blue color (fig. 6)—make it clear that becoming aware of autism in contemporary times is not only an ideological investment but also a monetary one.

As we invest in the understanding that autism is nothing more than a biological problem—a too-slow-to-develop body and an untimely population—the efficient way to proceed necessarily becomes to invest in biomedical research that will aim to bring about autism's solution (i.e., intervention treatments that target the autistic body and work to speed up its untimely growth and development by diminishing and/or eliminating 'too slow' or inflexible autistic ways of being). In this way, the resolution functions indirectly as an appeal to invest in the latest biomedical research focused on identifying autism's biological pathologies, uncovering its neurological etiologies, and developing effective treatments to diminish and/or eliminate autistic ways of being. *Invest money*, the document hints, but not indiscriminately. Under a neoliberal rule that abides by the logic of the market, money must be invested well. Put differently, money must be invested in such a way that provides good returns. In such a way that generates profit.

The UN's call for a global and globalizing commitment to (i.e., investment in) individual and social development was heeded in the fall of 2009 when a newly elected US president, Barack Obama, at the height of the so-called World Economic Crisis, held a press conference at the National Institutes of Health (NIH) to announce his administration's substantial monetary investment in health focused research as part of the American Recovery and Reinvestment Act (or 'stimulus package') (Government of the United States of America, 2009a). The five billion dollars in research money—as President Obama quipped at the press conference, "that's with a '*b*'"—represented, in Obama's words, "the single largest boost to biomedical research in history" (Government of the United States of America, 2009b, para. 5). The money was earmarked for studies that would apply knowledge and technologies derived from the Human Genome Project to "understand, prevent, and treat" cancer, heart disease, and autism; "diseases," in his words, "that have long plagued humanity"[6] (Government of the United States of America, 2009b, para. 5). At the press conference, the president spoke, in particular, about this "largest-ever infusion of funding into autism research"— approximately one hundred million dollars was specifically designated for autism research—where, said Obama, "grant recipients will have the opportunity to study genetic and environmental factors of a disease that now touches more than one in every 150 children" (Government of the United States of America, 2009b, para. 9). The research supported by the grants, Obama said, would "hopefully lead to greater understanding, early interventions, more effective treatments and therapies to help these children live their lives and achieve their fullest potential, which is extraordinary" (Government of the United States of America, 2009b, para. 9).

To invest in something (or someone) is to commit a valued asset—e.g., money or capital—in the hope of securing a profit, a more valuable return. In this way, any notion of investment is premised, first, on some version of an economy of exchange. If I was to invest in the stock market, for example, I might examine and appraise my investment options, weigh their potential risks against their potential benefits, and buy up those stocks that I think will, as time passes, go up in value so as to ensure that my initial investment will turn a profit. Applying this investment orientation to real estate, we might commit a certain amount of money upfront with the belief that, in time, the property value will grow and might be sold for a greater sum of money. Similarly, in neoliberal times, this investment orientation is also commonly applied to education. Investing in higher education means paying high tuition fees now with the expectation of better employment opportunities later. We invest money, but we also invest other valuable resources with the expectation of return. We invest, for example, time, love, and energy in children, in families, in friends, in partners, and so on. In each of these examples, sacrifices are made in the present time (we part with valuable resources), but only with the expectation of rewards in the future time (we gain desired outcomes). A key implication of this investment logic is that we do not necessarily invest in what is valuable now but, rather, we invest in what *could* be valuable in the future. In this way, investments have precisely to do with the imagining of futures and desirable ones at that.

It is interesting and certainly revealing to note that the subject of the autistic 'advocated for' is figured in Obama's remarks (as well as in the WAAD resolution and on the coffee cup) as a child. Indeed, the figure of the child is cited in all three examples as the primary focus and motivation for the need to invest in autism research and awareness. For example, the UN resolution states that autism "mostly [affects] *children*," that there is a "high rate of autism in *children* in all regions of the world," and finally that UN member states ought to take "measures to raise awareness throughout society . . . regarding *children* with autism" (United Nations General Assembly, 76 Plenary Meeting, 2008, *my emphasis*). Indeed, but for a single, brief mention of "all persons with disabilities," the resolution makes it clear that the autistic child, and not the autistic adult, is the focal point of and driving force behind World Autism Awareness Day. A similar story is told on the Starbucks' fact-to-be-consumed: recall that Wright tells us that one in every 150 *children* receives an autism diagnosis. At the NIH press conference, Obama, too, reinforces the common cultural understanding that only children are 'touched' by autism and that investment in autism research is necessary to ensure that these children can go on to live good lives and reach their 'full' potential.

This focus on the child is not surprising. The West has a long history of infantilizing the disabled subject. As Paul Longmore's (2013) extensive analysis of the cultural phenomenon of the telethon and the figure of the poster child makes clear: the image of the disabled child is central to the ideological and economic success of charity and advocacy work. Longmore demonstrates how the disabled child is figured by organizations as, at once, innocent and tragic, thus always confirming the necessity and virtue of paternalistic intervention. The representations of autism discussed in this chapter invariably appear against this historical backdrop. Indeed, in Western culture in general and in autism advocacy work in particular, autism is almost exclusively represented as a condition linked with childhood. According to an empirical study by Stephenson, Harp, and Gernsbacher (2011):

> Parents portrayed the face of autism to be that of a child 95% of the time on the homepages of regional and local support organizations. Nine of the top 12 autism charitable organizations restricted descriptions of autism to child-referential discourse. Characters depicted as autistic were children in 90% of fictional books and 68% of narrative films and television programs. The news industry featured autistic children four times as often as they featured autistic adults in contemporary news articles. (n.p.)

The dominance of cultural representations framing autism as a condition linked with childhood structure dangerous material exclusions for disabled/autistic adults. Stephenson, Harp, and Gernsbacher (2012) write of the infantilization of autistic adults:

> Adults with disabilities in general, and those with developmental disabilities in particular, have long been treated as childlike entities, deserving fewer rights and incurring greater condescension than adults without disabilities. The stereotype of the "eternal child" has burned a disturbing path through history and continues to wreak havoc in arenas ranging from employment discrimination to forced sterilizations (Osburn, 2009; Pfeiffer, 1994; Wolfensberger, 1972). (Stephenson, Harp, and Gernsbacher, 2012, n.p.)

Of course, autistic adults continue to contest the singularity of the figure of the autistic child, both formally (e.g., the Autistic Adult Picture
Project, Bev Harp's Late Intervention Campaign, and the work of self-
advocacy organizations like ASAN) and informally, by occupying this
culturally incoherent subjectivity. Throughout the remainder of this
chapter, I show how advocacy's move to center the autistic child (and its
subsequent effacement of the autistic adult) also has much to do with
neoliberal notions of time and timeliness. I turn now to an examination
of the temporal workings of the cultural figure of the child. I then move
to interrogate the particular significance of the temporally disruptive
figure of the autistic child and the related 'threat' of the autistic adult.

Cultural Investments in 'Better' Futures and
the Promise of the Child

It almost goes without saying that the figure of the child is conceptually bound to notions of futurity (Berlant, 1997; Edelman, 2004; Spivak, 2004; Muñoz, 2009; Berlant, 2011; Mollow, 2012). This sentiment
is repeated time and again in our culture; we hear it in song lyrics (e.g.,
Whitney Houston's declaration, "I believe that children are our future/
teach them well and let them lead the way" [Masser and Creed, 1984])
and political speeches (e.g., former president John F. Kennedy's famous
pronouncement that "children are the world's most valuable resource
and its best hope for the future" [Kennedy, 1963, para. 1]). We glean it
from commercials advertising healthy food products (e.g., Pediasure's
corporate tagline "Feed kids potential") and in the informational facts
printed on the sides of paper coffee cups. As Lee Edelman (2004) notes,
it is indeed almost impossible to speculate about future times without
the figure of the child. Edelman (2004) writes, "the Child has come to
embody for us the telos of the social order" (Edelman, 2004, p. 11); it
is, he says, the "preeminent emblem of the motivating end," compelling
and so propelling us toward the possibility of 'better' futures (Edelman,
2004, p. 13).

The ubiquitous presence of the figure of the autistic child within
discourses of autism advocacy (and the conspicuous effacement of the
autistic adult) is significant as it conjures a very particular—and highly
functional—temporal environment where notions of futurity get collapsed with the immediate present, where we must invest 'now' for better

'laters.' While the question of what childhood is is surely open to endless theorizing, in this Western/ized culture and in these neoliberal times, one way of understanding childhood is to understand it as a time. The normative time of childhood—understood simultaneously as a biological time of growth and development and a sentimental/nostalgic time of innocence, hope, and vulnerability—is precisely that time of seemingly infinite 'laters'. The child is positioned as 'early on' on the (normative) biological timeline and therefore is understood as having *more* time, *more* future yet-to-be-realized. In a neoliberal regime where 'time is money,' the child is figured as 'time-rich' and so represents a good investment opportunity indeed. Underscoring a logic of exchange—a logic that, as we have seen, is central to any conception of investment—the UN resolution, the Starbucks coffee cup, and Obama's remarks all resonate with the promise of better futures and the necessity of investing in (some) children in exchange for more profitable future returns. In all three examples, the better future evoked is characterized in terms of more timely economic development, both individual and social.

The WAAD resolution, as we have seen, paints a picture of an untimely child's body that poses "consequent development challenges" to governmental and nongovernmental initiatives and to the private sector (United Nations General Assembly 76 Plenary Meeting, 2008, para. 5). While the resolution does not explicitly say how the one (individual development) is connected to the other (social and economic development), we must assume its logic as a matter of commonsense. We might assume—and it would seem the resolution expects us to assume—that the logic goes as follows: the 'too slow'/inflexible developing (autistic) body represents an excessively costly body and this excessive cost works to slow down the development of, to quote the resolution, "long-term health care, education, training and intervention programmes" (United Nations General Assembly 76 Plenary Meeting, 2008, para. 5). The autistic body, the resolution suggests, represents the possibility of expensive social services, costly and ongoing medical evaluations and treatments, specialized education programs, and so on. Such an understanding resonates throughout our culture as autism is so often framed as an excessive economic burden. Consider the following examples:

- **News headlines:** e.g., *The New York Times* headline, "Tug of War over Costs to Educate the Autistic" (Fairbanks, 2009); *The Chicago Sun-Times* headline, "Families Confront Stiff Cost of Autism" (Ritter, 2005); "Autism Costs Society an Estimated $3 Million Per Patient,

According to Report" (*Science Daily*, 2007); "Fighting Autism Too Costly, Top Court Told" (Makin, 2004); "Autism a Lifelong Burden, Study Shows: Because Few Adults with the Disorder Can Work, the Economic Costs Continue" (Picard, 2007); "Mothers of Autistic Children Earn 56% Less Income, Study Says" (Jaslow, 2012); "The Lifetime Cost of Autism Tops $2 Million per Person" (Park, 2014); "Study Says Cost of Autism More than Cancer, Strokes and Heart Disease" (Siddique, 2014); "Autism Is the Most Costly Medical Condition in the UK" (London School of Economics and Political Science, 2012).

- **Journal articles and studies:** e.g., "Measuring the Parental, Service and Cost Impacts of Children with Autistic Spectrum Disorder" (Jarbrink, Fombonne, and Knapp, 2003); "The Lifetime Distribution of the Incremental Societal Costs of Autism" (Gantz, 2007); "Economic Cost of Autism in the UK" (Knapp, Romeo, and Beecham, 2009); "The Costs of Services and Employment Outcomes Achieved by Adults with Autism in the US" (Cimera and Cowen, 2009); "Implications of Childhood Autism for Parental Employment and Earnings" (Cidav, Marcus, and Mandell, 2012); "Economic Cost of Autism in the UK" (Knapp, Romeo, and Beecham, 2009); "Costs of Autism Spectrum Disorders in the United Kingdom and the United States" (Buescher et al., 2014).
- **Legal decisions:** e.g., Auton v. British Columbia (2004); Wynberg et al. v. Ontario (2006); McHenry v. PacificSource (2009).
- **International Research Summits:** Partnering with multinational investment banking firm Goldman Sachs and the Child Development Centre of Hong Kong, Autism Speaks organized the 2012 international summit, "Investing in Our Future: The Economic Costs of Autism" (Autism Speaks, 2012).
- **Government reports:** The Centers for Disease Control and Prevention ADDM reports (CDC, 2006; CDC, 2010; CDC, 2012; CDC, 2014); Canadian Autism Research Agenda and Canadian Autism Strategy: A White Paper (Autism Society of Canada, 2004).

Yet the resolution's logic does not end with the conceptualization of the autistic body as an excessive cost. The WAAD resolution optimistically reminds us that the need to invest in autism awareness is motivated, at least to some degree, by the promise of a better future where individual autistic children's bodies can be helped to 'grow and develop' in a more timely way by "early diagnosis and appropriate research and interventions" and presumably, in this way, be placed in a better position to more fully realize their human rights and fundamental freedoms (United Nations General Assembly 76 Plenary Meeting, 2008, para. 2, 6). Drawing on the UN Convention on the Rights of the Child and the UN Convention on the Rights of Persons with Disabilities, the resolution paints a utopic picture of a nonautistic future where all individuals are free to lead a 'full' and 'decent' life, to be 'self-reliant,' to 'actively' participate in the community, and so on.

Similarly evoking the utopic time of better futures, President Obama speaks of biomedical research holding "incredible promise for the health of our people and the future of our nation and our world," a promise that, in his words, "we've only begun to realize" (Government of the United States of America, 2009b, para. 4, 6). Obama states that by investing in biomedical research, "we" (i.e., nonautistic investors) are also and necessarily investing in a "brighter future" (Government of the United States of America, 2009b, para. 15). "We" are building, in his words, "a better world for ourselves, our children, and our grandchildren"—a world where autistic children are freed from autism and thus are free to "live their lives and achieve their fullest potential" (Government of the United States of America, 2009b, para. 11, 19).

Obama's remarks at the NIH press conference, together with the WAAD resolution, are suffused with a neoliberal rhetoric of potentiality, articulated in terms of individual rights and the freedom to become. The UN resolution suggests that investing in greater autism awareness—e.g., learning/identifying the 'warning signs' of autism and seeking to mitigate, if not eliminate autism—is necessary because:

> children with disabilities should enjoy a full and decent life in conditions which ensure dignity, promote self-reliance and facilitate the child's active participation in the community, as well as the full enjoyment of human rights and fundamental freedoms on an equal basis with other children. (United Nations General Assembly 76 Plenary Meeting, 2008, para. 2)

This of course begs the question: As we realize our freedoms and enjoy our human rights, what or who are we free to become? And what rights must we enjoy along the way? Rose (1999) points out, "only a certain kind of liberty—a certain way of understanding and exercising freedom, of relating to ourselves individually and collectively as subjects of freedom—is compatible with liberal arts of rule" (p. 62). There are, in other words, limited permissible ways of exercising our rights and freedoms in neoliberal times. Drawing attention to the ways rights discourse works to regulate particular historically specific cultural values and ideals, including those market-driven values and ideals of the contemporary neoliberal state, Jo Boyden (1990) observes: "the norms and values upon which this ideal of safe, happy and protected childhood are built are culturally and historically bound to the social preoccupations and priorities of the capitalist countries of Europe and the United States"[7] (p. 186). Thus, as Veena Das warns, discourses of human rights and freedoms can be "a means of sanctioning cultural authoritarianism" (as cited in Stephens, 1995, p. 39), an "alibi," following Spivak (2004), for a whole host of (historically/economically/politically mediated) interventions (p. 524). Far from being simply 'fundamental,' 'guaranteed,' or 'naturally endowed' to all humans, human rights and freedoms are granted or withheld or even revoked—they are, in other words, socially, historically, politically, and economically determined. And in this way they function to determine the necessary shape of their bearer. Returning to passage from the WAAD resolution quoted above, rights and freedoms are revealed as something other than what one simply has as a matter of nature or even as a matter of law. Rights and freedoms are, rather, framed as something one *should fully enjoy*. For a subject to be granted human rights and freedoms—and so to be regarded as living a full or good life—the subject must enjoy his/her rights and freedoms in particular, limited ways. Under neoliberalism, an individual is only recognized as 'fully enjoying' his/her human rights and freedoms if s/he moves in time with neoliberal values and its market rationalities; if s/he enjoys or consumes goods—coffee, for example—and so participates in the s/pace of production.

According to the WAAD resolution, there exists a pressing need for greater awareness of autism as a biomedical problem and for more biomedical research and corrective therapies, because all children, including children with autism, ought to be free/have the right to lead and enjoy 'full lives,' to achieve their full potential. What is more, children must do these things—as per a refrain of neoliberalism—independently (to be 'self reliant') and efficiently (abiding by a timely tempo of development and a time flexibility that invariably leads to 'actively participating' in the economic development of the greater global community). The child, in other words, is *made* free, but only to, following Ruth Lister (2003), become a "cipher for future economic prosperity and forward looking modernization" (p. 433). This imaginary of the "future worker-citizen," she points out is "the prime asset of the social investment state" (p. 433). The autistic child—conceived of as the child 'with' or tied to autism[8]—thus, becomes framed as needing to be freed from his/her autism so as to be free to become a good neoliberal subject, well positioned to enjoy human rights by participating in and, indeed, enjoying a 'full' life of production and consumption.

Most interestingly, as the advocate heeds the UN's encouragement and becomes more aware of autism, as she accepts the WAAD resolution's invitation and chooses to 'appropriately' observe April 2 (by ringing the bell at the stock exchange, for example, or by buying a WAAD T-shirt or a 14K gold puzzle piece necklace), as the advocate, in other words, exercises her freedom and realizes herself as a good advocate, she is also and simultaneously engaged in the realization of bodies that are less free. These bodies—autistic bodies—are characterized by the WAAD resolution as first requiring early diagnoses and interventions before being able to 'fully realize' and 'enjoy' their rights and liberties, bodies that need help to live their (good, neoliberal) lives and, in Obama's words, achieve their 'full potentials.' And so as the advocate realizes herself as an advocate, she also engages in the realization of herself as a good neoliberal subject—a timely (and so necessarily nonautistic) subject who consumes/enjoys goods while learning about the signs of good developmental timing; a subject, moreover, who is engaged in the work of producing the good neoliberal subjects of the future by working to develop/speed up autism's presumed 'bad timing.' In this way, the freedom and rights of autistic subjects are constructed as dependent (and thus contingent) upon the good choices of good advocates.

Investing in interventions that work to speed up untimely development and thus to ensure the flexible efficiency of children's bodies are investments with the expectation of good (i.e., profitable) return. As per the WAAD resolution, we ('civil society') must invest resources in the present to ensure the production of future-citizens that are both 'timely' (i.e., that make good use of time) and 'time-rich' (i.e., that still have much time). Of course, these are bodies that are also highly valuable—and indeed lucrative—to a market economy; they arrive on time to their milestones and thus are better positioned to flexibly, efficiently participate in the processes of production and consumption and to otherwise contribute to (or, at least, not slow down) the timely development (modernization) of the state. This logic not only assigns economic value to normative human development, transforming the body of the normatively developing child into a material asset. It also works to dangerously produce the non-normatively developing body as disposable: nonvaluable and, perhaps even, as nonviable in the contemporary market-driven economy, a notion that I will explore in more depth for the remainder of this chapter.

That autism's 'too slow' development represents a significant economic burden to the public and private sectors, and so poses a threat to better futures, indeed seems to be a fact that the WAAD resolution takes for granted. Yet if we attend carefully to Obama's remarks at the NIH press conference, it would seem that the business of investing in better futures needs—is absolutely dependent upon—the untimely autistic body and the time sensitive response of advocacy. Indeed, we might note how good, neoliberal versions of advocacy—populated by advocates who participate in and even enjoy the work of noticing the differences between autistic and nonautistic comportments and who produce and consume treatments for such differences—already represent a good, very profitable return on an awareness investment. Consider, for example, how the Obama administration's one hundred million dollar investment in autism research—a sizeable monetary investment, to be sure—was almost counter-intuitively announced in the midst of the greatest economic crisis since the Great Depression and that the money invested was sourced from the US recovery act—the stimulus package—the explicit purpose of which was to stimulate or 'recover'[9] a faltering market economy (encourage spending, create jobs, and so on). Investing in the *business* of treating and curing autism[10] is explicitly framed by the president as an investment in the future economic prosperity of the state. It is an investment that works to stimulate the economy by, 'improving' and 'saving' lives (i.e., rehabilitating autistic people and thus cultivating future producers and consumers), while 'creating' and 'saving' American jobs along the way. In Obama's words:

> we know that these investments in research will improve and save countless lives for generations to come [. . .] But we also know that these investments will save jobs, they'll create new jobs—tens of thousands of jobs—conducting research, and manufacturing and supplying medical equipment, and building and modernizing laboratories and research facilities all across America. (Government of the United States of America, 2009b, para. 12)

Lofty appeals to better children's futures through the development of children's bodies function as powerful and productive investment appeals. At once, this kind of appeal functions to secure more and better neoliberal body-assets better able to contribute to state and global economies as well as to entice the emergence of good, productive, and consumptive advocate-workers who realize their subjecthood by ensuring the development (production) of better (time efficient) citizen-workers of the future. What is more, such an appeal also works to stimulate the development of whole industries centralized on the production of the timely body, itself an economic commodity to be bought and sold (Albrect, 1992).

The Business of Autism

Despite the constant lament that autism is just too costly, a significant or even 'crippling' economic burden for the social whole, the production of the time-rich but not time-efficient body of the autistic child has generated a multibillion dollar 'autism industrial complex'—public and private investment interests that benefit economically from, and indeed whose very fiscal survival is reliant upon, the existence of the late body that needs help catching up to its milestones and so to its (and apparently everyone else's) better future. While Obama references several of these investment interests explicitly—biomedical researchers, private and public biomedical research facilities, medical equipment manufacturers and suppliers, and so on—there are surely many other economic interests that stand to benefit, directly and indirectly, from the president's and the UN's (as well as other major and minor players) rearticulation of the need to speed up autism's untimely development.

Harlan Lane (2007) writes about the existence of what sociologist Joseph Gusfield calls the "troubled persons industries," industries that, in Gusfield's words, "bestow benevolence on people defined as in need" (as cited in Lane, 2007, p. 81). For example, in recent decades there is an ever growing range of new and specialized jobs that absolutely depend on the construction of an untimely autism in need of 'speeding up' (i.e., specialist/expert doctors, teachers, professors, researchers, advocates, occupational and physical therapists, psychologists, psychiatrists, social workers, counselors, and so on). These and many other jobs are supported by a wide array of intervention therapies and the institutions where these are delivered. Many, if not most, therapies are privately offered and almost all seek to diminish autistic behaviors and/or 'cure' autism.

Autism treatment protocols on offer are as diverse as they are many—a sign of a 'healthy' market, to be sure. Therapeutic approaches range from being government endorsed, evidence-based, and FDA approved[11] to existing on the fringe of pseudoscience. Some therapies are, in no uncertain terms, violent and abusive (e.g., chelation, chemical castration, bleach therapies) and others can be very helpful for certain people (e.g., some communication programs, service animals, and so on). The list that follows is an incomplete snapshot of the treatments and therapies available for purchase on the market today (and this list is by no means exhaustive). My intent here is not to collapse the very real and material distinctions between therapeutic approaches but rather to provide the reader with a sense of the immensity and diversity of the autism industry. Beginning with the more mainstream products and services available on the market, there are a great many behavior therapy programs (e.g., Applied Behavioral Analysis and Intensive Behavioral Intervention) and schools; relationship therapies (e.g., Relationship Development Intervention, Son-Rise, Floortime, and SCERTS); social skills programs; neurofeedback therapies; occupational and physical therapies; communication therapies; electric shock therapies; and of course a wide variety of (approved and unapproved) pharmaceutical based drug therapies. There are a host of alternative, naturopathic, and homeopathic treatments including chiropractic therapies, craniosacral therapies, diet supplement therapies, nutrition therapies (e.g., casein-free and gluten-free diets), acupuncture therapies, massage therapies, music and art therapies, aromatherapy treatments, and animal assisted therapies (e.g., dolphins, dogs, and horses). There are also an overwhelming number of overtly hazardous pseudoscientific therapies on the market. Some examples include: bleach therapies (e.g., Miracle Mineral Solution), nicotine patch therapy, camel milk therapy, stem cell therapies, hormone injections, antifungal agent therapy, holding therapy, detoxification therapies (e.g., chelation and hyperbaric oxygen treatments, clay baths), shamanism therapies, chemical castration (e.g., Lupron protocol), and so on.

While whole industries have cropped up around treating and/or curing autism, other industries have discovered it can also be profitable to take the prevention route, marketing products that aim to prevent untimely bodies altogether and/or to enhance timely bodies by stimulating normal fetal and infant brain development (e.g., BabyPlus Prenatal Education System, Juicy Juice for Brain Development) and, as discussed in the previous chapter, an increasingly wide range of development toys (Nadesan, 2002). Other industries still have honed in on the autism niche market, marketing a plethora of communication tools and software (e.g., Dynavox Technologies, as we saw on the red flag poster in fig. 2), informational books and 'autism friendly' products/products marketed to help build 'appropriate' skills (e.g., Toys 'R' Us "Ten Toys that Speak to Autism" or the 2,000-square-foot retail store in California, Angels for Autism). Think your kid might be autistic? There's an app for that! Want to modify your child's behavior? There's an app for that too.[12]

"The 'cultural presence' of autism has grown vastly over the past few decades," note Mallett and Runswick-Cole (2012). Autism, they argue, has become a 'hot' commodity. Or to quote comedian Sasha Baron-Cohen (cousin of Simon Baron-Cohen of Theory of Mind fame), as vanguard fashion expert Bruno states—"chlamydia is out" and "autism is in." Heeding the UN's request that all of 'civil society' (including the private sector) engage in autism awareness raising, even industries that have little or nothing to do with autism in specific or childhood development more generally—coffee chains, designer boutiques—have thrown their philanthrocapitalist hats in the ring by promoting autism awareness on their paper coffee cups and in their window displays while, all the while, drawing a profit. As the Starbucks cup makes evident, Western/ized culture loves to consume autism. One can, for example, purchase a pair of Autism Speaks skate shoes or a bag of puzzle piece shaped pretzels (fig. 6). The autism 'brand' can be found anywhere from clogs to candles. It marks cufflinks, keychains, frying pans, wine bottles, baseball caps, T-shirts, balloons, bumper stickers, Champaign glasses, and thongs. The commonality and, indeed, outright popularity of the autism brand references a kind of cultural love of autism. Still, the often unambiguously violent messaging on these artifacts (e.g., 'solve autism,' 'fight autism,' 'beat autism') bespeaks a language other than love. If we, as a culture, are loving autism as a commodity, we are most certainly loving it (or even fetishizing it, as Mallett and Runswick-Cole argue) as something to hate (Mallett and Runswick-Cole, 2012).

No single organization exemplifies the lucrative interminglings of corporate interest and autism advocacy more clearly than Autism Speaks. Consider the Autism Speaks Marketplace website (Autism Speaks, 2011e), where patrons can learn about and purchase the latest autism products and therapeutic toys, choose from an expansive array of puzzle piece branded clothing and accessories, learn about the organizations multimillion dollar corporate partnerships (e.g., Toys "R" Us, T.J. Maxx, Chevrolet, Fox Sports, Home Depot, Zales Diamonds, and so on), or participate in the 'shop and give' initiative where they can buy nonautism related products (e.g., clothes from the Gap, Old Navy,

Fig. 6 A collection of 'autism brand' consumer products and corporate initiatives that reflect the marketization of autism.

Banana Republic, or Roots, flights from Expedia, books from Amazon, music from iTunes, and so on) and have a portion of the proceeds of the sale (between 1 and 12.5 percent) go to Autism Speaks. The Starbucks cup, the World Autism Awareness Day resolution, President Obama's speech, and the sheer breadth of the autism industrial complex all gesture toward the cultural fact that, under neoliberal rule, social and/or economic investment in the untimely autistic child is not just an investment in the realization of the future-citizen-worker but in the *potential* for its realization. In one unbroken—and clearly very lucrative—move, our market-driven times at once produce *and* regulate, create *and* constrain conducts that are beyond the norm.

Risk-Benefit Potentials

Throughout this chapter so far, I have been reading discourses of autism advocacy through the frames, logics, and temporalities of 'our times,' times that are characterized primarily in relation to the political and economic orientations of a global—globalized and globalizing—free market. I conclude this chapter by tracing how such free market orientations deliver us to commonsense understandings of worth and value (what and who constitutes a good investment or good 'stock' and what and who gets recognized as investment 'risk') via particular and culturally specific narratives of potentiality.

Insofar as it resides at the nexus of the 'now' and the 'later'—the point of collapse between present and future—the time-rich figure of the child is the figure of potentiality par excellence. If we imagine the child in terms of the biological, its body comes to represent the potential for growth and development, the potential for growing up, for getting older, becoming an adult, and so on. But, as we have seen, the child's body represents more than the potential for biological growth; it also comes to represent the potential for economic growth and development—it represents the potential for work, for social achievement, for economic success—potential that is closely related to the potential of a society, a nation, an empire.

In his essay "On Potentiality," Giorgio Agamben (1999) meditates on Aristotle's writings on the concept. In *Metaphysics*, Aristotle writes: "Impotentiality [adynamia αδυναμία] is a privation contrary to potentiality. Thus all potentiality is impotentiality of the same and with respect to the same" (as cited in Agamben, 1999, p. 182). Unpacking these observations, Agamben (1999) writes: "to be potential means: to be ones own lack. To be in relation to one's own incapacity. Beings that exist in the mode of potentiality are capable of their own impotentiality; and only in this way do they become potential" (p. 182). For Agamben, then, potentiality is "the presence of an absence" and the relation between the two (Agamben, 1999, p. 179). This centralization of the absent-present character of potentiality—that potential is both absent insofar as it is an imagination of not-yet future times but is also, and therefore made very present, actively structuring the present time—is crucial for critiques of development discourses as it permits an analysis of the ways in which children's bodies, themselves, become understood as both absent and present. These are present and ready-to-hand bodies-to-be-managed, bodies managed always in relation to their status as could-be but not-yet bodies of the future. Evans (2010) writes, "children's bodies are absent-presences within hoped-for utopias" but also, she continues, within, "threatening dystopias" (p. 34).

To echo one of the most rudimentary of stock market principles: the potential for gain bears within it the seed of potential loss. While potentiality is often oriented toward desired outcomes—the potential for better futures, economic gain, and so on—it is also, and because of this, vulnerable to risk. Time-rich and thus, as we have seen, ripe with the potential for good return, the figure of the child also comes to represent the potential for loss. The child might, as writes Stockton (2009), take on those "elegant, unruly contours of growing that don't bespeak continuance" (p. 13). In relation to stringent cultural ideals and their inflexible measures, the child might not grow in the 'right' direction;[13] s/he might fail to grow 'up,' might not move 'forward' on the developmental timeline fast enough, might not 'go far' in life. The child might squander his/her temporal riches with the rigid inefficiency of 'developmental delays,' and so 'wasting' 'full' potentials for culturally determined—and, as we have seen, in these neoliberal times this often comes to mean economically determined—notions of success and achievement. Thus, to borrow from Muñoz's (2009) critique of Edelman's child figure, "The future is only the stuff of some kids. Racialized kids, queer kids are not the sovereign princes of futurity" (p. 95). And to this list we must also add disabled kids (Mollow, 2012; Chen, 2012; Kafer, 2013). Indeed, under neoliberalism, categories of race, queerness, and disability are finely imbricated; such categories and the bodies they mark threaten to disrupt the forward motion of a normative (and so white, middle-class, heterosexual, able-bodied) development and the subsequent promise of a good, productive future time.

As is exemplified in both the WAAD document and in Obama's appeal to better futures, imagined utopias reflect the political commitments, the values and interests of a particular culture at a particular historical moment. Imagined dystopias, too, are marked by the particularities of culture and history. As Ericson and Doyle (2003) remind us: "risk [. . .] is a cultural code for expressing and defending interests. Nothing is inherently risky but anything can be treated as a risk if the party claims that it has the potential to adversely affect their interests and values" (p. 16). Culturally and historically specific investments call into being particular kinds of fears and thus particular conceptualizations of risk. As the timely body of the normative or 'normally developing' child gets inaugurated as the primary site of neoliberal investment, autism is introduced as a risk, a variable that might divert potential gain into potential loss. Autism, in other words, is framed as that risk which may—in the absence of biomedical control—potentially divert the normative, productive course of a time-rich child by causing them to squander their temporal wealth: by 'wasting' or 'losing' temporal riches with the rigid inefficiency of 'developmental delays,' by arriving late (or not at all) to milestones and so to productive and consumptive futures. This risk of a dystopic autistic future is indicated by Wright as he alludes to individual children's futures being 'at stake' in the absence of early biomedical intervention. The WAAD resolution broadens Wright's not-so-subtle threat by painting a picture of an 'underdeveloped' child that poses risks—"consequent development challenges"—to nation states, global communities, and the private sector.

Still, we cannot forget that, following Aristotle and Agamben, 'all potentiality is impotentiality'—the one contains the other and vice versa. Put differently, without the potential for loss, there can be no potential for gain. To make an investment is to live with risk and, in a market economy, invest we must. Simons (2006) notes: "risk is not immediately understood as the chance that some problems will arise, but is instead a chance or opportunity" (p. 533). Risk is thus not necessarily something to be avoided altogether. Recall, for example, the extent to which the market is dependent on the 'troubled person' (Lane, 2006). And so rather than something to be eliminated altogether, risk—and this, of course, includes those bodies constituted as 'risky' or 'at risk'—becomes something (someone) to be managed with the aim of maximizing gain.

In other words, something that must be measured, monitored, calculated, strategized about, manipulated, and above all, controlled.

Our contemporary times have witnessed the emergence of scores of tools and techniques aimed at assessing and managing the perceived risk of autism (e.g., empirical studies examining epidemiology or risk factors, informational facts about early warning signs, assessment tools, technologies and checklists, and so on). I now turn to a consideration of but one of these techniques: the systematic production and circulation of statistics that tell of autism's presence, or perhaps more accurately, its *prevalence*. Before I delve into some of the productive effects of statistics, it is important to first note how these are accomplishing something more than simply relaying information about a given risky phenomenon. Ericson and Doyle (2003) write: "Risk communication systems are not simply conduits through which knowledge of risk is transferred. Rather, they have their own logics and autonomous processes. They are themselves the producers of new risks, because it is through them that risks are recognized, subject to communication and acted upon" (p. 2). Statistical techniques of measuring, assessing, and managing risk provide the conditions of possibility for the appearance of a given risky phenomenon and are thus involved in the very constitution of what (who) gets recognized as risky in the first place. As Titchkosky writes: "to put disability into [statistical] text [. . .] is to enact its meaning" (Titchkosky, 2007, p. 76). In order to examine the productive effects of notions of investment within contemporary autism advocacy discourses, it becomes necessary to look to the ways in which understandings of risk get communicated and thus created. To do this, let us return, once again, to the central usages of this chapter: Bob Wright's Starbucks coffee cup statement, the UN World Autism Day resolution, and President Obama's one hundred million dollar investment in biomedical autism research.

Advocacy in a Time of Epidemic: The S/pace of the 'NOW'

Weaving together epidemiological narratives of prevalence and proximity and citing increasing odds in collapsing times, each of the three central examples from this chapter communicates and, indeed, actively works to constitute autism as a very specific kind of risk: particular usages of autism statistics in contemporary times invoke autism as a risky pathology threatening the benefit outcome (or 'health') of neoliberal investments. As we shall see, autism gets transformed into a risk-to-be-managed, while nonautism (normalcy) is reified as an investment-to-be-protected.

"Every 20 minutes," whispers your morning coffee, "— less time than it will take you to drink your coffee—another child is diagnosed with autism." Be "concerned" with your child's development, Wright instructs, for autism's untimely development is "much more common than people think, with one out of every 150 children diagnosed" (Autism Speaks, 2007). Obama, too, cites this '1 in 150' odd. Autism, he said at his 2009 press conference at the NIH, is "a disease that now touches more than one in every 150 children" (Government of the United States of America, 2009b, para. 9). While the United Nations World Autism Awareness Day resolution does not cite the '1 in 150' statistic, it nonetheless references it, stating that the assembly is "*deeply concerned* by the *prevalence* and *high rate* of autism in children in all regions of the world" (United Nations General Assembly 76 Plenary Meeting, 2008, para. 5, my emphasis). More than simply or transparently informing us of empirically derived numbers of individual autism diagnoses or the rates at which these diagnoses occur (processes that are themselves historically, politically, and economically mediated, to be sure), the production and circulation of statistical facts underscores the central and often taken for granted fact that autism represents a risk to contemporary investments, both ideological and economic.

But it is perhaps more interesting to ask the question: what kind of risk does autism come to represent? One way that autism gets statistically represented as a growing subpopulation is through the listing of numbers, climbing statistics meant to reflect the number of individual bodies being diagnosed at a given time. These kinds of statistics are most often found in scientific journals, in advocacy organization reports, or in government documents. For example, the Centers for Disease Control and Prevention (CDC) report from the Autism and Developmental Disabilities Monitoring (ADDM) Network entitled "Prevalence of the Autism Spectrum Disorders (ASDs) in Multiple Areas of the United States, 2004 and 2006" (2010), published a summary of its research findings that included statistical facts that showed autism's growing numbers in the United States during the two years studied:

Number of 8 year olds identified with an ASD [2004]: 172, 335
Number of 8 year olds identified with an ASD [2006]: 308, 038
(Centers for Disease Control and Prevention, 2010, p. 8)

Numbers such as these are seldom understood to be rhetorical. Commonsense tells us that numbers simply count up what is already there: autistic people. Yet recalling Ericson and Doyle (2003), techniques of measurement and modes of risk communication are no mere conduits. Numbers are rhetorical (Yergeau, 2010; Broderick, 2011; Titchkosky, 2007). The kinds of statistics that are deployed shape the kinds of risk that get recognized; they also shape the nature of the problem and thus anticipate and legitimize certain kinds of responses (Titchkosky, 2007). Autism is not some 'thing' that exists prior to the numbers that count it up. The process of counting, whose doing the counting, what counts as countable, how the count gets communicated, all these *social* processes shape the meaning of autism and our collective sense of the kind of risk it purportedly represents.

For example, the statistics from the 2010 CDC report cited above function to depict autism as a growing population: a population *trend* and, as we have seen, a risky one at that. More specifically, the risk that autism comes to represents in these statistics is the risk that its growth might not be stoppable, that it might grow beyond available techniques of management, that its growth is out of control. Yet, it is significant, to note that, at least in popular autism advocacy discourse, such growing numerical figures are not commonly cited. While these kinds of statistics might be found buried somewhere in an advocacy organization's annual report or as a bullet on a government fact-sheet, rarely are we confronted with the refrain: 'In the past two years, incidence of autism in eight-year-olds has increased from 172,335 to 308,038'; we do not encounter these kinds statistics on the streets, on our television screens, at the coffee shop. What we are confronted with is the extensive—excessive even—repetition of autism represented as a simplified ratio, a statistical odd (i.e., 'autism affects 1 in 110' as opposed to 'autism affects 308, 038'). As we go about our daily lives, odds are we'll encounter them. These odds are prominent in:

- **Newspaper headlines:** e.g., the *New York Times* headline "Study Puts Rate of Autism at 1 in 150 US Children" (Carey, 2007); a headline from Reuters India "With Autism at 1 in 110 Kids, Treatment in Demand" (Fox, 2009); "Autism Rates Now 1 in 68 U.S. Children: CDC" (Falco, 2014).
- **Media coverage:** e.g., MSNBC and NBC News' week-long coverage "Autism: The Hidden Epidemic?" (Autism Speaks, 2005);

CNN's day-long special, "Autism: Unravelling the Mystery" (Autism Speaks, 2008); Autism Speaks' political campaign "1 in 88 Can't Wait" (2013).

- **Advocacy Campaigns:** e.g., Autism Speaks "Learn the Signs" campaign (Autism Speaks, 2006b), Autism Speaks' "Times have Changed" PSA (Autism Speaks, 2010), National Autism Association's "Never Give Up" PSA (National Autism Association, 2010) all feature autism 'odds' prominently, but they are cited in almost every mainstream autism advocacy campaign of the moment.

Political debates. Presidential addresses. Celebrity interviews. And of course we might also encounter these odds as we are on the go with our morning coffee.

What different kinds of work are accomplished by these two similar yet divergent ways of statistically representing autism's presence (i.e., as a growing number or as a statistical odd)? Statistics that represent autism as a growing number count up individual untimely bodies, stack them up, one upon the other, growing them into towering bar graphs. As these teetering numbers (and the bodies they represent) shoot up and up and up again—172,335 . . . 308,038 . . .—they symbolically grow further and further away from us. The towering numbers are indiscriminate, faceless; they are someone else in some other place. What is more, as they continue to grow away from us they seem to move beyond the purview of the everyday; out of reach, beyond our control. Quite to the contrary, statistics that represent autism as an odd count up untimely bodies only to divide them out, distilling the numbers down to the most simple of ratios.[14] Rather than growing away, statistical odds grow inward. They close in: as the odds go up, the ratio gets smaller. 1 in 150; 1 in 110; 1 in 88, and most recently, 1 in 68. Like a countdown, increasing odds grow *toward us*. Where growing numerical figures are abstract, faceless, distant, and deeply impersonal, increasing odds are close, specific, personal, intimate.

It bears notice that with the odd, the number '1'—perhaps the most intimate of numbers—never changes over time. Autism's 1 never grows (we never are confronted with odds like '2 out of every 150'). As odds change over time, the variable number is the second number in the ratio—the number representing the population as a whole. According to the ADDM report released in the winter of 2010, autism no longer affects 1 in *150* children, but 1 in *110* (Centers for Disease Control and Prevention, 2010). In 2012, it was 1 in *88*. In 2014, 1 in 68. While increasing numbers function to expand out, increasing odds conjure an atmosphere of enclosure and confinement. Growing odds tell an allegorical story of a circle that is closing in, zeroing in on the '1,' which is, inevitably, your '1.' To borrow the tagline from a 2010 Autism Speaks PSA,[15] "autism is getting closer to home" (Autism Speaks, 2010c). Or in the words of Autism Speaks chief science officer Geraldine Dawson following the CDC's 2012 release of the 1 in 88 statistic, "as autism soars: no one is left untouched" (Autism Speaks, 2012b).

Obama, too, used this language of touch at the 2009 NIH press conference. Autism, he said, is "a disease that now *touches* more than one in every 150 children" (Government of the United States of America, 2009b, para. 9, my emphasis). Autism touches. Close. Recalling Wright, "It's much more common than people think." So 'close to home' is autism that it no longer waits on doorsteps but penetrates thresholds. It's making contact, grazing the fleshly borderlines of our children and thus the imagined path to our futures. These are not the only frontiers that autism is understood to be penetrating. Autism is narrated as leaky and indiscriminate, transgressing bounded spaces of identity and identification: as the WAAD resolution states, autism "affect[s] children [. . .] irrespective of gender, race or socio-economic status." It is seeping across state lines with neither restriction nor restraint: autism is, according to the WAAD resolution, concerning because of its prevalence and high rates among children all over the world. And as the odds count down, as the numbers close in and our borders are breached, each of these examples agrees on the necessary course of action: do something, do it quickly, and do it for the children. "Learn the early warnings signs," says Wright, "early intervention could make a big difference in your child's future" (Autism Speaks, 2007). "Early diagnosis," says the WAAD document, and "appropriate" (read: biomedical) "research and intervention is vital to the growth and development of the individual" (United Nations General Assembly 76 Plenary Meeting, 2008, para. 6). We need more biomedical research, declares the Obama administration, research that will lead to, in the words of the president, "greater understanding,[16] early interventions, more effective treatments and therapies to help these children" (Government of the United States of America, 2009b, para. 9). These representations also seem to agree: the adults are already lost to time. I will pick up on the deadly consequences of this interpretive move in the book's final chapter.

Insofar as these examples draw upon epidemiological tropes of 'high rates' of contact and indiscriminate spreading—not only is autism 'touching' us, according to Obama, it's 'plaguing' us—they comprise a story of autism that might be characterized in terms of what Priscilla Wald (2008) refers to as an "outbreak narrative," a narrative that, in her words, "follows a formulaic plot that begins with the identification of an emerging infection, includes discussion of the global networks through which it travels, and chronicles the epidemiological work that ends with its containment" (p. 2). This outbreak narrative is a familiar one; it is, indeed, another real 'sign of the times,' as it were. This is evidenced by a vast variety of contemporary artifacts du jour that take up this narrative including:

- **Films and television:** e.g., *Outbreak* (Petersen, 1995); *Quarantine* (Dowdie, 2008); *The Andromeda Strain* (Salomon, 2008); *The Stand* (Garris, 1994); *28 Days Later* (Boyle, 2002); *Carriers* (Pastor and Pastor, 2009); and HBO's *The Walking Dead* (Darabont, 2010) and *Contagion* (Soderbergh, 2011).
- **Video games:** e.g., *Resident Evil* (Mikami, 1997); *Pathologic* (Ice-Pick Lodge, 2006); *Left 4 Dead* (Turtle Rock Studios, 2008); and *Dead Nation* (Housemarque, 2010).
- **Books:** e.g., José Saramago's *Blindness (1999)*; P. D. James's *Children of Men (2006)*; Daniel Kalla's *Pandemic (2005)*; Cronin's *The Passage* (2010); Malcom Gladwell's *The Tipping Point (2002)*; Hamilton and Dennis's *Affluenza* (2006); and so on.

To quote Harold Varmus of *The New York Times*, "microbial plagues have displaced nuclear winter in the public's mind of the way the world will end" (as cited in Lavin and Russell, 2010, p. 66). The predictable worry-laden storyline of a dangerous-and-threatening-contagion-to-be-stopped often, if not always, underpins and indeed organizes (ever popular) discussions of contemporary viral diseases (e.g., AIDS, SARS, West Nile, Avian Flu, HIN1, and the range of diseases/illnesses associated with bioterrorism): how we understand these, how we fear them, how we react to their presence, and so on. The outbreak narrative also serves as a metaphoric way of understanding and orienting contemporary social problems—phenomena that are medically and morally constructed as undesirable and, as such, threatening.

In contemporary times we often hear talk of, for example, an 'obesity epidemic,' a 'smoking epidemic,' a 'violent crime epidemic,' or a 'junk food' epidemic. Child abuse. Schoolyard bullying. Pornography. Poverty. Homelessness. Suicide. Eating disorders. And so on and so forth, ad infinitum. As Lavin and Russill (2010) point out, "Americans *[and I think here we can also include all of us residing in the western and westernized countries]* have become increasingly prepared to view the world through the lens of infection and contagion" and adopt a kind of, in their words, "'epidemiological imaginary' in which individuals make sense of a time of spatial disruption through the terms of infectious disease" (p. 66, my editorial). And so it comes as no surprise that autism, too, is widely articulated and so understood in contemporary times as not only a risk but a particular kind of risk: a risk of epidemic proportions.

As I mentioned earlier, autism odds have been increasing rather rapidly. Prior to the winter of 2009–2010, the often cited 'odd' of having a diagnosis with autism was '1 in 150.' Over the course of that winter, however, two major scientific studies were released with more timely statistical odds. According to a major study published in *Pediatrics*, autism was now as common as '1 in every 91' children, while according to a study published by the CDC, '1 in 110' children had autism (Centers for Disease Control and Prevention, 2010; Kogan et al., 2009). Since then, there have been several new CDC reports, each publishing higher odds. '1 in 88' in 2012 and '1 in 68' in 2014 (CDC, 2012; CDC, 2014). Somewhat comically, one MIT researcher has even predicted that 1 in 2 children will have an autism diagnosis by 2025 (Meyer, 2014). As the odds change over time, what remains consistent is the unwavering notion that increasing odds represent a social threat. Around the globe, news of increasing odds is reported as 'shocking,' 'staggering,' 'striking,' 'alarming,' sending 'waves' through autism communities everywhere. Just what is shocking or staggering about these numbers is not in question. Vis-à-vis these statistics, we tacitly know that what is alarming is this: the numbers are saying that autism's prevalence is high, that its prevalence is too high, that it's getting higher. Autism is getting closer. Autism is closing in. 'Epidemic!' advocates cried.

According to the CDC, "[Autism Spectrum Disorders] are conditions of urgent public health concern," warranting a "coordinated response" (Center for Disease Control and Prevention, 2010, p. 27). Responding in 2009 to increasing prevalence statistics, Kelly Vanicek, board member of the National Autism Association, said "we hope these new numbers will create an immediate shift in priorities [. . .] this nation's children need the CDC's full attention, and we are again asking President Obama to declare autism an epidemic and a national health crisis" (National Autism Association, 2009, para. 3, 5). "Well these are staggering numbers," said Autism Speaks cofounder Suzanne Wright, "it's really uncomprehensible [sic] to think that so many families . . . *so many families* . . . in our country are suffering with autism [. . .] this is a whole generation of children being lost to autism. This is not acceptable" (Autism Speaks, 2009d).

The notion that autism is sweeping in, spreading through the population, immediately threatening the good normative lives and futures of loved ones fuels a sense of moral panic. In dominant discourses of autism advocacy, this collective sense of panic is routinely amplified through the circulation of affective and affecting analogies that frame autism as a fatal illness or even as death (Gross, 2012; McGuire, 2012). Autism is so often likened to potentially fatal diseases like cancer, AIDS, and cystic fibrosis (Gross, 2012; Broderick and Ne'eman, 2008). Autistic people are readily framed as lost, kidnapped or otherwise missing as is made explicit in Suzanne Wright's quote above as well as in her statement from the opening epigraph (Gross, 2012; McGuire, 2012). In 2009, the heads of two major US advocacy organizations, on two separate occasions, likened autism to the H1N1 influenza outbreak. National Autism Association vice president Ann Brasher stated: "The focus on the propaganda-driven swine flu 'pandemic' is outrageous considering the very real epidemic of autism" (National Autism Association, 2009, para. 5). In Bob Wright's (of Starbucks fame) words: "The statistical aspect of autism is just staggering. If we had 1 in 58 boys getting swine flu, the country would be crazy" (Brooks, 2009, para. 3). Of course, everyone knows autism is neither contagious nor fatal. Even the claim that there is an epidemic has been thoroughly troubled by social scientists and clinical scientists alike (Gernsbacher, Dawson, and Goldsmith, 2002; Timimi, Gardner, and McCabe, 2011). It is tempting to write off statements such as Brasher's and Wright's as merely bad analogies or instances of hyperbole. Yet we can trace out a kind of logic that underpins the moral panic that is fueling autism advocacy discourse today. It is a logic that ties us back to the contemporary ruling logic of the global(ized) free market. In *Empire*, Michael Hardt and Antonio Negri (2000) write that "along with the common celebrations of the unbounded flows of the new global village, one can still sense also an anxiety about increased contact and a certain nostalgia for colonialist hygiene" (p. 136). We can perhaps glean this so-called nostalgia in the contemporary neoliberal fixation with, and production of, a vast variety of risky social problems including the social problem of untimely individual and social development. If in colonial times problem bodies were understood and devalued via discourses of pathology (as we saw in chapter 3), in a fast-paced globalized and globalizing neoliberalism, problem bodies are, quite fittingly, understood via the logic of a *moving pathology*—the logic, in other words, of the epidemic. In this way, following Hardt and Negri (2000), "the age of globalization is the age of universal contagion" (p. 136).

To consider this further, let us return to an important interpretive effect of the odd. As we have seen, functionally a ratio is a relation: the 1 is not a 1 on its own but rather exists in relationship with the 150 or the 91 or the 110. In this way, the statistical odd underscores the relationship between autism's 1 and the whole of the population, touching these oppositions together. This is indeed the etymological root of contagion. From the Latin, con-tagio: to touch together. In the ratio, as autism rates are understood to be increasing, the autistic 1 stays the same; it is rather the nonautistic population that seems to be getting smaller—149, 109, and so on. The ratio works, in effect, to structure a rivalry or competition—a kind of Foucaultian "agon" or contest—between constructed oppositions: autism/nonautism, pathology/health, underdevelopment/development, cost/benefit (Foucault, 1980, p. 207).

The logic of this ratio goes as follows: as an (undesired) autistic population gets bigger, the (desired) nonautistic population is compressed. As autism demands (costly, timely) resources, those valuable resources of the whole are diminished. As autism arrives late, the whole is held back. Autism, the logic continues, becomes some 'thing' that for the good of (or even in some rhetoric the 'health' of) the normative whole—'civil society' perhaps—must be suppressed. In this way, the work of advocacy in contemporary times often gets taken up as the work of protecting, preserving, or recovering nonautism; the normative work, in other words, of (biological) securitization.

The logic of free competition—a logic that is shared, incidentally, by both global capitalism and contemporary discourses of contagion—delivers us security as a necessary response (Foucault, 2009, p. 48). Faced with the risk of a spreading contagion that threatens the health of the body, we take security measures to lower our risk. We wash our hands, sneeze into our sleeve, wear a condom, and so on. Faced with a risky stock, we also take measures. We lower our risk portfolio, protect our investments. What is more, when we are working to secure something—be it bodies or assets or body-assets—we do not wait until tomorrow, next week, next year. When confronted with a free roaming, fast-acting, uncontrolled risk, we install security measures. And we do it now.

As is evidenced in the examples throughout this chapter, discourses of autism advocacy are often situated in contemporary times at the point where the logics of contagion and the market converge.[17] And as the story of autism gets reforged in times of capitalism and outbreak, autism's meaning is transformed into a too-quickly spreading epidemic of 'too slow' bodies to be left behind by an accelerated neoliberal modernity. This story of autism conjures a very particular temporality that, in turn, works to speed up the s/pace of autism advocacy, producing a frenzied sense of urgency: a temporality that sweeps advocate and advocated for up, shapes their meanings, endows them with particular im/possibilities.

Within dominant discourses of autism advocacy, the autistic subjectivity—located simultaneously in the perpetual past (e.g., developmentally 'too slow' and always late) *and* the future (e.g., yet-to-be developed)—is discursively foreclosed from *being (existing)* in the privileged and agentive time of the 'now'. Via a kind of time-sensitive investment logic, autism is understood not as a being but as a happening—a costly body, a disruptive threat, a risky trend, and so on—a happening, moreover, that is happening fast. Every twenty minutes. Vis-à-vis understandings of drawn-out pasts and dwindling futures, the neoliberal 'now' becomes the time for responding to autism's perceived 'happening.' It is a time for action and reaction. Paradoxically, and as we have seen throughout this chapter, such timely actions and reactions are regulated and regulating—surveil particular kinds of behaviors, notice particular behaviors as signs of 'deviance,' discipline and restrict these behaviors, seek out biomedicine to ensure timeliness—but they are also entrepreneurial, creative, and creating—uncovering more ways of noticing and charting the minutia of human difference, generating more ways of classifying behaviors as abnormal or deviant, coming up with more and more ways of treating or preventing autism, more and more ways of raising awareness about its pathological state of underdevelopment. As it both stimulates and regulates conducts beyond the norm, the neoliberal 'now' is a time for ('good') autism advocacy.[18]

Advocacy's temporality of the 'now' does more than manage bodies and stimulate the economy, however. Slavoj Zizek (2008) writes that "there is a fundamental anti-theoretical edge to [. . .] urgent injunctions. There is no time to reflect: we have *to act now*" (p. 6). 'Now' is a temporality that forecloses the often slow or not time-efficient possibilities of contemplation, critical thinking, debate, deliberation, disagreement and in so doing functions to normalize and even naturalize neoliberal discourses in which notions of rights and understandings of (good) life are mediated and even determined by one's timely ability to 'fully' partake in and 'enjoy' market-driven processes of production and consumption. Embracing a non-normative autistic time—being untimely as it were—might permit us to notice still another risk, a risk that is, itself, animated by understandings of autism as a risk to be secured. What the examples in this chapter present to us is the risk of better futures where bodies must keep pace with the unyielding tempo of the market or be left behind. Most significantly, the better futures being envisioned here are futures without autism's difference. Throughout this chapter, we have seen how—to borrow from Roger Stahl's (2009) discussion of evocations of urgent temporalities in the US war on terror—"dominant voices use temporal rhetorics to shape a public environment hostile to deliberative possibilities," creating a temporal environment of control that is, he argues, a central characteristic of war discourses (p. 74). I turn now to a critical consideration of the strategies and tactics of representation that have emerged out of what has often been referred to as advocacy's war on autism.

CHAPTER FOUR

"We Have Your Son . . ."

Frames of Terror in Advocacy's War on Autism

———— ❧ ————

"We are a community of warriors."
—"Voice of advocacy," Alfonso Cuarón (2009), *I am Autism*

"This way of life is worth defending."
—George W. Bush (March 19, 2004), Remarks on the
Anniversary of Operation Iraqi Freedom

"Whose lives count as lives?"
—Judith Butler (2004), *Precarious Life: The Powers of Mourning
and Violence*, p. 20

In December 2006, following considerable pressure from autism advocacy organizations and parent advocates, the US Senate and House of Representatives unanimously passed a bill officially titled the "Combating Autism Act" (CAA) (S. 843) (fig. 7). The bill was first introduced by pro-war Republican senator Rick Santorum and signed into law by President George W. Bush (US law 109–416). It authorized the formation of the Interagency Autism Coordinating Committee (IACC), which was, in turn, tasked with overseeing all autism-related activities of the Department of Health and Human Services and research and policy carried out through the Centers for Disease Control and Prevention (CDC) and the National Institutes of Health (NIH). Over the course of a five-

Public Law 109–416
109th Congress

An Act

To amend the Public Health Service Act to combat autism through research, screening, intervention and education.

Dec. 19, 2006

[S. 843]

Combating
Autism Act of
2006.
42 USC 201 note.

Be it enacted by the Senate and House of Representatives of the United States of America in Congress assembled,

SECTION 1. SHORT TITLE.

This Act may be cited as the "Combating Autism Act of 2006".

SEC. 2. CENTERS OF EXCELLENCE; IMPROVING AUTISM-RELATED RESEARCH.

(a) CENTERS OF EXCELLENCE REGARDING RESEARCH ON AUTISM.—Section 409C of the Public Health Service Act (42 U.S.C.284g) is amended—

(1) in the section heading, by striking "AUTISM" and inserting "AUTISM SPECTRUM DISORDER";

(2) by striking the term "autism" each place such term appears (other than the section heading) and inserting "autism spectrum disorder"; and

(3) in subsection (a)—

(A) by redesignating paragraph (2) as paragraph (3); and

(B) by striking paragraph (1) and inserting the following:

"(1) EXPANSION OF ACTIVITIES.—The Director of NIH (in this section referred to as the 'Director') shall, subject to the availability of appropriations, expand, intensify, and coordinate the activities of the National Institutes of Health with respect to research on autism spectrum disorder, including basic and clinical research in fields including pathology, developmental neurobiology, genetics, epigenetics, pharmacology, nutrition, immunology, neuroimmunology, neurobehavioral development, endocrinology, gastroenterology, and toxicology. Such research shall investigate the cause (including possible environmental causes), diagnosis or rule out, early detection, prevention, services, supports, intervention, and treatment of autism spectrum disorder.

"(2) CONSOLIDATION.—The Director may consolidate program activities under this section if such consolidation would improve program efficiencies and outcomes.".

(b) CENTERS OF EXCELLENCE GENERALLY.—Part A of title IV of the Public Health Service Act (42 U.S.C. 281 et seq.) is amended by adding at the end the following:

Fig. 7 United States Public Law 109–416, the "Combating Autism Act of 2006," signed by President George W. Bush on December 19, 2006.

year period,[1] CAA released close to a billion dollars earmarked for bio-medical autism research, research that, for the most part, was focused on discovering cures for autism, treatments for it, and strategies to prevent it. Autistic self-advocates were—and continue to be—deeply critical of the act (see for example the Autistic Self Advocacy Network's #stopcom-batingme campaign and the subsequent Stop Combating Me flash blog initiative), denouncing the lack of autistic representation on the IACC[2] as well as the lack of diversity in the research that it is funding.

The Combating Autism Act was immediately dubbed—by many autism advocates and reporters alike—as the US government's 'war on autism.' "Congress declares war on autism," read an American televi-sion network news headline from the winter of 2006 (O'Keefe, 2006). "This is a battle plan to win the war against autism," said federal lobbyist Craig Snyder, who continued by noting that "it's now the law of the land" (Scelfo and Kantrowitz, 2006, para. 6). "This bill is a federal declaration of war on the epidemic of autism," confirmed John Shestack in an Autism Speaks press release, noting that the bill "creates a congressionally man-dated roadmap for a federal assault on autism" (O'Keefe, 2006, para. 6). The significance of these speech-acts that link autism and war extends well beyond their existence as metaphor-laden sound bites. In a histori-cal moment when autism is officially legislated in the United States as an outlaw at large—a state enemy-within to be 'combated,' 'assaulted,' 'battled'—the rhetorical appeal to actual wars in order to motivate social projects designed to eliminate autism from individual and collective life should not remain unexamined.

In this chapter, I trace the contours of a militaristic turn within domi-nant contemporary forms of autism advocacy, a turn distinguished by advocacy's reliance on the rhetoric of combat in order to express a mate-rial desire for life without autism and, indeed, to achieve this end. By drawing on Foucault's (1997) discussions of the vitalizing force of bio-political war, I show how the call to war in the name of (normative) life situates the war on autism within a greater cultural context of liberal war-fare. It is therefore both appropriate and necessary to attend to the war on autism alongside a brutally enduring transnational war on terror, the latter of which is characterized by the US-led invasion and occupation of Iraq and Afghanistan, by ongoing military operatives in the Middle East, and by heightened domestic surveillance policies and practices. The historical simultaneity of these two wars is not mere happenstance, nor are the striking resonances in their war-time rhetorics, rationalities, and technologies. To the contrary, the war on autism and the war on terror, as well as their respective oppositional figures of terrorist and warrior, are intimately connected and even dependent upon one another, functioning continuously to define, secure, and surveil the borders of a liberal normativity. As a way to reveal how discourses of autism and terror have converged into a shared (liberal, biopolitical) frame, I begin by examining three recent high-profile autism advocacy campaigns that cast, on the one hand, autism as a terrifying threat to normative life and, on the other, advocacy as what must, above all, eliminate this threat.

Terrorizing Autism

In the summer of 2005, the Autism Society of America (ASA) unveiled a "new arm to fight autism," a "jarring new initiative" called "Getting the Word Out" that was, according to a press release, aimed at "combat[ing] the rising statistics of autism diagnosis" by "talk[ing] about the harsh realities of living with Autism Spectrum Disorders" (Autism Society of America, 2005a, para.1). To this end, an elaborate new website was launched, complete with a dramatic opening Flash sequence that features a tragically grayscale photograph of a small child with what appear to be his parents (fig. 8). To the far left of the photographic frame, two adults—a man and a woman, both appear to be people of color—appear with their backs facing one another. Their postures and the expressions on their faces suggest upset, worry, exhaustion, and concern. To the far right of the frame is a young black child with his head resting in his hand. The boy stares pleadingly at the viewer: his body deflated and hopeless, his eyes wide with sadness.

The Flash sequence begins as a small tear is made in the top edge of the photograph. The following statement appears: "1 in 166 children are born with it." The photograph tears a little more, and then the words: "24,000 will be diagnosed with it this year." The tear extends deeper into the center of the photograph, now beginning to cleave the parents from the child. "It is more common than multiple sclerosis, cystic fibrosis and childhood cancer. Combined." Tear. "It is growing at a rate of 10–17% each year." Tear. "Currently there is no cure for it." As the tear reaches the bottom edge of the photograph, these words appear: "It can tear a family apart." The sequence ends as the left side of the photograph— the side with the image of the parents—is completely torn off and discarded. Only the torn image of the boy remains and the words: "It is . . . autism" (Autism Society of America, 2005a). This opening sequence in

It can tear a family apart.

Fig. 8 Detail of Autism Society of America's (2005) "Getting the Word Out" campaign website. Photographs by Eduardo Trejos, 2011. Reprinted with artist's permission.

turn delivers us into the website's inner pages that provide further details about the presumed origin of torn families and ripped photographs—information about, in other words, autism.

The section "Autism 101" (fig. 9) provides readers with information quite similar to information featured in those advocacy campaigns examined in previous chapters (Autism Society of America, 2005b). Reminiscent of the red flag campaigns explored in chapter 2, the webpage presents readers with biomedical evidence of autism's pathology. Readers are informed, for example, that "autism is a neurological disorder that effects the functioning of the brain impacting the normal development of the brain in the areas of social interaction and communication skills" and "children and adults with autism typically have difficulties in verbal and non-verbal communication, social interaction and leisure and play activities" (Autism Society of America, 2005b, para. 1). And much like the 'odds' campaigns explored in chapter 3, the site cultivates a growing sense of urgency by offering viewers statistical evidence of swelling numbers of autism diagnoses in collapsing temporal/spatial frames. "Roughly 1 out of every 166 children is diagnosed with Autism Spectrum Disorder" the text from the webpage tells us, "that's 66 children per day, nearly three an hour, one every 20 minutes" (Autism Society of America, 2005b, para. 2). Next to this biomedical and statistical information—facts that, as we have seen, work to frame autism as nothing more than a common deficit and a spreading pathology—another key piece of information is entered into evidence. The webpage features one-half of a torn black and white photograph—much like the one from the opening sequence—of what appears to be a young, white (presumably autistic) girl.[3] The girl in the photo is collapsed into a ball, her bare toes curled inward and her face obscured, buried in her knees. She is photographed cowering against a nondescript wall and tightly clenching a stuffed toy. Based on the opening animation, we must assume that the terrified, crumpled girl in the torn image has been wrenched away from those who love her, and—corralled within the tight confines of the photographic frame—she appears held captive by an unseen, but not unnamed, aggressor. "It is autism,"[4] the site reminds us. The text adjacent to the photograph confirms her captors identity, providing viewers with a kind of behavioral profile: "Autism knows no racial, ethnic or social boundaries," the text reads, "it doesn't care how much money you make, what kind of lifestyle you lead or what your education level is. For more information on understanding autism, treatment and/or education, please visit [the ASA website] autism-society.org" (Autism Society

Fig. 9 [Top] Detail of "Autism 101" web page from the Autism Society of America's (2005) "Getting the Word Out" campaign website. [Bottom] Detail of Autism Society of America's (2005) poster for the "Getting the Word Out" campaign. Photographs by Eduardo Trejos. Reprinted with artist's permission.

of America, 2005b, para. 3). Finally, at the very bottom of the page, the statement appears: "Helping to get the word out."

In the "Getting the Word Out" campaign—which belongs, as we shall see, to a whole genre of similar campaigns—autism is not strictly characterized as some 'thing'—a series of pathological behaviors, for example, or a risky statistic—and is surely not understood as a someone—a viable embodiment, a way of being, an identity. Out of a normative background image of the heterosexual, nuclear family and childhood innocence, autism emerges as a threatening 'Ripper' figure: a tearer of photos and families. As it tears, this figure of autism terrifies and terrorizes: pulling apart families, isolating children from their loved ones, holding (what we must presume to be otherwise nonautistic) kids captive. Autism is made faceless, hidden and ubiquitous, lethal and out of control. One part biology—striking at the body indiscriminately and spreading quickly ("Roughly 1 out of every 166 children is diagnosed with Autism Spectrum Disorder. That's 66 children per day, nearly three an hour, one every 20 minutes . . ."). One part (a)morality—cruel and uncaring, unmoved by the fiercely guarded social boundaries of privilege and position ("Autism knows no racial, ethnic or social boundaries. It doesn't care how much money you make, what kind of lifestyle you lead or what your education level is"). Autism is delivered to us, then, as an anthropomorphized threat. Half metaphor. Half corporeal. And very real.

This terrifying and terrorizing figure of autism solicits the emergence of still another figure, and an oppositional one. Out of the metaphorical scene of the tear, and in opposition to the tearing, terrifying, and terrorizing figure of autism, materializes a very particular figuration of autism advocacy. In the ASA's "Getting the Word Out" campaign, the figure of the advocate—the viewer of the photograph—is framed as witness to autism's terrible deeds, a neutral (and so necessarily nonautistic) bystander who happened upon the scene of autism's crime. Vis-à-vis tragic, captive children and torn up families, the figure of the advocate is therefore framed as he who should help, she who should intervene, they who ought to defend innocence and protect families by 'getting the word out' about this threatening figure of autism: what it looks like, how it behaves, where it hides, how to treat it.

The campaign was met with cries of protest by many autistic activists and bloggers. One such intervention, for example, was Amanda (Mel) Baggs's brilliantly disruptive counter-campaign "Getting the Truth Out" (Baggs, 2005). In her critique of the ASA campaign, Baggs curated a series of black and white photographs, frozen frames depicting her own autistic movements. The photographs counterposed the visual and textual rhetorics of the ASA campaign with her own politicized autistic accounts. In one greyscale image, for example, Baggs shows herself seated on the floor, her head in her hands. The adjacent text reads: "the young woman in this picture has autism, a debilitating developmental disorder that effects communication, socialization and behaviour" (Baggs, 2005). This same image appears again, this time with a different caption: "this is what I look like when I'm trying to relax, or zone out a little, or shut off vision so I can hear what is going on around me" (Baggs, 2012). Her approach worked to effectively unsettle the ASA campaign by exposing its representational tactics as both inaccurate and oppressive.

The ASA campaign ended in the summer of 2007. Though it was never formally retracted, its controversial website was taken down from the web. It bears repeating that the ASA has, in recent years, made a much more concerted effort to engage autistic perspectives, collaborate with leaders in the autism self-advocacy community, and challenge the oppressive rhetoric that it once was involved in promoting (see for example ASA's chief operating officer Scott Badesch's 2013 disavowal of the rhetoric of autism as threat and/or burden) (Autism Society of America, 2013).

In the winter of 2007, a few months after the "Getting the Word Out" campaign was dismantled, New York University's Child Studies Center (CSC) launched another controversial public awareness campaign, entitled "Ransom Notes." Appearing on billboards, kiosks, and in various online and print media sources, the campaign materials were aimed to "[alert] Americans to the silent public health epidemic of children's mental illness" (New York University, 2007b, para. 1). Figure 10 depicts the umbrella advertisement released by the CSC, which displays a towering urban billboard in the form of a large ransom note. The note's text—composed of words that appear to have been cut out from a variety of different print sources and pasted hurriedly together—delivers the message, "12 million kids are held hostage by a psychiatric disorder" (New York University, 2007a). The campaign referenced various 'psychiatric disorders' including Attention Deficit and Hyperactivity Disorder, bulimia, depression, and Obsessive Compulsive Disorder. Autism, too, was featured in the "Ransom Notes" campaign, appearing in two separate advertisements.

"We have your son," declares one such print advertisement (fig. 11). The advertisement, which was designed to look like a typed ransom note,

Fig. 10 Detail of New York University Child Study Center's (2007) "Ransom Notes" campaign umbrella advertisement. Photograph by Eduardo Trejos. Reprinted with artist's permission.

continues: "We will make sure he will not be able to care for himself or interact socially as long as he lives. This is only the beginning." The note is signed: "autism" (New York University, 2007a). Figure 11 also depicts another NYU CSC advertisement. Similar to the previous one, this advertisement is also made to look like a ransom note and begins with the terrifying pronouncement "we have your son." Its message, which appears to have been hastily scrawled by hand, continues: "we are destroying his ability for social interaction, and driving him into a life of complete isolation" (New York University, 2007a). This time, the note is signed: "Asperger's Syndrome." Superimposed at the bottom of both ransom note advertisements is the NYU CSC logo and the statement: "Don't let a psychiatric disorder take your child. The NYU Child Study Center is dedicated to giving children back their childhood by preventing, identifying, and treating psychiatric and learning disorders" (New York University, 2007a).

In "Ransom Notes" we encounter, once again, the anthropomorphized threat from the "Getting the Word Out" campaign. The terrifying and terrorizing figure of autism has struck again: still aggressively ripping apart families. Still faceless, still hidden, still lethal, and still out of control. And as such still generating the need for an oppositional figure of

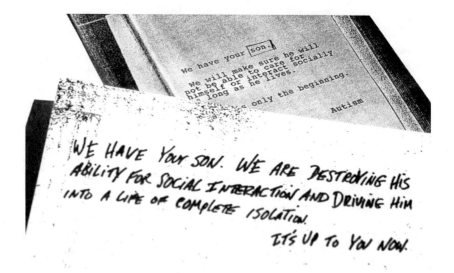

Fig. 11 Detail of New York University Child Study Center's (2007) "Ransom Notes" campaign posters "Autism" and "Asperger's Syndrome." Photograph by Eduardo Trejos. Reprinted with artist's permission.

the advocate who should take action not *for* autism, as the term 'autism advocacy' might seem to suggest, but *against it.* Yet the background story out of which these two figures emerge has been slightly altered in the "Ransom Notes" campaign, alterations that invariably work to shape and reshape the figures of autism and advocate anew.

In "Ransom Notes," autism's crime hits closer to home, it's more personal now, more intimate. The ransom notes are addressed to a 'you.' No longer a third party bystander merely witnessing autism's crime, the figure of the advocate is now framed as one of autism's many victims. 'Your' (presumed nonautistic) child has been ripped away from you and is now in the grasp of a masked villain (autism) who means him great harm, who intends to leave him isolated and alone, starving him of social interaction for as long as he lives. And "this," promises the figure of autism, "is only the beginning."

Vis-à-vis a threatening and violent figure of autism that is attacking and attacking close—tearing apart not just any family but your family, taking not just any child but your child—the figure of the advocate can no longer be s/he who *should* act, but is reformed and reborn as s/he who *has no choice but to act.* In "Ransom Notes," the viewer is confronted with a veritable ultimatum issued by the NYU CSC[5]: "Don't let a psychiatric disorder take your child." With 'your' child's life on the line, it is no longer enough to merely 'help' to 'get the word out' about autism's pathology or its rates of growth; the figure of the advocate is now positioned to embark upon a kind of reconnaissance mission aimed at recovering a taken child—a necessarily nonautistic child—from behind autism's enemy lines. As a way of 'giving children back their childhoods,' the advocate must, according to the campaign, search autism out, 'identify' it, 'treat' its pathology, and 'prevent' any future harm its presence invariably promises.

Shortly after this campaign was launched, and following wide-spread protests from an autistic community growing in numbers and also in power, the NYU CSC decided to retract the campaign (New York University, 2007c). As Kras (2012) writes in his analysis of the response to "Ransom Notes": "although the Ransom Notes campaign began and ended in New York City, the response to the campaign came from around the world. Ari Ne'eman and ASAN used the speed and penetration of the Internet to forge alliances with other disability rights organizations to quickly shut down the Ransom Notes campaign" (n.p.) (ASAN, 2007). ASAN's resistance campaign was reported in *The New York Times, The Washington Post,* and the *Wall Street Journal.* Members of neurodiversity and disability/crip communities also made use of myriad other creative resistance strategies (see for example Bev Harp's satirical series of Photoshopped posters—a wanted poster reminding the NYU that "kidnapping is a federal offence," a missing poster searching for respect, and a mock *Newsweek* magazine cover with the headline "what if they ran an ad about you calling you imprisoned?") (Harp, 2007).

In the fall of 2009, a year and a half after the "Ransom Notes" campaign was taken down, Autism Speaks produced a strikingly similar initiative, this time in the form of a short film entitled *I am Autism* (Cuarón, 2009). The film, which was written by Grammy-nominated songwriter Billy Mann and directed by Academy Award-winner, Alfonso Cuarón—both parents of autistic children—premiered to an audience of 150 first spouses and dignitaries from across the globe gathered for the Second Annual World Focus on Autism to raise greater awareness about a 'global autism epidemic' (Autism Speaks, 2009c). The film is divided into two carefully choreographed parts.[6]

The first part of the film features home video footage of individual autistic children, each filmed alone. A small boy sways at home plate, looking around without apparent focus or purpose with a blue plastic baseball bat idly propped on his shoulder. Another boy is alone at the beach, buried up to his chest in sand. A young girl repetitively runs her hands back and forth over a placemat. A man at the beach stands still looking down on a village of sandcastles. And so on. The isolated images are tied together by an ominous horror-film style soundtrack—complete with hollow echoes of children's cries—and the deep and sinister voice of 'autism.' The voice rumbles:

> I am autism. I'm visible in your children, but if I can help it, I am invisible to you until it's too late. I know where you live, and guess what? I live there too. I hover around all of you. I know no color barrier, no religion, no morality, no currency [. . .] I move very quickly. I work faster than pediatric AIDS, cancer, and diabetes combined [. . .] And if you are happily married, I will make sure that your marriage fails. Your money will fall into my hands and I will bankrupt you for my own self-gain. I don't sleep, so I make sure you don't either. I will make it virtually impossible for your family to easily attend a temple, a birthday party, a public park, without a struggle, without embarrassment, without pain [. . .] I am autism. I have no interest in right or wrong. I derive great pleasure out of your loneliness. I will fight to take away your hope. I will plot to rob you of your children and your dreams [. . .] And the truth is, I am still winning, and you are scared, and you should be. I am autism. You ignored me. That was a mistake.
> (Cuarón, 2009)

We can recognize immediately this disembodied voice. We have heard it before in typed words and in torn up images. This, we know, is the terrifying inflection of the 'tearer' of family photographs, the architect of ransom notes, and it is still threatening the family, still hiding in the shadows. Like the "Ransom Notes" campaign and the "Getting the Word Out" campaign before that, *I am Autism* evokes a familiar background story ripe with childhood innocence and the purity of (normative versions of) family, and it is out of this pleasant scene that the figure of autism emerges as a threat. Yet, let us note once again, the key changes in the telling of the story of this terrorizing figure and its terrifying transgressions.

I am Autism is narrated from autism's own perspective, and so the viewer is offered an intimate glance at the inner machinations of the mind of this monstrous figure. Still ensuring a personal tie with the viewer advocate—still addressing a 'you'—the figure of autism draws 'you' closer still. Unlike previous campaigns, in the film the figure of *autism speaks* (pun intended). And while photographs and notes tell us little of proximity, the voice is always nearby. Autism lurks close. Maintaining the shape of a hostage taker, as seen in previous campaigns, autism thus takes on the added dimensions of a kind of stalker: autism is next door or even in your very home. It is watching your family movies, intimately, malevolently plotting its next transgression.

And, most disturbingly, in *I am Autism* we are confronted with an autism that is growing bolder, its words are not merely addressing the viewer advocate but are taunting them. Happily married? Autism jeers, I'll fix that. Have money? it hisses, not for long. "I'm still winning," provokes autism, and you can't stop me. In this way, the figure of autism formulates a kind of challenge, shaping up a novel version of advocacy that takes up the role of adversarial opponent, the role of warrior. As the terrifying and terrorizing figure of autism devolves, the figure of the intervening advocate evolves. And necessarily so.

The second part of the *I am Autism* film shifts dramatically in tone and tempo. The hollow children's cries are replaced with full-bodied giggles, the eerie percussion traded for an upbeat tempo of a guitar being plucked, the singular menacing voice called 'autism' silenced by a chorus of voices called 'advocacy.' Those same children who moments earlier appeared alone are now seen surrounded by family. As she is tickled by her mother, the little girl's hands stop their repetitive movement; a brother or a friend drapes his arm around the boy buried in the sand; the kid playing baseball, now focused and smiling, is seen with a whole family behind him, cheering him as he readies himself to hit the ball. Accompanying these happy images is a medley of voices of advocates that seem to recollect the CSC's admonition, "Don't let a psychiatric disorder take your child." And take it further still:

> And to autism, I say: I am a father, a mother, a grandparent, a brother, a sister. We will spend every waking hour trying to weaken you [. . .] I am a parent riding toward you, and you can push me off this horse time and time again, but I will get up, climb back on, and ride on with the message [. . .] Autism? You forget who we are. You forget who you are dealing with [. . .] We are Qatar. We are the United Kingdom. We are the United States. We are China. We are Argentina. We are Russia. We are the European Union. We are the United Nations [. . .] We

are coming together in all climates. We call on all faiths. We search with technology and voodoo and prayer and herbs, genetic studies and a growing awareness you never anticipated [. . .] We speak the only language that matters: Love for our children. Our capacity to love is greater than your capacity to overwhelm [. . .] We are a community of warriors. We have a voice. You think that because some of our children cannot speak, we cannot hear them? [. . .] You think that because my child lives behind a wall, I am afraid to knock it down with my bare hands? [. . .] Autism, if you are not scared, you should be. (Cuarón, 2009)

As the figure of autism is seen to be devolving in the three campaigns described above—as it is depicted as an entity that is growing bolder, hitting harder, moving closer—let us also note how the dominant cultural figure of the (always and already nonautistic[7]) advocate is changing too, its own oppositional figure shaped anew. Over the course of the three campaigns, we have watched as this figure has shifted from the shape of a neutral witness charged with the task of *helping* to spread the word about autism's criminalized deeds, to an invested victim who *has no choice but to protect and defend* against this figure, and now finally *to a victim-no-longer*—to, in other words, a militant warrior who not only reactively defends and protects but who actively and even pre-emptively engages in battle. I would like to mark out these latest—and very related—figural incarnations of a terrorizing-autism and its advocate-warrior for further exploration in the pages to follow.

As with the first two campaigns detailed earlier, the premiere of the *I am Autism* film was met with an eruption of protest from the neurodiversity movement. A petition circulated by the Autistic Self Advocacy Network (ASAN) accumulated thousands of signatures, and autistics and their allies came together to organize a number of grassroots interventions including a nationwide series of protests at Autism Speaks events. A variety of Internet campaigns swept around the globe including several YouTube videos parodying the film—for example, "I am Autism Speaks" and "I am Socks" ("I am Autism Speaks," 2009). These campaigns, petitions, and protests caught the attention of mainstream media. Local news covered many of the protests and ASAN president Ari Ne'eman's condemnation of the film was discussed in *Time* magazine (Wallis, 2009). In response to this negative reaction, Autism Speaks almost immediately removed the video link from their website. No formal retraction was made.

Offense and Apology

In the three autism advocacy initiatives detailed above, we are introduced, reintroduced, and introduced again to a terrifying and terrorizing figure of autism. The "Getting the Word Out" website, the "Ransom Notes" advertisements, and the *I am Autism* short film work together to sketch out a kind of composite image of a dangerous figure, highlighting various key characteristics to facilitate quick and easy recognition. The campaigns seem to say: 'Look at this figure of the ripper, this hostage-taker, this stalker. Observe its malevolent ways, scrutinize its immoral intentions, witness its devastating wake: this IS autism.' In response to these assertions, as we have seen, various interested and implicated folks came together and importantly declared this terrifying figuration of autism to be inaccurate, inflammatory, oppressive, and even dangerous. They (we) said: 'Autism is going down for a crime it did not commit. This figure of autism is not autism. The campaigns represent a case of mistaken identity.' In response to such critical responses, Autism Speaks and NYU's Child Studies Center evoked the notion of public debate, a move that ultimately worked to depoliticize the critical responses to their respective campaigns. For example, in a press release announcing the retraction of the "Ransom Notes" advertisements issued by the CSC, the Center's director, Dr. Harold Koplewicz, framed the campaign as nothing more or less than a hotly debated topic: "While many people praised the campaign and urged us to stay the course, others were troubled by it" (New York University, 2008, para. 2). Autism Speaks executive president Peter Bell took a similar approach in framing the critical responses to the *I am Autism* film. In an interview with *Time*, Bell is quoted as saying that while the video received many "positive" responses from the autism community, "we realized it did hurt a certain segment of the population, which is why we removed the video link from our website" (Wallis, 2009, para. 6).

Political acts of contestation and resistance—acts of contestation and resistance that were led, we must note, by autistic people for autistic people—were rationalized in the campaign retractions as mere opinions, one side in a good old fashioned debate. And while generating debate was certainly a central objective of these and similar campaigns—as Koplewicz stated, "we wanted a campaign that would grab people's attention, break through the clutter, and serve as a wake up call to what we believe is America's last silent public health crisis"—

the decision to dismantle the campaign was taken as (too) "much of the debate centered on the ads instead of the issues" (New York University, 2008, para. 1, 2). Such is the nature of an empirical debate, the NYU and Autism Speaks retractions suggest. Some are 'for' while others are 'against.' Some consider autism to be terrorizing children and families while others believe it to be a valuable and viable way of being in the world. Some have been empowered by the 'jarring' advocacy initiatives while others were offended. And, the logic extends, in the end we are all entitled to our own opinion. Agree to disagree. Yet, we must note, how the rhetoric of equal opinion and neutral debate frame dominant ideologies and acts of resistance to these ideologies as if on even political terrain, an interpretive move that both effaces the uneven nature of the power structures grounding dominant discourses of autism and depoliticizes acts of resistance to such discourses. The retractions from NYU and Autism Speaks rationalize critical voices of dissent as merely opinions that we may or may not agree with, thus making it possible to dismiss these opinions entirely.

Following Koplewicz's line of reasoning, the central problematic of these campaigns was not the moral figuration of autism as a vicious and violent hostage-taker, it was not the problematic discursive figuration of autism as somehow separate from the autistic person, nor was it the repetition and propagation of a dominant ideology that re/asserts that life with autism's difference is a terrifying and terrible life indeed. Rather the problem with the campaign was understood as nothing more or less than an instance of poor delivery. As Koplewicz suggests with respect to "Ransom Notes," what was creating too much debate was the advertising vessel carrying the campaign's message—the posters and billboards, their bold new design, and so on—and not the message itself. This understanding, of course, works to reiterate and affirm the campaign's central message—that autism is taking away the lives of children and terrorizing loved-ones—as itself nondebatable. It thus became possible to simultaneously announce the campaign's retraction, express regret about the 'hurt' and 'offense' it caused 'a certain segment,' while all the while repeating the message: 'psychiatric disorders' rip children away from their families. This message is quite evident in the NYU press release as it concludes by stating: "we would like to move forward and harness the energy that this campaign has generated to work together so that we do not *lose one more day in the lives of these children*" (New York University, 2008, para. 4, emphasis mine). And so even as the billboards were taken down and the advertisements plucked from circulation, it was, to use the language of the ransom note, 'too late:' very particular figures of autism and advocacy were fortified and released into our culture. And we continue to encounter these figures again and again, each time in slightly altered form. For the remainder of this chapter, I examine how dominant terrifying cultural figurations of autism continue to be made possible. If autism is going down for a crime it did not commit, I ask: how is it being framed? In the following section of this chapter, I use framing theory and Michel Foucault's discussions of biopower in order to address these questions. In particular, I demonstrate how dominant contemporary discourses of autism and advocacy are surrounded and contained by historically and culturally specific frames of terror.

Framing Autism

Frames direct our gaze, guide our perception. Following the work of Erving Goffman (1986), Judith Butler (2009), and others interested in the interpretive practices of framing, I use the concept of the frame to denote that which marks the limits of a scene—the shifting and contingent epistemological scaffolding that is logically and temporally prior to a phenomenal field (Minh-ha, 1992; Titchkosky, 2007; Merleau Ponty, 2002). To be framed is a prior condition of any appearance: "whatever appears," writes Titchkosky (2007), does so only and always insofar as it is "conditioned by the possibility of appearance" (p. 17). A condition of appearance, the frame also and necessarily conditions appearances. There can be no appearance, no image, no phenomenon, no figure in the absence of a conditioning frame, that shifting, contingent scaffolding that comes before and rests beneath a phenomenal field. That which anticipates it, collects it, renders it intelligible.

Let us take the example of a classical painting. In classical painting, the frame demarcates for the viewer an essential whole of the painting. The painting is all that is collected inside the frame. In a 1639 letter, French painter Nicolas Poussin presents a theory of the classical frame. In a letter to a patron, he writes:

> Once you have received your painting, I beg you, if you think it a good idea, to adorn it with some framing, for it needs it: so that when gazing at it in all its parts, the rays of the eye are retained and not scattered outside in the course of receiving the *espèces* of the other neighboring objects, which, being jumbled with the depicted things,

confuse the light [or the space: *confondent le jour*]. It would be very fitting that the said frame be gilded, quite simply, with mat gold, for it
unites very sweetly with the colors without clashing with them. (Poussin, 1639 quoted in Lebensztejn, 1988, p. 37)

For Poussin, the classical painting is not composed, in any essential way,
of that which lies outside of the limits of the frame. The meanings that
are attributed to its depicted image, in other words, are fundamentally
not made of, in, or by the spaces that display it, for example, or the viewers who find themselves before it, or the histories it was born of or the
culture in which it invariably dwells. To the contrary, for Poussin, that
which lies outside the limits of the framed painting is nothing more than
a distraction that 'jumbles' and 'confuses' an originary image and its
static meaning. If you wish to look at the painted representation, Poussin
suggests to his patron, look here, within the frame, and not elsewhere.
The classical frame, then, as Poussin conceives of it, functions normatively by gathering and directing the 'scattered' gaze of the viewer. It is
a construct that tames and regulates our lines of perception, guides our
modes of recognition.

As he reminds us how processes of classical framing function normatively, Poussin also reminds us something of the character of such normative functions. He informs his patron that while the frame is absolutely necessary to regulate the gaze, not just any frame will do. For Poussin,
the frame must be self-effacing, inconspicuous. It should be, he writes,
"guilded quite simply, with mat gold." It must blend, in other words, with
the background image of the painting itself, 'sweetly uniting' with its
colors. Conceived of in this way, as Lebensztejn (1988) writes: "the [clas-
sical] frame acts as a scaffolding: once it has helped to build the depicted
space, it should disappear as much as possible, so that the depicted space
appears naturally self-contained" (p. 37). Thus, Poussin's frame appears
only to disappear. It normatively regulates space and perception, only
to efface its own construct. And as the frame is obscured, the image it
frames and the organized character of our lines of perception and our
modes of recognition are forgotten, reified as natural.

Much like the scene of a painting, or indeed like any scene at all, the
'scene' of autism advocacy is surrounded by (multiple) frames: historical
frames, geopolitical frames, economic frames, moral frames, frames of
charity and frames of biology, frames of love and frames of war. These
frames are integral to the scene that they frame and, as in Poussin's
description of the classical frame, function to direct and so regulate the

ways in which we come to regard autism and advocacy. And much like Poussin's frame, the cultural frames encasing discourses of autism advocacy, too, very often escape our attention, 'sweetly uniting' with—and so disappearing into—the colorful, taken-for-granted landscape of everyday life. As the variety of possible interpretive frames diminishes, dominant ways in which to regard autism and advocacy become rendered as natural, given, and self-evident, transformed from their status as sociopolitical constructs to the way that things naturally are and have always been. Because processes of framing typically function normatively, that is to say, because a given frame appears only to disappear through a process of naturalization, regulating space and perception in ways that efface its own construction, to pay critical attention to the multiple frames that condition the phenomenon of autism advocacy today is a disruptive act indeed. "To call the frame into question," writes Judith Butler, "is to show that the frame never quite contained the scene it was meant to limn, that something was already outside, which made the very sense of the inside possible, recognizable" (p. 9). In the midst of disappearing frames and naturalized, taken-for-granted understandings, the critical task, according to Butler, is to connect the scene before us—in this case, the scene of autism advocacy and the figures that dwell within this scene—to the often taken-for-granted interpretive frames that contain the scene and the figures within it, giving them shape and possibility.

Since the appearance of any given image, object, or other phenomenon relies upon a prior frame, the task of the cultural critic is to give an account of the kinds of frames that are installed around certain scenes or certain figures, as well as an account of how these frames differentially allocate and deny power and privilege. Butler (2009) reminds us:

> 'To be framed' is a complex phrase in English, a picture is framed, but so too is a criminal (by the police) or an innocent person (by someone nefarious, often the police), so that to be framed is to be set up, or to have evidence planted against one that ultimately 'proves' ones guilt [. . .] if one is 'framed', then a frame is constructed around ones deeds such that one's guilty status becomes the viewer's inevitable conclusion. (Butler, 2009, p. 8)

While contesting the validity or accuracy of a given figuration often provokes, as we have seen, the infinite regress of an empirical debate, thinking of the figure as framed—to 'frame the frame,' to borrow from Trinh Minh-ha (1992)—both accounts for the situated ways in which certain bodies are produced as always and already guilty *and* opens up space for critically attending to and engaging the multiple social processes, or interpretive social frames, that work to regulate our perceptions and structure our modes of recognition such that, from Butler, a "guilty status" becomes an "inevitable conclusion" (p. 8). One powerful interpretive frame that structures the war on autism and the militaristic turn in autism advocacy more broadly is the frame of liberal biopolitics. By critically attending to the biopolitical frames that currently encase autism advocacy discourses, we are better positioned to understand how autism is made into a figure of terror, as well as to understand how the subsequent militaristic advocacy response to it is naturalized and normalized.

Biopolitical Frames of Life

In a lecture delivered at the Collège de France on March 17, 1976, Foucault argues that the eighteenth century witnessed an important transformation in the way that power came to be exercised over the subject. With the rise of liberalism (and its attendant investments in notions of progress and the overall betterment of human life), a new form of power materialized, a 'biopower' concerned with the management of 'life itself' (Foucault, 1997). Foucault grounds this concept of biopower against the backdrop of a classical theory of sovereignty. Whereas the power of the sovereign is, in Foucault's articulation, the power to "take life or let live," biopower is the power to "make live" and "let die" (p. 241). The distinction between a sovereign power that "*lets* live" and a biopolitical power that "*makes* live" is an important one (Foucault, 2007, p. 241, my emphasis). Under sovereign rule, life is a privilege of the subject: one lives because the sovereign has not yet exercised his power to kill. Whereas sovereign power is essentially a morbid power defined by, and contingent upon, the sovereign's right to inflict death, biopower is a vital power with the principal vocation of making life live. Biopower targets life so as to improve it, optimize it, and above all, ensure it. In the here and now of liberalism, 'to live' (and, of course, here we must read, to live 'better' and 'more' according to normative liberal standards and values) is the rule.

Technologies of biopower take as their referent the living biological individual, but only insofar as this individual lives in relation to— and thus alters and effects—the overall life of a greater living biological entity: the 'vitality' of the species. As the population (itself a product of biopower) emerges as a political and economic problem, biopower produces a host of regulatory mechanisms—e.g., health statistics, birth to death ratios, and rates of illness and disability—whose functions are to measure, monitor, evaluate, and ultimately manipulate coefficients of life in order to secure and even augment the 'good life' of the (liberal) social whole. As these regulatory mechanisms work to "establish a sort of homeostasis" of the social body, they simultaneously normalize populations and condition the emergence of, and indeed the proliferation of, categories of abnormalcy: problem populations in need of normative interventions (Foucault, 1997, p. 246). This hyper-attention to, and meticulous classification of, species life—this "fragment[ation]," in Foucault's words, "of the field of the biological"—has altered modern conceptualizations of the categories of life and death (Foucault, 1997, p. 255). Under biopower, life has been extended into a kind of vital spectrum, with many gradations.

There are also, it follows, many shades of death. Foucault describes a "gradual disqualification of death" under biopolitical rule and, along with it, a shift in the overall conceptualization of the category of death (Foucault, 1997, p. 247). "Death," writes Foucault, "[is] no longer something that swoop[s] down on life" but rather is "now something permanent, something that slips into life, perpetually gnaws at it, diminishes it, weakens it" (Foucault, 1997, p. 244). Death is no longer that which takes life all at once but rather is a kind of pathology that penetrates life's frontiers. Death infiltrates, spreads, wastes—even terrorizes. It is the murky underbelly of vitality, the expression of life's absences, a kind of biopolitical nonlife or "necropolitics," to use Achille Mbembe's (2003) term. Under a liberal rule of life, the threat of this relationally negative space of nonlife is (and indeed must be) understood and articulated in and through the terms and tropes of vital (biological) invasion, in and through discourses of pathology. This resignification of death as a pathological relation of life rationalizes certain forms of human difference as vital and, as such, in need of protection and preservation, while simultaneously casting other forms of human difference as life-threatening and, as such, in need of neutralization and/or elimination.

Of primary importance to any discussion of liberal life is the question: what (who) constitutes 'life'? As life is installed as a governing rule of liberal society, what (whose) life comes to be understood as securing or even optimizing the overall vitality of the species and what (whose) life gets read as inherently threatening to species life? Conceptions of life are, as Foucault emphasizes, always normatively defined, measured and organized (Foucault, 1997). Dillon and Reid observe:

> If you wish to make life live, as Foucault teaches us that liberalism does, you must embark on a rigorous and continuous assaying of life. What are the properties of the species? Which properties are compatible with the welfare of the species? Which properties endanger the species? How do these life processes work? (Dillon and Reid, 2009, p. 43)

This hyper-attention to and meticulous taxonomy of species life—this, following Foucault, "fragmenting" of "the field of the biological" into subspecies populations—is a necessary function of a biopolitical regime, for it allows for the identification of those forms of life that promote or optimize the life of the species and those forms of life that inhibit or threaten it. Yet what often escapes attention is how this process of fragmenting the biological (e.g., splitting the field of the human into developmentally 'normal' and 'abnormal' species types) is a process that is at once politically determined (i.e., determined or motivated by, for example, social, historic, and/or economic factors) and morally coded (i.e., certain species types are coded as 'good' or 'beneficial,' while others are coded as 'bad' or 'threatening') (Titchkosky, 2007). What also, and very commonly, escapes attention is how such divisions inaugurate certain lives as nonvital: lives that—while technically alive—are not recognized as performing the normatively defined process of living and so are cast as pathologically life-threatening, as draining the life of the normative whole (Butler, 2009).

Let us return now to the contemporary scene of autism advocacy, a scene that is born of and framed by liberalism and its biopolitical rule of life. It is not a coincidence that the emergence of the diagnostic category of autism coincides with the rise of liberal governmentalities (on the diagnostic style of reasoning and liberal governmentality, see Tremain, 2010). Indeed, liberal concerns with the contours of life—and the resultant proliferation of diagnostic categories under this regime—have made possible dominant contemporary versions of autism and advocacy; while liberalism shapes life as conditional, autism emerges as one of life's conditions. As I have argued, autism is predominantly framed as always and already guilty of terrorizing and terrifying: guilty, in other words, of not necessarily taking away life per se but infiltrating it, destroying it, ruining it, 'spoiling' it (Goffman, 1963). Indeed, a life with autism—conceived of in the sense of both a person 'with' autism as well as a collective 'with' autism[8]—is being ushered into contemporary intelligibility as a kind of biopolitical death. Autism is found guilty, time and again, of pathologically 'gnawing' at life, guilty of ruining life, of lowering the 'quality of life,' of diminishing life's viability, and so on.

Considering the three examples of advocacy initiatives described in the beginning of this chapter, as well as other campaigns and initiatives detailed in earlier chapters, autism is, time and again, conceived of as nothing other than an undesirable and even dangerous individual biological pathology. The evidence is in and it is damning: 'bad' biology, 'mis-wired' brains, devolving development, histories of red flags. It is, as was explored in chapter 1, 'bad' genes or damaged pathways leading to, as examined in chapter 2, abnormal behaviors and underdeveloped bodies and minds. It is preventing, as in chapter 3, the full enjoyment of liberal rights and freedoms. Autism is dominantly conceived of, in other words, as a pathological threat to (normative, liberal versions of) individual life and is even framed as actively spoiling/wasting away this life.

At the same time as dominant enactments of advocacy narrate autism as a threat to *individual life*, they also and simultaneously depict an autism that is infiltrating the frontiers of the (normative) *life of the whole*, wasting it away, bit by bit. As we have seen in both this chapter and the previous one, autism is represented in epidemiological terms, a spreading epidemic moving through the greater population, working faster, to borrow a very commonly evoked phrase, "than AIDS, cancer, and diabetes combined" (Cuarón, 2009). Such an epidemic not only spoils individual lives but threatens to spoil the life of the whole. First, it's the diminishment of the 'good life' of the liberal (middle class, heteronormative) nuclear family—high rates of divorce, depleted bank accounts, disrupted leisure activities, ruined birthday parties—and then it's the erosion of the vital life of the liberal society as a whole—disappearing independence, (too) costly social supports, and so on. With such frames, autism's "guilty status" is *made* an "inevitable conclusion" (Butler, 2009, p. 8). And there is plenty of guilt to go around.

Insofar as autism and its advocate are invariably tied together in discourses of advocacy, the frames that present autism as always and already guilty of acts of terrorizing life shore up the advocate as always and already suspect. Recalling the red flag campaigns from chapter 3 and the Starbucks cup from this chapter, the advocate is continuously being framed as *potentially guilty*—potentially guilty of not learning the signs,

potentially guilty of not being vigilant in watching for red flags, potentially guilty of, in other words, being a 'bad' advocate and so aiding and
abetting an already guilty autism and becoming complicit in autism's
crimes against life.

Vis-à-vis guilty and potentially guilty figures that threaten the frontiers of liberal life, a whole host of security mechanisms must be erected
so as to safeguard 'life,' protect it, and indeed ensure it by keeping non-
normative (autistic) life at bay. As biopower frames autism as a pathological threat that for the 'good' or the 'health' of normative liberal
life requires neutralization or elimination, advocacy materializes as that
which—at all cost—must protect, preserve, and/or recover nonautism.
The work of autism advocacy thus becomes the normative and normalizing work of (biological) securitization. Foucault writes:

> Regulatory mechanisms must be established to establish an equilib-
> rium, maintain an average, establish a sort of homeostasis and com-
> pensate for variations within this general population and its aleatory
> field. In a word, security mechanisms have to be installed around the
> random element inherent in a population of living beings so as to
> optimize a state of life. (Foucault, 1997, p. 246)

We have encountered such 'security measures' time and again throughout the previous chapters. In contemporary times, the perimeters of normative life are clearly staked out by red flags (e.g., the posters from chapter 2) and systems of early warning (e.g., the CDC-sponsored "Autism
A.L.A.R.M." document in figure 12 that unmistakably resembles a kind
of emergency procedures document). We (as a culture) calculate and
recalculate the odds of a security breach (e.g., the discussion of odds in
chapter 3). And when breaches in security happen, as they invariably
do—when the flags go up, when the alarm sounds, when the odds close
in—when, in other words, the imagined frontiers of normative life are
penetrated and normative life is understood to be under attack, we go
to war.

The War on Autism

There can be little doubt that we live in the midst of a global—and
globalizing—war on autism. In a contemporary moment when the
notion that autism ought to be eliminated from human life is written

Autism is prevalent
* 1 out of 6 children are diagnosed with a developmental disorder and/or behavioral problem
* Approximately 1 in 150 children are diagnosed with an autism spectrum disorder
* Developmental disorders have subtle signs and may be easily missed

Listen to parents
* Early signs of autism are often present before 18 months
* Parents usually DO have concerns that something is wrong
* Parents generally DO give accurate and quality information
* When parents do not spontaneously raise concerns, ask if they have any

Act early
* Make screening and surveillance an important part of your practice (as endorsed by the AAP)
* Know the subtle differences between typical and atypical development
* Learn to recognize red flags
* Use validated screening tools and identify problems early
* Improve the quality of life for children and their families through early and appropriate intervention

Refer
* To Early Intervention or a local school program (do not wait for a diagnosis)
* To an autism specialist, or team of specialists, immediately for a definitive diagnosis
* To audiology and rule out a hearing impairment
* To local community resources for help and family support

Monitor
* Schedule a follow-up appointment to discuss concerns more thoroughly
* Look for other conditions known to be associated with autism (eg, seizures, GI, sleep, behavior)
* Educate parents and provide them with up-to-date information
* Advocate for families with local early intervention programs, schools, respite care agencies, and insurance companies
* Continue surveillance and watch for additional or late signs of autism and/or other developmental disorders
* Continue to provide a medical home

For More Information: www.medicalhomeinfo.org

The recommendations in this document do not indicate an exclusive course of treatment or serve as a standard of medical care. Variations, taking into account individual circumstances, may be appropriate.

This project is funded by a cooperative agreement between the American Academy of Pediatrics and the National Center on Birth Defects and Developmental Disabilities at the Centers for Disease Control and Prevention

August 2007

Fig. 12 American Academy of Pediatrics A.L.A.R.M. document (2008) outlining screening and surveillance procedures for pediatricians. Poster rights belong to American Academy of Pediatrics, 2008. Reprinted with organization's permission.

into US law and public policy, many disparate soldiers are taking to the trenches of a war. "Progress is slow in war against autism," screams a 2009 CNN headline (CNN, 2009). "Pediatricians are receiving new marching orders in the war against autism," reports a CBS medical correspondent (CBS, 2007). Larry King discusses it (Douthit, 2009). Oprah endorses it (Winfrey, 2007). The Pentagon funds it (Kirby, 2008). And having had a change of heart, Yoko Ono has decided to give this war a chance (Autism Speaks, 2009a).

Indeed, we find ourselves in a contemporary social context where doctors, professional athletes, celebrities, politicians, journalists, parents, 'stakeholders,' and concerned civilians from around the world are coming together 'against' autism; where we can walk, run, row, fish, shop, or take a cruise to 'fight' autism, or read up on the latest research study taking 'aim' at autism (York University, 2010). In these (war) times, it is possible to pass a stranger on the street wearing a T-shirt with the image of an armed child in military fatigue and the words "welcome to my war on autism," and we might flip on the TV and tune in as celebrity advocate Jenny McCarthy—author of *The New York Times* best-selling book on parenting autistic children called *Mother Warriors*—teams up with World Wrestling Entertainment for an "autism smackdown" (fig. 13 depicts Eduardo Trejos's digital collage, "In the Name of the Normal," which offers a visual sampling of this war and its linguistic and representational targets and tactics).

Of course, our times have not only given birth to this war on autism but also and most glaringly to the war on terror. But there are many other wars still. We are living in the midst of a 'war on child abuse,' a 'war on obesity,' a 'war on mental illness,' and an (ever ironic) 'war on bullying.' Indeed, in contemporary times, war has been declared on such disparate targets as cars, poverty, bed bugs, crime, ignorance, greed, drugs, germs, cancer, and of course on war itself. And while it seems almost reasonable to assert that these days there is, as Richard Ericson puts it, a "war on everything" (Ericson, 2007, p. 214), such a cynical assertion fails to adequately account for the politically uneven grounds that give rise to such militaristic metaphors and their very material targets. Even as the 'war on' lexicon is applied and applied liberally to a whole gamut of disparate targets, war is never waged indiscriminately. War is never waged, for example, on that which is desired and valued in a culture. Government reports are not calling for a war on literacy and doctors are not waging a battle against mental health. The call to war inflects the contours of life. As Dillon and Reid (2009) observe: "wars have always been fought

Fig. 13 "In the Name of Normal" (2011) Digital Collage, Eduardo Trejos. Reprinted with artist's permission.

in the name of whatever different forms of life have been made sacred" (p. 35) [In this way, war performs the dual function of protecting that which is desired and valued in and by a culture by targeting that which is perceived as threatening to this.]

Under biopolitical rule, (a normative liberal version of) life is what is of primary value; it must be accounted for and monitored, protected and secured against a terrifying and pathological nonlife. And when it is threatened, life must be battled for. I turn now, and for the remainder of this chapter, to a consideration of the existence and persistence of two significant contemporary wars—the war on autism and the war on terror—and I suggest that the fact that these two wars are appearing at the same moment is not mere historical happenstance. To the contrary, the war on terror and the war on autism—and their resonant oppositional figures of terrorist/warrior—are intimately connected, even dependent upon one another, for they both share a very particular (liberal, biopolitical) war frame.

War Frames

As we attempt to better understand these war frames, it becomes necessary to first ask: how is it possible to wage war and so to expose *life* to the possibility of harm—under a biopolitics *where life is what is of primary value*? Under a politics that privileges and even enforces life, war seems counterproductive, itself a transgression of the vital rule. Foucault asks:

> How can [biopower] kill,[9] if it is true that its basic function is to improve life, to prolong its duration, to improve its chances, to avoid accidents, and to compensate for failings? How, under these conditions, is it possible for a political power to kill, to call for deaths, to demand deaths, to give the order to kill, and to expose not only its enemies but its own citizens to the risk of death? (Foucault, 1997, p. 254)

In response to his own questions, Foucault suggests that liberal war—and the harm it invariably causes—is and can only be made possible when waged in the name of life (Foucualt, 1997, p. 256). As (normative) life itself comes to be understood under liberalism as both what is of value and what is at stake, war, and its inherent violence, emerges almost counterintuitively as a kind of 'vital' force charged not with the taking of life but with the protecting, promoting, and ensuring of it. Following Foucault, liberal wars are "no longer waged in the name of a sovereign who must be defended, they are waged on behalf of the existence of everyone; entire populations are mobilized for the purpose of wholesale slaughter in the name of life necessity: massacres have become vital" (Foucault, 1990, p. 137).

What is more, Foucault asserts that this vital technology of liberal war must be conceptualized in racist terms. Indeed, he asks: "how can one not only wage war on one's adversaries but also expose one's own citizens to war [. . .] except by activating the theme of racism?" (Foucault, 1997, p. 257). Here, Foucault conceptualizes racism not as an ideological commitment per se but rather as, in his words, "a way of introducing a break into the domain of life that is under power's control" (Foucault, 1997, p. 254). Indeed, this 'break' in life's domain, this constitution of a "negative ontology" (Patterson and Hughes, 1997; Kumari Campbell, 2005, p. 108), this liberal process of breaking up and marking out vital and pathological species types through the organization of superior and inferior ways of being human, or perhaps more accurately, viable and nonviable ways of *living humanness*, is, for Foucault, the primary technology of contemporary racism. "The first function of racism," he writes, "[is to] to fragment, to create cesuras within the biological continuum addressed by biopower" (Foucault, 1997, p. 255).

It is this racist organization that is, Foucault argues, an essential feature of liberal war, a kind of war not premised on military confrontation per se but rather is established as a kind of "biological-type relationship" where inflicting harm or even death on an individual life (or even on many individual lives) is rendered intelligible as necessary for the preservation of the life of the whole (Foucault, 2007, p. 255). Via biopolitical frames of racism, certain bodies are coded as 'nonvital' types and emerge as always and already guilty of crimes against life. Such types are thus rendered vulnerable as necessary casualties of (liberal) war. "Enemies who have to be done away with," writes Foucault, "are not adversaries in the political sense of the term; they are threats, either external or internal, to the population and for the population" (Foucault, 1997, p. 256). Nowhere is this vital logic more striking than in the war-time rhetoric of former US president George W. Bush (Reid, 2006; Dillon and Reid, 2009; Butler, 2009). Let us consider, for example, how biopolitical logics are structuring the following speech delivered by Bush on March 19, 2004. In commemoration of the one-year anniversary of the US-led war in Iraq—a particularly bloody year of war with a death toll of more than one hundred thousand troops (Roberts et al., 2004)—Bush offered the American public a few remarks about the value of life. He said:

> there is a dividing line in our world, not between nations, and not between religions or cultures, but a dividing line separating two visions of justice and the value of life. On a tape claiming responsi-

bility for the atrocities in Madrid, a man is heard to say, "We choose death, while you choose life." We don't know if this is the voice of the actual killers, but we do know it expresses the creed of the enemy. It is a mind-set that rejoices in suicide, incites murder, and celebrates every death we mourn. And we who stand on the other side of the line must be equally clear and certain of our convictions. We do love life, the life given to us and to all. We believe in the values that uphold the dignity of life, tolerance, and freedom, and the right of conscience. And we know that this way of life is worth defending. There is no neutral ground—no neutral ground—in the fight between civilization and terror, because there is no neutral ground between good and evil, freedom and slavery, and life and death. (Bush, 2004, p. 411)

In his speech, Bush divides up many things. His words work hard to create caesuras: splitting outside from inside, limit from possibility, death from life. In her discussion of representational frames delimiting the field of appearances in the war on terror, Butler (2009) characterizes these "war frames" as "the ways of selectively carving up experience as essential to the conduct of war" (Butler, 2009, p. 26). For Butler, the frame is made through a carving up of the field of experience, the sculpting of the field of phenomena. The meaning of such a field, for Butler, is not self-evidently there, as it was for Poussin, but is rather conditioned by and conditional to a process of framing. Let us examine how Bush engages in the 'carving up' of a field of experience he calls 'the world.' Let us examine, in other words, how he is engaged in the work of framing understandings of the world anew. Rejecting other familiar (and equally artificial) ways of carving up the world (e.g., as a series of nation states or along the lines of religion), Bush's speech cuts yet another dividing line deep into the world, carving it up into two parts—allies and enemies, an 'us' and a 'them'—distinguished, not coincidentally, by oppositional 'visions' and 'values' with respect to life.

One world—the 'we' of America, we must presume, and its allies—is sculpted by Bush as an essentially vital world, populated by thriving figures who "love life, the life given to us and to all," figures who demonstrate their vitality, moreover, by adhering to liberal norms and values (i.e., 'life' is constituted in Bush's speech as not merely living but as 'civilized,' 'free,' 'tolerant,' and so on). Meanwhile, the other world—the 'they' of al-Qaeda, collected by a figuration of a Muslim who is always and only a terrorist—is framed as having fallen outside of the frame of liberal norms and values or even as existing in opposition to these frames (i.e., where Bush's 'we' are 'civilized,' his 'they' are 'terrorists'; where his 'we' are 'good,' his they are 'evil'; where his 'we' are 'free,' his 'they' are 'slaves'; and so on). And so out of a racist act of inserting a break in the continuum of life comes a Middle Eastern "death world" (Mbemebe, 2003; Puar, 2007) populated with pathologically morbid Muslim terrorists who "[rejoice] in suicide, [incite] murder, and [celebrate] every death we mourn." Following Foucault, where Bush's 'we' makes live, his 'they' takes life, and so while his 'we' is always (or at least until expelled) inside the rule of life, his 'they' is always, firstly, guilty of transgressing it.

By making reference to a tape that was released by a group claiming responsibility for the 2004 train bombings in Madrid, Bush described a malignant voice issuing terrifying threats to (normative, liberal versions of) life, telling us that a man's voice can be heard on the tape saying: "We choose death, while you choose life." "We do not know if this is the voice of the actual killers," the former president admitted, reminding us that ultimately this burden of proof did not matter. It did not matter whether or not this was the voice of the actual culprit behind the bombings, for within Bush's liberal frame of life and death, the voice on the tape—cathected to death—materialized from the start as breaking the rule of life. The voice on the tape was the life-draining voice of the already guilty that spoke a (racially inflected) "creed of the enemy." Under a liberal biopolitics, where transgressions of the rule of (normative) life are encoded not merely as deviant but also as pathological and indeed as life-threatening, this voice spoke the need for its own elimination. From within biopolitical frames of war, American military invasion and occupation were henceforth reencoded as (life-saving) threat elimination in the terms of which the casualties that these operations invariably produced, and continue to produce, were and are framed as "necessary violence" (Foucault, 1997; Butler, 2009). There is something familiar in the malignant voice in Bush's speech, a voice speaking terrifying threats of biopolitical death. It is faceless, hidden, lethal, out-of-control. Recall that the terrifying and terrorizing figure of autism, too, materializes as speaking threats to the normative (social and individual) body. Autism, too, is framed as always and already guilty of speaking a "creed of the enemy" and, as such, calling for its own elimination, its own eradication. The figure of autism, much like the figure of the terrorist—or perhaps more precisely *alongside* this figure—is made the necessary casualty of a vital and vitalizing war.

Let us note the striking resonances between the rhetorical devices that have given shape to, and continue to give shape to, both the war on terror and the war on autism, as well as give shape to the particular ally and enemy figures that these war stories generate. The startling ease with which the war-time rhetoric of the war on terror blends with the dominant rhetoric of autism advocacy is instructive. The racist figuration of a death-driven Muslim terrorist and the ableist figuration of a terrifying autism are tied together in a tale of terror drawn from, and made intelligible within, an historically and politically specific discursive formation ruled by the ascendency of liberal versions of life.

In the following section, I conclude this chapter by considering Bush's characterization of the post-9/11 terrorist 'enemy' and the construction of a necessary response to this enemy against the autism/advocacy narrative put forward in the *I am Autism* film. In so doing, my intent is not to make a simple analogy or comparison between the respective figurations of terrorists and warriors but to attend to the shared (racist/ableist) biopolitical war frame that pulls these figures together and allows them to appear as they do. The move to acknowledge continuities between categories of disability and race under biopower holds important implications for critical analysis and intervention: attending to the biopolitical production of race and racism can clarify understandings of disability and systems of ableism (and vice-versa). Framed by biopower as a primary threat to (normative) species life, the category of autism— and that of disability more broadly—has become a crucial component of modern forms of racism just as the category of race has become necessary to the modern workings of ableism (for more on the biopolitical continuities between categories of disability and race see McWhorter, 2009; Tremain, 2012; Chen, 2012). This process of clarification is made all the more evident as we piece apart and analyze the biopolitical logics underpinning liberal warfare. Biopower functions to both disable *and* racialize the figure of the terrorist and the figure of autism producing them as the proper targets (and necessary casualties) of wars aimed to "eliminate . . . biological threat" so as to "improve . . . the species or race" (Foucault, 1997, 256). Contemporary discourses of autism advocacy and terror share a liberal, biopolitical frame, a frame that conditions into possibility the very particular appearance of pathologically terrifying and terrorizing enemy-figures and, in so doing, delimits the range of possible reactions and responses to those bodies marked as/conflated with such figurations. Vis-à-vis this life-threatening/life-draining enemy figure—be it the figure of autism or the figure of the Muslim terrorist—a very particular and historically specific kind of response is naturalized as obvious and necessary. In the face of terror, what is required are immediate militarized acts of intervention and rehabilitation, invasion and occupation. In the name of life, the figure of death must be stopped up, silenced, eliminated at all cost. In this way, the war on autism and the war on terror can—and I argue should—be read as continuous biopolitical wars committed to a single aim of defining, preserving, and securing the borders of a normative homeland (or liberal versions of it) through the marking out of threatening types that (or rather who) require absolute eradication in the name of the life of the whole. I turn now to the former president's characterization of the contemporary 'terrorist' enemy and read this characterization against the narrative put forward in the dominant enactments of autism advocacy described throughout this chapter.

Pathologized Enemies and Vitalized Allies

Just a day after September 11, 2001, in what was a watershed moment in the formation of contemporary understandings of terrorism, Bush delivered a now infamous speech in which he characterized the figural shape of the terrorist. He said: "We are facing a different enemy than we have ever faced." Then he continued:

> This enemy hides in shadows, and has no regard for human life. This is an enemy who preys on innocent and unsuspecting people, runs for cover. But it won't be able to run for cover forever. This is an enemy that tries to hide. But it won't be able to hide forever. This is an enemy that thinks its harbors are safe. But they won't be safe forever. (Bush, 2001, p. 1100).

Bush introduces us to a new, or at least different, kind of enemy figure whose threatening character is understood in terms of a particular kind of pathological threat, a threat that hides, spreads, circulates, infiltrates, and gets closer to home. Out of, and in relation to, this (ostensibly) different kind of enemy emerged a different kind of allied response. "The United States of America," continued Bush:

> will use all our resources to conquer this enemy. We will rally the world. We will be patient, we will be focused, and we will be steadfast in our determination. . . . We will not allow this enemy to win the war by changing our way of life or restricting our freedoms. America is united. The freedom-loving nations of the world stand by our side.

This will be a monumental struggle of good versus evil, but good will prevail. (Bush, 2001, p. 1100)

With these remarks, Bush referenced a terrorist 'enemy' that could be anywhere, blending in, moving unnoticed through borders in diffuse global networks, lying low in deviant 'cells.' This figuration of the terrorist that travels in (to borrow from Puar's genealogy of the terrorist subject) "rhizomic, cell-driven, non-national, transnational networks that have no self-evident beginning or finite end" (Puar, 2007, 52) is understood by way of racist/orientalist notions of infiltration and contamination and, necessarily, by way of an inherently ableist conception of biological contagion. Puar demonstrates how the mode of characterizing the movement of terror along the representational lines of cellular contagion is "often sublimated (against the foil of the western liberal rational subject) through the story of individual responsibility and personal pathology" (p. 52). The cellular, epidemic-like movement of the terrorist is reified, in other words, by the notion that the terrorist subject possesses (is possessed by?) a pathological biomedical impairment. Acts of terror are dominantly framed—explicitly and implicitly—as nothing more than, nor anything less than, the destructive effects of the individual (psycho)pathology of the Muslim terrorist, as well as the collective (psycho)pathology of a Muslim "death world" (Puar, 2007). Recall that, in Bush's 2004 speech, the "creed of the enemy" is not a doctrine, nor an ideology per se. It is rather, in his words, a death-driven "mind-set" (Bush, 2004, p. 411).

Indeed, the minds and movements of the terrorist have been psychologized through and through. This is evidenced in the proliferation of a vast variety of books, articles, reports, and whole academic disciplines that embark on a search after the pathological origins of a terrifying mind or mind-set and that engage in the ongoing project of observing and classifying its deviant/dangerous 'terrorist' behaviors. Some examples of these include:

- *Crusaders, Criminals, Crazies: Terror and Terrorism in Our Time* (Hacker, 2007);
- *Origins of Terrorism: Psychologies, Ideologies, Theologies, States of Mind* (Reich, 1998);
- *Psychology of Terrorism* (Horgan, 2005);
- *The Mind of the Terrorist: The Psychology of Terrorism from the IRA to al-Qaeda* (Post, 2008);

- "The Psychology of Terrorism: A Case for the 21st Century" (Crenshaw, 2000);
- "Psychology of Terrorism" (Borum, 2007).

One US federal report, entitled "The Sociology and Psychology of Terrorism: Who Becomes a Terrorist and Why?," provides a literature review of a whole host of contemporary research examining the pathological psychosocial origins of terrorist behaviors (Hudson, 1999). The report cites, for example, a model for the genesis of terrorist inclinations, developed by psychologist Eric D. Shaw. Shaw's "Personal Pathway Model" suggests that terrorist behavior originates from:

> a selected at risk population who have suffered from early damage to their self-esteem [. . .] who appear to have been unsuccessful in obtaining a desired traditional place in society, which has contributed to their frustration. The underlying need to belong to a terrorist group is symptomatic of an incomplete or fragmented psychosocial identity. (Hudson, 1999, p. 25)

The report continues by presenting a great many other theories of the psychology of terrorism. The research cited in the report argues that terrorism might be caused by:

- **'Mental illness'** (e.g., Post's postulation of a "terrorist psychologic" or the linking of "depressive aspects" of an individual's personality with "the terrorists' death-seeking or death-confronting behaviour" [Hudson, 1999, p. 28]);
- **Lack of empathy** (e.g., Strentz's postulation that leaders of terrorist organizations are marked by their "oblivious[ness] to the needs of others and [are] unencumbered by the capacity to feel guilt or empathy" [Hudson, 1999, p. 37]);
- An unsettling and it seems equally pathological **'extranormativity'** (e.g., Crenshaw's allegation that "the outstanding common characteristic of terrorists is their normality" [Hudson, 1999, p. 30] or Fried's suggestion that the terrorist "may be perfectly normal from a clinical point of view [. . .] he may have a psychopathology of a different order" [Hudson, 1999, p. 31]).

Significantly, what has materialized and ultimately solidified the figure of the Muslim terrorist as so utterly terrifying is the notion that the pathol-

ogy threatening the frontiers of the liberal life world might not be immediately apparent. Bush's enemy figure possesses the dangerous combi-
nation of a (near) normative outward appearance and a pathological
death-driven inner impairment. Of course, the figure of autism is framed
as possessing/possessed by a wide range of pathological impairments—
biomedical pathologies like 'mis-wired' brains, as we have seen, or bad
genes that lead to deviant behaviors. Alongside the figure of the terrorist, the figure of autism, too, is understood to derive its terror from a
purported 'lack of empathy' or 'mindblindness' (Baron-Cohen, 1995;
McGuire and Michalko, 2011). And time and again the ultimate threat
of autism is narrated, precisely, in terms of its invisibility. Awareness campaigns repeatedly tell us that the 'disorder' of autism may be hard to
notice for it lies in otherwise normative bodies. As per the terrorist narrative, the story of autism is told as a kind of 'spreading' pathology, infiltrating normative populations in an epidemiological, cellular fashion:
an epidemic "work[ing] faster than pediatric AIDS, cancer and diabetes
combined" (Cuarón, 2009). Knowing no borders or barriers, autism is
framed as learning languages, infiltrating homes, moving next door, and
hiding in otherwise normative bodies. Figures of terror, in Bush's words,
"hide in shadows" (Bush, 2001, p. 1100). Says the voice of autism in
Cuarón's film: they are "invisible until it is too late" (Cuarón, 2009).

Betrayed by pathological movements and behaviors, the contemporary figure of terror—be it the terrifying figure of the Muslim terrorist or the terrorizing figure of autism—emerges as a racially inflected
(life-threatening) figure whose pathological character is not only understood as biologically abnormal but also as essentially amoral. Whereas,
for example, a pathological inner impairment drives the figure of the
Muslim terrorist to perform acts of (in Bush's words) "evil," to "[prey]
on innocent and unsuspecting people," and to "rejoice in suicide" and
"celebrate death," notions of autism as neurological disorder give shape
to a figure who stalks families, plots to rob (liberal) hopes and dreams,
takes and holds kids hostage, and does so with—as per *I am Autism*—"no
interest in right or wrong," "no morality" (Bush, 2001, p. 1100; Bush,
2004, p. 411; Cuarón, 2009).

As discourses of terror shape the biopolitical enemy as both life-
threatening and amoral, they also work to delimit the terms of responses
to it as both necessary and moral. Vis-à-vis a death-driven enemy, a life-
loving, and life-saving allied warrior is born. Confronted with an enemy
that hides in plain sight, the 'ally' must increase its surveillance techniques, fortify its borders, and hone its technologies of war. Said Bush

to terrorism: "The United States of America will use all our resources to conquer this enemy," "we will be patient, we will be focused, and we will be steadfast in our determination" (Bush, 2001, p. 1100). We will watch where you run, find where you hide, and uncover your 'safe harbors.' Said the autism advocates to autism: "We will not rest until you do," we will search for you "with technology and voodoo, prayer and herbs genetic studies and a growing awareness you never anticipated," we will "knock down" your "walls" with our "bare hands," and "if you are not scared, you should be" (Cuarón, 2009).

Faced with a life-threatening global network of enemies—a moving and hidden pathology that contaminates and spreads through the social and individual body—allied soldiers and civilians draw together in the establishment of a homogenous, normative 'we.' The establishment of biopolitical threat—whether figured in the shape of autism or of a Muslim terrorist—secures a collective 'we' with a kind of vital and vitalizing patriotism. "America is united," stated Bush, "and we will rally the world," "the freedom-loving nations of the world stand by our side" (Bush, 2001, p. 1100), "We are a community of warriors," said the Autism Speaks advocates, "We are Qatar. We are the United Kingdom. We are the United States. We are China. We are Argentina. We are Russia. We are the European Union. We are the United Nations" (Cuarón, 2009). It should not be surprising that the war on autism and the war on terror both evoke this kind of loving patriotic response. Indeed, the very notion of patriotism betrays the intermingling of the geopolitical and the biological. Patriotism—the love of and for the *patris*, or 'fatherland'—is a devotion to a *living* nation, a 'homeland' that also constitutes a lineage, an inheritance, a family, a body. Faced with the life-threatening figuration of a terrifying and terrorizing enemy (be this enemy the figure of the terrorist or the figure of autism), the 'ally'—the proper advocate, the respectable citizen, the good soldier—is constrained as a militant warrior, as the fiercely loving protector and defender of the borders of a kind of normative homeland (which is at once a political paradigm, a nation, a family, a child), and is charged with the task of securing and, indeed, ensuring normative life no matter what the cost and, as I explore in the next chapter, regardless of the casualty.

Insofar as it upholds the value of normative liberal versions of life and indeed works to ensure it within the borders of the nation, the war on autism reifies the necessity to protect 'this [read: normative white, patriarchal, able-bodied, middle-class, heterosexual] way of life' from other terrifying and terrorizing external threats. The implication is striking:

autism has become a galvanizing figure in the war on terror just as the figure of the terrorist is bolstering the war on autism. The intermingling of political agendas can be gleaned in the *I am Autism* film, for example, as the sole Muslim-majority country that is incorporated into Autism Speaks' vital fold of nations united against autism is Qatar—a state with significant political and military ties to the United States and one that is home to the largest US air base in the Middle Eastern region as well as a host of other military installations. With this in mind, it becomes ever more crucial to acknowledge the materiality of the production and circulation of terror figures.

Securing the Normative Homeland

I end this chapter—and begin the next one—by acknowledging how the creation of enemy figures is, itself, a productive move that ushers particular bodies (read: actual autistic, disabled, and/or racialized people) into recognition as always and already guilty of terrorizing life. While biopolitical war frames function to govern the ways in which we come to regard all embodied movements and behaviors as potentially terrifying and terrorizing, some 'racialized disabled' bodies and/or 'disabled racialized' bodies are differentially positioned within such frames so as to appear as always and already deviant: death-driven and life-threatening (Watts and Erevelles, 2004). Such ways of regarding bodies as legible sites ever in danger of betraying the profile of the terror figure lead to increased security and to the installment of a wide range of surveillance techniques[10] at normative borderlands and state frontiers—security checkpoints and prenatal screening, behavioral assessment reports and threat assessment reports, watch lists, registries and identity cards.

While the range of security measures targeting the bodies, minds, and movements of the terrorist subject has been well theorized (Puar, 2007; Razack, 2008; Thobani, 2007), it is certainly instructive to consider the securitization of the autistic subject. Mainstream autism advocacy organizations are, here again, powerfully involved. In 2011, in response to pressure from advocacy organizations (most notable, the NAA and Autism Speaks) and as a direct result of the Combating Autism Act, the Centers for Disease Control and Prevention (CDC) added a specific diagnostic code for 'wandering behavior' in the International Classification of Diseases, Ninth Revision, Clinical Modification (ICD-9-CM). This addition was "intended to capture information about individuals, with any condition classified in the ICD, who wander [. . .] to provide a way to document, understand, and improve the situation for individuals who are at risk of injury or death due to dangerous wandering" (CDC, 2011). The move to diagnostically code 'wandering' was opposed by a great many autistic and disability rights advocacy groups, including the Autistic Self Advocacy Network (ASAN), the Arc, TASH, the National Association of State Directors of Developmental Disabilities Services (NASDDDS), and the National Disability Rights Network (NDRN). In a letter to the CDC that was cosigned by forty disability rights organizations, ASAN lists three major concerns with respect to the new code: (1) the code offers no way of differentiating wandering as a medical symptom from wandering as an individual choice and therefore limits self-determination rights of disabled people; (2) for all disabled people and, perhaps, especially disabled people who do not/cannot speak, leaving a situation is an important communication strategy as well as a crucial mode of self-protection; and (3) the codification of 'dangerous wandering' could be used as a way to justify violent restrictions of movement and freedom (ASAN, 2011). Many autistic activists have expressed concern about how this information will be used; the codification of 'dangerous wandering' can serve a way to collect data and track autistic/disabled movements. Of course, recalling the previous chapter's analysis of the booming autism industrial complex, the wandering code has opened up a whole niche market geared toward securing the wandering autistic subject. Such 'life-saving' safety products range from temporary lost and found tattoos; to door and window alarm systems; to GPS locators and other tracking devices; to a variety of heavy-duty door locks, such as the ever alarming Guardian security lock, which, according to the NAA, "is difficult for even our most talented little escape artist to get through" (NAA, 2011).

There are still many other examples of how a (our) culture at war with autism has sanctioned unparalleled incursions into the lives of autistic people in the name of personal and collective security. Western/ized advocacy organizations, for example, have lobbied local governments to institute autism registries where parents can register autistic individuals to be 'flagged' in the 911 system (see for example the Autism Society of America's "Take Me Home" program or the Autism Society of Ontario's "Autism Registry"). In response to the truly terrifying numbers of autistic people who have been detained, violated, and sometimes killed at the hands of police officers, security guards, or first responders, a great many advocacy organizations are organizing training workshops and producing informational materials to enable quick and easy recognition of autism's 'red flag' pathological traits (see for example Autism Speaks' Family Services Autism Safety Project or the National Autism Association's *Big Red Safety Toolkit*—"Be RED-y to find a child with autism"). Many organizations also offer (read: sell) 'Autism Alert' cards, which typically list the biomedical signs and symptoms of autism and are intended to be presented by the autistic person to an authority in event of a detention or encounter.

While I do not want to underplay the strategic material utility/necessity of police training, identity cards, or registries: a sensitized or aware officer or a card offering a biomedical origin story may well serve to stave off violence for particular bodies (e.g., bodies that bear the signs of class or race privilege). However, as we have seen time and again throughout this book, the process of pathologization so often provides the very explanatory frameworks that rationalize violence as a necessary and even normal response. While more biomedical information *may* deter prison/jail incarceration (though this is, in and of itself, an unrealistic claim, as according to Ben Moshe (2011), in 2005 more than 50 percent of inmates in US prisons or jails are classified as having "mental health problems"), it can also work to ensure psychiatric incarceration (p. 387). Identity registries and alert cards make it the responsibility of the individual with autism (or their caregivers) to ensure a biomedically authorized explanatory framework is provided in order to legitimately expect to avoid mistreatment or even violence at the hands of public authorities. They dangerously suggest that violence against autistic people is an individual matter and, by extension, work to efface the cultural fact that 'combating,' 'fighting,' 'beating' autism is systemically authorized in this culture and is even promoted. We cannot engage with the metaphors of war without engaging in their very real materiality. Born of a culture 'against' autism, the so-called war on autism renders very real people differentially and disproportionately vulnerable to intervention, detention, incarceration, as well as other violations and violences enacted in the name of life (Butler, 2009; Puar, 2005). I explore the materiality of these violences in the following chapter.

In the summer of 2010, less than a year after the *I am Autism* film was removed from the Autism Speaks' website, the organization launched their new public service announcement entitled "Closer to Home" (Autism Speaks, 2010c). The PSA, which was designed pro bono by the advertising conglomerate BBDO—the same agency that, three years earlier, came up with the NYU "Ransom Notes" campaign—opens with the appearance of a young, middle-class white man wearing a jean jacket who appears to be in a college dorm room. Against the whining background music of a violin, he speaks:

"I think someone in my friends' school has this thing called autism . . ."

Before the eyes of the viewer, the man's face changes. He appears older now—a young professional with a smart haircut and a crisp polo shirt. He speaks:

". . . my friends' brother's son has autism . . ."

The man ages once again, his hairline receding slightly, his polo shirt replaced with a crisp dress shirt:

". . . my neighbor's son has autism . . ."

The man now makes a final transformation, his hair dusted with grey:

". . . my son has autism."

With this proclamation, the camera pans out and a young child, a boy, enters the frame. Against the backdrop of a middle-class living room, the two embrace. A voice-over says: "Autism is getting closer to home. Today, 1 in 110 children is diagnosed with autism. That's a 600 percent increase in the last twenty years. Learn the signs at autismspeaks.org."

The terrorizing figure of autism is completely disappeared from this advertisement. And the truth is we no longer need gory threats or menacing confessions. We are well aware of the terrifying and pathological character of this, now prominent, cultural figure. We have been educated. And so we know this: its invisibility and its quietness only means it is all the more dangerous. Autism—still figured as terrifying and terrorizing—"is getting closer to home" (Autism Speaks, 2010c).

Banal by comparison, but consistent in message and meaning, "Closer to Home" did not follow the same trajectory as "Getting the Word Out," "Ransom Notes," and *I am Autism*. It did not elicit any widespread public outcry and, at the time of this writing, the campaign remains in circulation.

CHAPTER FIVE

Collateral Damage

Normalizing Violence and the Violence of Normalcy

———— ❦ ————

"She was a tough nut to crack . . ."
　　—Dr. Karen McCarron, videotaped confession played at her
　　2008 trial for the murder of her daughter, three-year-old
　　Katie McCarron (McDonald, 2007, p. B1)

In contemporary times and in Western/ized spaces, there seems to be a collective, cultural fixation on—or perhaps even obsession with—'life with' autism (Broderick and Ne'eman, 2008; Mallett and Runswick-Cole, 2012). Indeed, these words, 'living' and 'with,' are so commonly strung together in relation to autism in everyday life that they appear everywhere from newspaper articles to government reports, from scientific studies to celebrity appeals, from fundraising initiatives to self-help books. Consider but a few of a vast number of recent examples:

- A *Vancouver Sun* headline: "*Living with* Autism" (McMartin, 2007);
- A BBC headline: "*Living with* Autism in the UK" (Guerry, 2008);
- An article published in *Redbook* magazine: "*Living with* Autism: Losing my Little Boy" (Rones, 2009);
- A common phrase: "1 out of every 110 children is *living with* autism";
- A parent resource: "*Living with* Autism: Practical Strategies for Supporting People with Autism Spectrum Disorders" (Autism Association of Western Australia, 2007);

- An *Evening Herald* headline: "Breakthrough brings fresh hope for families *living with* autism" (Connor, 2010);
- Kathleen Dillon's (1995) book: *Living with Autism: The Parents' Stories;*
- An oft repeated "fact" that "1 to 1.5 million Americans *live with* Autism Spectrum Disorder";
- A 2008 Easter Seals study "*Living with* Autism";
- A *Daily Press* article: "*Living with* autism disconnects kids from the world" (Freehling, 2001);
- An edited collection of stories: *That's Life with Autism: Tales and Tips for Families with Autism* (Ross and Jolly, 2006)
- The common biomedical observation: "many persons *living with* autism have significant communication challenges";
- Elizabeth Attfield and Hugh Morgan's (2006) book: *Living with Autistic Spectrum Disorders: Guidance for Parents, Carers and Siblings;*
- A talk show episode: "*Living with* Autism" (Winfrey, 2007).

Given the sheer ubiquity of the understanding that autism is a condition that is not lived but 'lived with' and as this way of articulating the condition of autism seems to roll so quickly off the tongue and drift so easily across the page, I want to conclude this book with a discussion of the meaning of the condition of 'living with.' And so I ask, once again, the same question I have been asking throughout the previous pages but now in a different way: what does it mean to be 'living with' autism and autistic difference in contemporary times and in Western/ized spaces?

Living with Autism

Perhaps the most literal way of reading the meaning of the phrase 'living with autism' is as an instance of person-first language—a dominantly used and widely accepted system of naming disability that places the 'person' before the 'disability' (e.g., 'person with a disability' or 'people with autism'). When confronted with the phraseology 'living with autism,' we might reasonably and literally understand it as referencing an individual life 'with' autism, as referencing, in other words, a person with autism. Indeed, there are many instances where the 'living with' phraseology is evoked precisely in this way. To draw on a few examples from the list above: "1 to 1.5 million people in the US *live with* an Autism Spectrum Disorder" or "many persons *living with* autism have significant communication challenges" or "*living with* autism disconnects kids from the world." Each of these statements suggests that the condition of 'living with autism' is a condition of the individual 'with' it.

As a great many disability studies scholars and activists have demonstrated, far from being merely a politically correct system of naming, the person-first lexicon also functions to organize disability meanings in particular ways (Linton, 1998; Sinclair, 1999; Overboe, 1999; Michalko, 1999; Titchkosky, 2001). In her critique of person-first language, Titchkosky (2001) observes: "Wherever and however this ['person-first'] lexicon appears, it always recommends that disability should be spoken of as something that comes along 'with' people" (p. 126). Indeed, if 1 out of every 110 children is a 'child *with* autism,' it follows that autism—at least in some sense—can only be located with that 1 child. It is, in other words, discursively forbidden from being with the other 109 children. Statements such as "many persons *living with* autism have significant communication challenges" suggest that communication challenges do not, in any essential way, belong to all of us—to the realm of social interaction—but rather belong to persons afflicted with a biomedical condition: persons with autism (McGuire and Michalko, 2011). Far from being merely a politically correct system of words or names, the person-first lexicon functions to systematically organize disabled people as 'just people'—regular, ordinary people who happen to have a disability (Michalko, 1999; Overboe, 1999; Titchkosky, 2001; Brown, 2011). In organizing disability (and so autism) in this way, the person-first lexicon functions to localize disability squarely in the individual, thereby forbidding any conceptualization of its existence outside of the individual: in the sociocultural environment, for example, or in intersubjective relations.

The solidification of disability's status as an individual condition is not, however, the only interpretive move made by person-first language. Person-first language does, as Brown (2011) suggests, possess quite a bit of "attitudinal nuance" (para. 8). Problematizing the specificity of the phrase 'person with autism,' Sinclair (1999) offers us three critiques. First, he says, the phrase 'person with autism' suggests that person and autism are somehow separate entities. He writes:

> I can be separated from things that are not part of me, and I am still the same person. I am usually a "person with a purple shirt," but I could also be a "person with a blue shirt" one day, and a "person with a yellow shirt" the next day, and I would still be the same person,

because my clothing is not part of me. But autism is part of me. (Sinclair, 1999, para. 2)

What Sinclair reminds us, in other words, is that the phrase 'person with autism' suggests that autism is not essential to personhood. He continues:

> Characteristics that are recognized as central to a person's identity are appropriately stated as adjectives, and may even be used as nouns to describe people: We talk about "male" and "female" people, and even about "men" and "women" and "boys" and "girls," not about "people with maleness" and "people with femaleness. (Sinclair, 1999, para. 3)

Lastly, Sinclair argues that the person-first nomenclature presumes a state of bad-ness or wrongness. In his words, "It is only when someone has decided that the characteristic being referred to is negative that suddenly people want to separate it from the person" (Sinclair, 1999, para. 4).

Further examining the phraseology 'person with autism,' the preposition 'with'—wedged between person and autism—functions discursively to separate the ideological category of 'person' from a biomedical condition of 'autism.' And, in a culture 'against' autism, it creates an artificial disconnect between the ('good') individual person and the ('bad') autism that comes to be associated 'with' it as an add-on to this person. To be 'with' autism (and not, for example, to be 'of' it or 'in' it) is to locate autism with the individual while asserting its essential separation from it (Michalko, 1999). The 'with' thus performs a paradoxical act of separation *and* association. As a person-first lexicon organizes autism into some 'thing' located squarely in the individual, it also and simultaneously forbids it from being understood as entwined with or integral to a person's personhood (Linton, 1998; Michalko, 1999; Overboe, 1999; Titchkosky, 2001; Sinclair, 1999; Brown, 2011).

As we analyze the social significance of the 'living with' phraseology in terms of a person-first lexicon, we must account for the meaningful slippage between the expression 'person *with* autism' and its vital permutation: 'person *living with* autism.' While these two expressions are certainly related linguistic technologies that seem to be utilized interchangeably in everyday talk, they are not precisely equivalent formulations and, as such, the interpretive work they perform is not identical. While in the former phraseology, the word 'with,' alone, is wedged between the person and the autism, in the latter, two words—'living with'—are wedged between and this difference is significant. While the 'with' posits autism as some kind of a personal possession or appendage that has become associated with or tied to an individual person, the 'living with' underscores autism as an appendage that has become attached to *the life* of the person. Where the phrase 'person with autism' renders autism as some (undesirable, pathological) 'thing' some people happen to have, the phrase 'person living with autism' renders autism as some (undesirable, pathological) 'thing' some people have to live with.

Most interestingly, let us note how the vital permutation of person-first language has opened up the condition of being 'with' (the individualized pathology of) autism to not only include persons living with autism as this is conceived of in the strictest sense but also to include people who, quite literally, have autism in their lives. Indeed, we are, for example, seemingly constantly confronted in the media, in advocacy initiatives as well as in everyday conversation, with parent narratives that characterize their relationship with their autistic child in terms of a 'life with autism.' Families as well as communities, nations, and indeed the United Nations are, as we have seen in earlier chapters, all commonly understood—both implicitly and explicitly—as 'living with autism.' In fact, while each of the examples of cultural artifacts appearing in the long list above succeeds in confirming autism's taken-for-granted status as an individual condition, very few of them articulate 'living with autism' as a condition of the individual alone. For example, Dillon's (1995) book *Living with Autism* does not recount stories of individuals living with autism, as its title would seem to suggest. Rather, the book tells the stories of individuals (parents, in this case) living with individuals living with autism. Oprah's (2007) "Living with Autism" episode focused on the narratives and perspectives of neurotypical parents, siblings, advocates, and physicians—people who, in some way, had autism in their lives. Likewise, the Easter Seal study "Living with Autism" surveyed over 1,600 parents of autistic people about their life with autism (Easter Seals, 2008). With these examples, it becomes quite evident: another way the phrase 'living with autism' comes to be employed and understood in contemporary times is as a way to describe a collective condition of 'life with' the individualized condition of autism. This vitalized person-first system of meaning produces autism (as is invariably embodied by an individual autistic person or a group or subpopulation of individual autistic people) as a condition afflicting the whole, as some pathological element that is separate from this whole, and that has, as a matter of misfortune, become attached to collective life.

The hegemonic conceptualization of autism as some pathological 'thing' that is not 'lived' but 'lived with'—where 'living with' autism is understood as something done by *both* individuals and collectives—points to a significant and central *animus* underpinning and orienting dominant neoliberal versions of autism produced and circulated within the field of advocacy. Moreover, this vital *animus* is generating particular and significant consequences, both ideological and material. Going along with the grain of linguistic technologies that characterize autism as something that is not 'lived' but 'lived with,' dominant representations of autism produced and circulated within the contemporary field of autism advocacy singularly depict autism as an undesirable pathological condition of the (social and individual) body, a condition that is conditional to particular (unfortunate) individuals and their (equally unfortunate) families, communities, and nations. This pathologization of autism is endemic to dominant enactments of autism advocacy: in fact, it is by no means an exaggeration to assert that every mainstream advocacy initiative explored in this book has been premised on the assumption that autism is some 'thing' one 'has' and not someone who 'is.'

Autism is not a person, we are assured, time and again, although some people do 'have' it. It is not a person . . . it is a puzzle (Harp, 2012; McGuire and Michalko, 2011). Autism is having one's puzzle out of order—a puzzling dis-order that handicaps and isolates, prevents 'fitting in' (Harp, 2012; McGuire and Michalko, 2011). Autism is not a person; it is, as shown in chapter 1, a series of 'tendencies.' It is a characteristic 'trait' declared Bleuler back in 1911. It is a collection of 'symptoms' calculated Kanner in 1943; it is 'echolalia,' 'stereotypy,' 'literalness.' It is 'extreme aloneness.' Autism is not a person, promised a 1960s-era Bettelheim; it is a prison, a shell. It is a 'withdrawal' from 'humanity.' A chilling effect of a cold mother. Autism is not a person said Lovass; it is an exhibition of 'inappropriate behaviors.' It is a mind blind to intentionality, according to Baron-Cohen. A lack of emotion. A misfiring of neurons. A miswired brain. It is too high levels of mercury. It is to be in possession of 'bad' genes. Autism is, as we were informed by the examples in chapters 1 and 2, to have a body that develops too slowly, unnaturally, undesirably. Autism is not a person but a 'red flag.'

And so it is repeated in posters and slogans, in newspaper articles and in media broadcasts, in novels, in blockbuster films, in advocacy initiatives, in scientific studies, and on fast food containers; to 'live with' autism (whether it be collectively or individually or both) is to bear pathology. As the living person, or perhaps life more broadly, is discursively made to come before and so to exist as separate from autism, and as autism is transformed into some pathological 'thing' that is not '*of*' the living person but has, as a matter of misfortune, come to be affixed to this life, we can observe how the vital category of the living person—the vital category of life itself—is emptied in some essential way of any possibility of being autistic.

Autism is not an essential part of life, as per the repeated refrain of advocacy. It is rather a condition of life; it is that which life must 'live with.' It is, as we saw in chapters 2 and 3, that which threatens the 'good life' of neoliberal development, that which prevents children, adults, communities, and nations from living 'fully.' It is, we are promised by world leaders and international structures of governance, that which gets in the way of production and consumption. Autism is not life; it is afflicting life, a disease of epidemic proportions. It is that which infiltrates life's borders. It is not life, as per the advocacy campaigns analyzed in chapter 4, it is that which grabs hold of life, builds a wall around life, holds it hostage. It is ruining birthday parties, bankrupting nations, causing divorce. Autism is not life, it rips life apart; it is scrawled threats writ large on the living. It is, we are told by advocacy over and again, life's terrifying and terrorizing opponent. Autism is not life; it is nothing more than the ticking sound of life running out.

Life, in other words, is being made a condition of nonautism. And while life is always life, the condition of 'life with' autism comes to be immediately understood as a life that bears the origin of its own undoing. It is a life under threat and so is no kind of life at all. As it 'lives with' this maligned and malignant version of autism—an autism that is not a person but a pathogen afflicting a person, an autism that is not lived but is threatening to life—how can advocacy not come into being as that which, as we witnessed in the previous chapter, must wage a (life-saving) war *against* autism? How can advocacy be anything other than, as in chapter 2, that which must watch out for autism's presence and work to eliminate its signs of difference? How, in other words, can advocacy live anything other than a (good, neoliberal, and necessarily nonautistic) life of fighting for—and so securing, attaining, recovering—the vital being of nonautism? How, when any alternative to the nonautistic life is so carefully and so thoroughly framed as not life at all?

When autism is not a person but a 'puzzle,' advocacy must (at least try to) 'solve' it, put order to its inherent dis-order. It must fund, seek out, support, and conduct studies to better know its pathological origins so as to eliminate these origins and neutralize their puzzling effects.

When autism is not a person but a puzzle, advocacy must not dwell or desire or deal in puzzling uncertainties (McGuire and Michalko, 2011). Advocacy becomes that which deals with and in the uncomplicated certainty of neat fits and good fitness. The advocate is, as in chapter 2, the surveiller of bodies and the noticer of red flags. It is that which must be aware, be wary and beware of particular behaviors, certain ways of moving, of acting, of reacting. When autism is not a person but a flag, advocacy becomes that which sees autism and, of course, sees red. And yet advocacy sees more than just red. When autism is not a person but a sign or a symptom, advocacy can see red but is also positioned to see beyond this, to see beyond the appendage of autism to the vital promise of an underlying nonautism. When autism is not a person but a sign or a symptom, advocacy can reasonably understand and orient to autistic ways of being as naturally occurring unnatural human deviances that can and must be identified, corrected, and unlearned. Advocacy becomes, in other words, that which intervenes early and teaches (or, at least, ensures the teaching of) the moral conduct of 'proper' human development.

When autism is denied status as a living someone and when those lives that 'live with' a (life-threatening) autism are cast as at stake, advocacy therefore and necessarily goes to war and does so, moreover, in the name of the normative promise of nonautism. When autism is not coterminous with life, when it is rather understood as a drain on the (good, neoliberal) processes of living, the work of advocacy becomes the vital and vitalizing work of first protecting/defending the normative borders of nonautistic life and, second, rescuing and recovering those (otherwise nonautistic) individuals or collectives that 'live with' autism. When autism is not a life but a spreading epidemic—a terrifying network of pathological cells—advocacy becomes, as in chapters 2, 3, and 4, the search for ways to eliminate autism. Advocacy becomes redirection, rehabilitation, restraint, recovery, or cure. It becomes security measures and preemptive strikes. When autism is not a life but a partition blockading life, the mission of advocacy is to tear autism down with hands bare. When autism is not a cohesive 'living person' but a fragmented condition of a 'person living with,' advocacy can see underlying bodies without symptoms, minds without blindness, brains that don't misfire. When autism is not a life but a shell surrounding life, advocacy is positioned to see normal kids, as per the opening epigraph, that simply need to be 'cracked' out.

What sensibility of life do such contemporary representations of autism permit us to think, or better, what do they inaugurate? Vis-à-vis all

"normative violence"

that is recounted in the paragraphs above and all that has come in the pages before, one thing is clear: in our contemporary culture, to 'live with autism' is not to dwell in it or be of it. It is not to desire it, cultivate it, or love it. It is not to advocate *for* it. Within dominant contemporary discursive spaces of advocacy, to live with autism is to long for life without it. As (normative) acts of living as well as living people are relentlessly and meticulously made and kept separate from an extraneous and pathologically threatening autism, advocacy is delivered to us, as we have seen, time and again, as that which can—and should—ensure autism's minimization or even it's eradication from collective and individual life. And as I have also suggested throughout this work, this way of conceptualizing autism and advocacy—and the relationship between the two—is thick with danger.

Life without Autism

As a way to both address and assess this danger, I turn next to a critical consideration of fatal acts of violence against autistic people that have been reported and circulated through the popular Western/ized news media in the past decade, instances that include but are certainly not limited to those that follow. The column below holds together the names of people who were killed for being autistic—cases where the victim's status as autistic was a detail relevant to their murder. I have made the decision to limit this list to include only those deaths that occurred during first decade of the 2000s—the same decade that, I argue, gave rise to an ongoing cultural war on autism. However, the names of the dead continue to appear with an aching frequency in Western/ized news media, and many disability and autism activists, bloggers, scholars, community members and allies, including myself, continue to be actively watching and documenting these headlines. The ellipses at the end of the column represent a call for all us to join in this important work of bearing witness. Joel Smith's website This Way of Life (archived since 2006) was foundational in this respect insofar as it opened up a virtual space to acknowledge and connect instances of autism violence and track their judicial outcomes. It simultaneously provided a space for collectively mourning the victims of autism violence. The task of bearing witness has, in many ways, become central to the work of self-advocacy.[1] While Smith's site is now archived, other autistic/ally community members have continued this difficult work of monitoring and mourning (see for example the work of Kerima Çevik and her website The Autism Wars). In 2012, ASAN (in collaboration with other disability organizations such as Not Dead Yet and the National Council of Independent Living) held a "Day of Mourning," remembering disabled people who were killed by a parent or caregiver. In a statement on the ASAN website, Zoe Gross writes: "On March 30th, 2012, we held vigils in 18 cities to remember those we have lost, and to remind the world that their lives had value. On March 31st, 2012, a 4-year-old autistic boy named Daniel Corby was drowned in a bathtub by his mother." This work is ongoing. The "Day of Mourning" is now marked annually with vigils held around the world (Brown, 2013).

While the phenomenon of autism violence is well known, felt, and documented in autistic communities, in mainstream culture the names of victims of autism violence are seldom linked together. Even less often are these names linked to a broader culture 'against' autism, an act of forgetting that is also an act of violence in and of itself. This column—this tenuous thread of names, dates, and details—is a gesture toward the violent materiality of a cultural desire for 'life without autism.' Each of these names is a trace of a violence that belongs to a culture . . . *our* culture 'against' autism: our culture that wars against autism, fights it, combats it, smacks it down. Our culture—of which advocacy is a powerful and influential part—that imagines and treats life as conditional and autism as (one of) its condition(s).

Willie Wright, fifteen years old. Willie was asphyxiated on March 4, 2000, while being restrained by hospital staff at Southwest Mental Health Center in San Antonio, Texas ("Child Restrained", 2000).

Justin Malphus, five years old. Justin was severely beaten to death by his mother, Joyce Malphus, on April 12, 2000, in Georgia. Malphus then threw his body into the family pool (Lowery, 2002).

Wayne Winter, thirty-nine years old. On January 15, 2001, Wayne was asphyxiated while being restrained by three employees at a residential facility in Ontario, Canada (Churchill, 2001).

Gabriel Britt, six years old. Gabriel was reported missing on March 3, 2001. His body was found eight days later in a pond near his family's home in South Carolina. Terrence Britt, Gabriel's father, was convicted of his death (Ferrell, 2004).

Mark Owen Young, age eleven. Mark was murdered on September 17, 2001, in Durham, United Kingdom. His mother, Helen Rogan, gave her son and herself prescription drugs, slashed both of their wrists, and jumped off a bridge in Derwent Valley ("Mother killed herself and son", 2002).

Brahim Dukes, eighteen years old. Brahim was starved to death on December 29, 2001, in the home of his stepmother, Audrey McDaniels, in Philadelphia(Soteropoulos, 2002).

Matthew Goodman, fourteen years old. Matthew died on February 6, 2002, of respiratory complications and blood infection caused by physical and chemical restraints used by his residential program in New Jersey (Peterson, 2002).

Lillian Leilani Gill, four years old. Lillian was murdered in March of 2002 by her mother, Sharon Michelle Gill, in Big Bear City, California (Berry, 2006).

Dale Bartolome, twenty-seven years old. Dale was murdered on July 29, 2002, in California. Dale was shot by his father, Delfin Bartolome, in a van in a parking lot outside his school. His father then turned the gun on himself (Tran and Anton, 2002).

Craig Sorger, thirteen years old. Craig was beaten and stabbed to death on February 15, 2003, in Ephrata, Washington, by two of his playmates, thirteen-year-olds Drake Savoie and Jake Lee Eakin (Dininny, 2006).

Eric Bland, thirty-eight years old. Eric starved to death on February 24, 2003, in California by his sister and caregiver, Delores Johnson (Nelson, 2004).

Nozomu Shinozaki, twenty-two years old. Over the course of three hours on February 25, 2003, Nozomu—a Japanese student going to school in New Zealand—was beaten to death by a mob of nine or more of his schoolmates ("Autistic student killed in three-hour gang attack", 2003).

Jason Dawes, ten years old. Jason was strangled to death by his mother, Daniela Dawes, in New South Wales, Australia, on August 4, 2003 (Lamont, 2004a).

Terrance Cottrell, Jr., eight years old. On August 22, 2003, Terrance—"Junior"—was asphyxiated to death in Milwaukee by the Reverend Ray Hemphill at a faith healing ceremony at Faith Temple Church of the Apostolic Faith. Hemphill was attempting to release "demons" from the boy ("Conviction upheld for man who killed boy at church", 2006).

Angelica Auriemma, twenty years old. Angelica was killed on December 5, 2003, by her mother, Ioanna Auriemma, in Brooklyn, New York. Auriemma drowned her daughter in the bathtub and then attempted to kill herself (Gallahue and Messing, 2003).

Scarlett Chen, four years old. Scarlett was drowned in a bathtub by her mother, Xuan Peng, on July 12, 2004, in Toronto (Small, 2007).

Patrick Markcrow, thirty-six years old. Patrick was killed by his mother, Wendolyn Markcrow, on March 29, 2005, in Buckinghamshire, United Kingdom. Markcrow drugged and suffocated her son and attempted to kill herself (Johnston, 2005).

Tiffany Pinckney, twenty-three years old. Tiffany died on April 2, 2005, in an upscale neighborhood in Mississauga, Canada, due to starvation and gross neglect at the hands of her sister, Allison Cox, and Cox's husband, Orlando Klass (Mitchell, 2008).

Abubakar Nadama, five years old. Abubakar died of a heart attack on August 23, 2005, following a radical experimental 'chelation therapy' procedure that was intended to 'cure' him of his autism in Pennsylvania (Smith, 2005).

Hansel Cunningham, thirty years old. Hansel died after being tasered and restrained on November 17, 2005, by Des Plaines police officers at his residential treatment facility in Illinois (Higgins, 2006).

Hevin Dakota Jenkins, two years old. Hevin was killed in December 2005 in Huntington, West Virginia by his aunt, Tonya Sloan. Sloan and her boyfriend, Anthony Milam, then placed Hevin's body in a trash bag and threw it into a river. The boy's body was never recovered (Long, 2007).

Ryan Davies, twelve years old. Ryan was murdered in Humberside, England, on April 12, 2006, by his mother, Alison Davies, who also committed suicide. Closed circuit TV cameras show Davies took Ryan with her as she jumped off a 100-foot bridge in Humberside (Fernand, 2006).

Katie McCarron, three years old. Katie was suffocated to death with a plastic garbage bag by her mother, Dr. Karen McCarron, in Illinois on May 13, 2006 (Sampier, 2008a).

Sean Miles, thirty-five years old. Sean was beaten with a golf club, stabbed in the head, and then drowned in the Thames River in Oxford, England, in May of 2006 by Edward Doyle, Terry McMaster, and Karen Fathers (Wilkinson, 2007).

Marcus Fiesel, three years old. Marcus was murdered in September 2006 in Cincinnati, Ohio, by his foster parents, Liz and David Carroll, Jr. The couple pinned the boy's arms behind his back, wrapped him in a blanket, bound him with tape, and left him in a closet as they went on vacation (Hassert and White, 2007).

Ulysses Stable, twelve years old. Ulysses was murdered in Bronx, New York, on November 22, 2006, by his father, Jose Stable. Police officers found Ulysses's naked body in the bathtub with his throat slit. Said Stable to the police: "I terminated the life of my autistic son" (Burke, Gendar, and Moore, 2006).

Jonathan Carey, thirteen years old. Jonathan died on February 15, 2007, in upstate New York while being restrained. Two employees of the residential facility where he lived, Edwin Tirado and Nadeem Mall, were charged with manslaughter (Morgan Bolton, 2007).

Brandon Williams, five years old. Brandon died in Arizona at the hands of his mother, Diane Marsh, and her friend, Flower Tompson on March 21, 2007. The two fed Brandon a cocktail of sleeping pills and painkillers. An autopsy later revealed that the cause of Brandon's death was a skull fracture (Smith, 2008).

William H. Lash IV, twelve years old. William was shot to death in July of 2006 in Fairfax County, Virginia, by former assistant secretary of commerce in the George W. Bush administration, William H. Lash III (Jackman and McCrummen, 2006).

Lakesha Victor, ten years old. Lakesha was found dead in her family's home on August 20, 2006. An autopsy revealed Lakesha died of malnutrition and dehydration. Lakesha's mother, Ludusky Sue Hotchkiss, was charged with second-degree murder and second-degree manslaughter (Martinez, 2009).

Unnamed girl, seven years old. Died in November of 2007 in Hawk's Nest, Australia. The girl was grossly neglected by her parents and was found starved to death in her own excrement ("Starvation murder trial: girl was autistic", 2009).

Mohammad Usman Chaudhry, twenty-one years old. Mohammad was shot three times in the chest by Los Angeles police officer Joseph Cruz on March 25, 2008, in Los Angeles. Mohammad was unarmed (Rubin, 2011).

Gabriel Poirier, nine years old. Gabriel suffocated to death on April 17, 2008, at his school in Quebec, Canada. Gabriel was making loud noises in the classroom when his teacher wrapped the boy four times in a weighted blanket and left him immobilized on the classroom floor for twenty minutes (Alphonso, 2008).

Jacob Grabe, thirteen years old. Jacob was shot several times, including once in the head, on September 11, 2008, by his father, Allen Grabe, while he was sleeping in his home in Colorado (Shockley, 2010).

Kyle Dutter, twelve years old. Kyle was shot to death in Wisconsin by his father, Ryan Dutter, on November 18, 2008. Dutter then shot and killed himself ("Father accused of killing son served in navy, former fire-fighter", 2008).

Terrell Stepney, nineteen years old. Terrell was murdered on February 27, 2009, in Cheasapeke, Virginia, by his grandmother, Constance Stepney, who gave him an overdose of prescription pills. Stepney also committed suicide (Davis, 2009).

Jeremy Fraser, nine years old. Jeremy died in March of 2009 in Salem, Massachusets after his mother, Kristen LaBrie, withheld at least five months of chemotherapy treatment ("Mom sentenced to 8–10 years", 2011).

David Cox, eighteen years old. David was beaten to death in the street in June 2009 by a group of teenage strangers in Doncaster, United Kingdom (Taylor, 2009).

Michael Vonheath Becht, Jr., ten years old. Michael was killed on July 6, 2009, in St. Paul, Minnesota, by his mother, Patti Becht, who gave him a drug overdose. Becht also attempted, unsuccessfully, to kill herself (Simons, 2009).

Jeremy Bostick, eleven years old. Killed on September 27, 2009, in Edmonton, Canada by his thirty-nine-year-old father, who then killed himself ("Dad in murder-suicide had sought help for autistic son", 2009).

Unnamed Crestline boy, nine years old. On October 18, 2009, an unnamed boy from Crestline, California, was shot to death by his grandmother and caregiver, Denise Snyder. Snyder also shot herself (Pinion-Whitt, 2010).

Tony Khor, fifteen years old. Tony was murdered on October 25, 2009, in Mississauga, Ontario, Canada by his mother, Seow Cheng Sim, in a hotel room (Tambar, 2009).

Fabián Duque, sixteen years old. Fabián was fatally shot on November 9, 2009, in a car in Philadelphia by his father, Segundo Duque. Duque then shot and killed himself (Farr, 2009).

Walter Knox Hildebrand, Jr., twenty years old. Walter died on November 19, 2009, malnourished and assaulted, in California, allegedly at the hands of his brother and caregiver, Stuart Allen Hildebrand ("Man arrested in death of brother", 2010).

Timothy Aleshire, twenty-seven years old. Timothy died January 1, 2010, after being restrained by four individuals at his state operated workplace in Eden Prairie, Minnesota (Walsh, 2010).

Jude Mirra, eight years old. Jude was murdered on February 5, 2010, by his mother, Gigi Jordan, in a room at the Peninsula Hotel in New York

City. Jordan allegedly gave Jude a cocktail of ground-up prescription pills and then attempted, unsuccessfully, to kill herself (Baker and Hughes, 2010).

Ajit Singh, twelve years old. Ajit died in London, England, on February 9, 2010, after being forced by his mother, Satpal Kaur-Singh, to ingest a cup of bleach. Kaur-Singh also attempted to kill herself (Gill, 2010).

Steve Eugene Washington, twenty-seven years old. On March 21, 2010, Los Angeles Police Department gang enforcement officers Allan Corrales and George Diego reported that Washington looked 'suspicious' and appeared to be removing something from his waistband. Corrales and Diego both fired shots at Washington; one bullet hit him in the head. He was unarmed (Rubin, 2011).

Roland Campbell, twenty-one years old. Roland died suddenly on April 18, 2010, while in police custody in Kentucky. It was ruled that there would be no further inquest in the cause of his death (Kegley, 2010).

Benjamin McLatchie, twenty-two years old. Benjamin was shot and killed on April 27, 2010, in Portland, Oregon, by his father, Daniel McLatchie. McLatchie then shot and killed himself (Hench, 2010).

Rylan Rochester, six months old. Rylan was smothered to death in Colorado on May 31, 2010, by his mother, Stephanie Rochester, when Rochester began noticing 'early warning signs' of autism (McGhee, 2010).

Christopher Melton, eighteen years old. Christopher was murdered by his mother, Tracy Hawks, on June 4, 2010, in Howard County, Maryland. Hawks used a gas generator to suffocate herself and her son (Carson, 2010).

Zain Akhter, five years old. Zain was strangled with a wire in Irving, Texas, by his mother, Saiqa Akhter, on July 19, 2010. Akhter then called 911 and said: "I killed my kids [. . .] both are autistic. I don't want my kids to be like that [. . .] I Want normal kids . . ." (Golstein and Eiserer, 2010; "Mother to 911—'I Killed My Kids'", 2010).

Faryaal Akhter, two years old. Faryaal was strangled with a wire in Irving, Texas, by mother Saiqa Akhter. Faryaal died a day after the death of her brother, Zain (above), on July 20, 2010 (Goldstein and Eiserer, 2010).

Kenneth Holmes, twelve years old. Kenneth was shot and killed on July 28, 2010, in New York by his mother, Michaela Jackson, who subsequently shot herself (Schram and Bain, 2010).

Jawara Henry, twenty-seven years old. Jawara was asphyxiated on December 5, 2010, at New York State-run South Beach Psychiatric Center on Staten Island. Henry's death has been ruled a homicide (Karoliszyn, Parascandola, and Paddock, 2010).

This list of names is misleading: it is an artifice of cohesion, a singular and uniform gloss for many differences, departures, and incongruencies. The many-ness of these names and their stories span countries and continents, a vast breadth of material and social differences and uneven vulnerabilities, all of which I have[2] uneasily—and perhaps even unjustly—brought together into a single column of violence. Indeed, there are many ways we could (and reasons we should) consider these cases individually, examining and weighing their similar or dissimilar properties and thinking through the ways violence is differentially structured by material and social differences. However, in strategic resistance to the many ways violence against autistic people is systematically and repeatedly splintered and effaced through discourses of individualization, the towering column above and the analysis to come seek not to simply or easily compare or contrast one individual story against another. Rather, I attempt to curate these stories against a backdrop of culture, to let them touch in such a way that neither conflates them into one singular and monolithic story of violence nor permits us to forget the dangerous repetition and aching frequency with which such violences are occurring in the contemporary West. In the pages to follow, then, I examine how dominant cultural systems of understanding and practices of organizing difference—systems and practices that, always and invariably, as we have seen, structure inequity in unequal and so racist, sexist, heterosexist, classist, and ableist terms—provide for a particular, contingent, and often near imperceptible shared cultural backdrop that shapes the boundaries of life and the differential acceptability of acts of violence.

However similar or dissimilar these individual stories are, each belongs to and is born of a global and globalizing culture of puzzling threats and eclipsing futures, a culture of red flags and global epidemics, a culture where we are told, time and again, that the only way that non-autism and autism can live with one another is if we believe ourselves to be cleanly split, respectively, into 'living people' and 'threatening pathologies,' into 'warriors' and 'enemies.'

Vis-à-vis a culture fixated on notions of 'life with' autism, I turn now to three specific stories of life without it. I look at the murder of ten-year-old Jason Dawes, killed by his mother, Daniela Dawes, in 2003, then the murder of four-year-old Jia Jia "Scarlett" Chen, killed by her mother, Xuan Peng, in 2004, and lastly at the murder of three-year-old Katherine "Katie" McCarron, killed by her mother, Karen McCarron, in 2006. Each are stories of an 'individual living with autism' who was murdered by a nonautistic individual 'living with' an 'individual living with autism.' In all three of the stories, autism was articulated as the target of—and the underlying reason for—violence.

The Murders of Jason Dawes, Scarlett Chen, and Katie McCarron

On August 4, 2003, ten-year-old Jason Dawes was suffocated in New South Wales, Australia. His mother, Daniela Dawes, admitted to holding the boy's mouth and nose shut until he was dead (Lamont, 2004). She then attempted to kill herself, but was discovered and revived. Dawes was subsequently arrested and charged initially with murder, a charge that was soon reduced to manslaughter when the Crown accepted that the defendant was experiencing depression at the time of the killing. To this charge of manslaughter due to diminished responsibility, Dawes plead guilty.

Following a series of articles covering Dawes's sentencing hearing that ran in the *Sydney Morning Herald*, autism was at the center of this case. "She was a good mother," *Herald* reporter Leonie Lamont writes, "Dozens of people said so. From her teenage daughter and estranged husband, to the staff at the bank and local video store" (Lamont, 2004a, para. 1). "How then," Lamont continues, "could this good mother, Daniela Dawes, grip her child's nose and mouth shut, and hold the struggling child until his last, terminal, breath?" How? Autism, it is suggested. "Jason Dawes had severe autism," reports Lamont, and Dawes—described in the article as a "a crusader for her son"—"battled doggedly for years to get the educational, behavioral, and medical support her son needed. The family left Ballina, and returned to Sydney in search of better services—which they didn't get" (Lamont, 2004a, para. 8–9). The notion of Jason's potentiality and his future outlook became central to the focus of the articles reporting on the Dawes hearing and its aftermath. Senior councillor James Bennett spoke at the hearing about a mother growing increasingly concerned about her son's impeding adulthood. He is quoted in the *Herald* as saying: "In the exchanges between the offender and her husband in weeks preceding these events they both expressed their despair at the future—how were they going to care for this young boy as he entered puberty?" (Lamont, 2004a, para. 23).

On June 2, 2004, the Parramatta District Court ruled that Dawes be immediately released on a five-year good behavior bond for the manslaughter of her ten-year-old son. "Her son died at her own hand," reports the *Herald*, "but a judge ruled yesterday that Daniela Dawes had been through too much to be sent to jail" (Lamont, 2004b, para. 1). As the sentence was handed down, Justice Roy Ellis told the court:

> This offender has suffered enough and the circumstances of this offence are so exceptional as to justify the imposition of a noncustodial sentence. All the evidence leads to the inevitable conclusion that this offender will punish herself significantly for the rest of her life [for] taking the life of her beloved son [. . .] This offender was required to educate, feed, toilet, bathe, entertain and love Jason. She [also] loved and cared for her daughter. She constantly lived with the fact that her son had lost his best chance of acquiring greater life skills because of the failure of authorities to provide appropriate intervention during his early formative years. (Lamont, 2004b, para. 3, 10)

Addressing Daniela Dawes directly, Justice Ellis then said: "I wish you all the best" (Lamont, 2004, para. 2).

On July 12, 2004, four-year-old Jia Jia "Scarlett" Chen was drowned in her family's bathtub in Toronto, Canada. Nearly six months later, the Toronto police arrested the child's mother, Xuan Peng, charging her with the first-degree murder of her daughter, a charge which was dropped to second-degree before the case was tried (Huffman and Keung, 2005, p. B01). At her trial, which began in November 2007, Peng plead not guilty.

A series of *Toronto Star* articles covering the Peng trial described the case put forth by the prosecution as a case of autism: "a mother increasingly frustrated with caring for her autistic daughter deliberately drowned the four-year-old in a bathtub in the family home," writes *Star* reporter Peter Small of the prosecution's allegations (Small, 2007, p. A8). Addressing the Superior Court, Crown prosecutor Joshua Levy is quoted as saying: "Scarlet was a child that required constant supervision [. . .] a child in her own world"—a child who was described by her mother, according to the *Star*, as having "no sense of danger, [a child] who would run into traffic, jump from high places and would only communicate with gestures" (Small, 2007, p. A8). The court heard of a mother with severe depression who was having trouble managing the care of her daughter.

In a key moment of the trial, the prosecution revealed that mere hours before Scarlett was drowned, the family attended a follow-up appointment with pediatrician Dr. James Leung to discuss the results of some tests Scarlett had had regarding her "developmental delays" (Small, 2008a, p. A16). According to the *Star*, "Leung told the court the results of the CT scan were normal [. . .] he told the family there was nothing to be done for the girl surgically" (Small, 2008a, p. A16). Leung told the court that "Peng and her mother peppered him with questions [. . .] asking whether there was any hope" (Small, 2008a, p. A16). "They were disappointed, he said, adding that was a typical reaction for families" (Small, 2008a, p. A16). In the cross-examination, the defense pressed the doctor, who emphasized that he never suggested to the family that there was no hope for Scarlett. "There are all kinds of programs," he said, "to help her adjust to the reality that she would always be developmentally delayed" (Small, 2008a, p. A16). According to *Star* reporter Donovan Vincent, "her parents were informed that while Scarlett would never function normally, she was only mildly autistic and there was potential for major improvement" (Vincent, 2009, p. GT4). Scarlett was found two hours later, drowned in the bathtub, her body naked and covered in vomit (Vincent, 2009, p. GT4).

On March 1, 2008, a jury found Xuan Peng guilty of the second-degree murder of her daughter and she was sentenced to life in prison with no chance of parole for ten years (Powell, 2008, p. A12). However, just over a year later, this sentence was overturned by the Ontario Court of Appeal on account that the original trial judge excluded the jury from the possibility of reaching a lesser verdict of manslaughter. Faced with a new trial for manslaughter, Peng, who had up until then maintained her innocence, now plead guilty. The *Star* reports the story of the death of Scarlett Chen, agreed upon by prosecution and defense, as follows:

> The 33-year-old mother was trying to put her daughter to sleep so she could do some chores—cleaning and soaking baskets and a shower curtain in the bathtub—but Scarlett wouldn't sit still, let alone lie down. Exhausted, Peng called her husband—more than a dozen times—asking when he would be coming home to relieve her. It was the middle of July, and hot. Earlier in the day, a doctor told Peng and

her husband there would be no "quick fix" for their daughter, who still wasn't speaking. Scarlett would need assistance for the rest of her life and would never function "normally." "Fascinated" by the water, Scarlett wanted to get in the bath. She took off her clothes and tried again and again to climb in the tub. Then, "at her wits end after a day of bad news and the extreme stress of taking care of her autistic child," Scarlett's mom "snapped." She pushed her daughter's head underwater and held it down until she stopped struggling. (Kennedy, 2010, p. GT7)

Based on this version of events, counsel from the Crown and the defense reached a plea agreement on a five-year sentence that granted Peng two-for-one credit for the eighteen months she had already spent behind bars (Kennedy, 2010, p. GT7). "Given her unique circumstances, especially given the stresses in her life and her mental state, a five-year prison sentence seemed the appropriate range," said assistant Crown attorney Joshua Levy (Friday, 2010, p. A11). Peng was immediately released from custody to serve three years probation. Outside a Toronto courthouse, a newly freed Peng addressed reporters: "I miss my daughter every day," she said. "I still love my daughter. I hate autism" (Friday, 2010, p. A11).

On May 13, 2006, three-year-old Katherine "Katie" McCarron was suffocated in her grandmother's home in Morton, Illinois. Katie's mother, Dr. Karen McCarron, confessed that she suffocated Katie with a plastic garbage bag. Hours after Katie's murder, McCarron attempted suicide. She survived. McCarron was arrested and charged with murder in the first degree, to which she pleaded not guilty by reason of insanity.

The McCarron murder trial, which took place in Tazewell County in January of 2008, seemed to revolve around Katie's autism. *Peoria Journal Star* reporter Kevin Sampier writes, "All of the witnesses who knew Karen McCarron, a former pathologist, said she was a woman obsessed with curing her daughter's autism and was a perfectionist who would not accept the fact her daughter wasn't 'indistinguishable' from her peers"[3] (Sampier, 2008b, p. B1). In a videotaped confession played at the trial, McCarron describes, according to the *Journal Star*, "the moment she learned Katie had autism and how it changed everything". McCarron is quoted as saying: "I cried hard when she first got her (autism) diagnosis. Then I stopped crying. I was always trying to figure out how to cure it." "I tried very hard to lessen the effects of autism," she continued "I sent her to a very good school" (Sampier, 2008c, p. A1). Shortly after

Katie's diagnosis of autism, she and her father, Paul McCarron, spent eighteen months in Raleigh, North Carolina, so that Katie could attend a clinic that specialized in treating autism. According to the *Journal Star*, the defendant's husband took the stand to testify that Katie's autism was "not severe" and that she "wasn't prone to kicking, screaming, biting or behavior sometimes associated with more severe autism cases" (Sampier, 2008a, p. A1). "Katie was always a well-behaved little girl," he said, adding that she was developmentally behind for her age but [had] learned the alphabet, knew shapes and colors, and recognized various animals" (Sampier, 2008a, p. A1). While Katie's father was pleased with the developmental progress she was making, McCarron was dissatisfied. "I didn't know what to do," said McCarron in her videotaped confession, "she was not learning at a rate I would expect . . ." (McDonald, 2007, p. B1). "Everything I tried to do didn't help her," she said, "[Katie] was a tough nut to crack" (McDonald, 2007, p. B1). Indeed, according to the *Journal Star*, family members and friends who testified at the trial reported that "the progress Katie made was never good enough for McCarron, who was constantly critical of the girl" (Sampier, 2008c, p. A1). According to the *Journal Star*, "the topic of every conversation with her revolved around curing Katie's autism. Negativity and hatefulness were ceaseless when she discussed the child, who they say she never hugged, kissed or praised after she was diagnosed with autism" (Sampier, 2008b, B1). "It was never good enough," testified family member Jennifer McCarron, "She looked at Katie as a problem, and she got rid of her problem. There's nothing more to it than that" (Sampier, 2008b, p. B1).

Yet McCarron's own testimony suggests there was something more going on than 'simply' understanding Katie as a problem. Most notably, in her videotaped confession, McCarron is seen to identify autism—and not Katie—as the source of her problem—the object even of a deep hatred. She said: "I loved Katie very much, but I hated the autism so, so much, . . . I hated what it was doing to her. . . . I just wanted autism out of my life" (Sampier, 2008c, p. A1). Of her decision to kill Katie, she said: "maybe I could fix her this way, and in heaven she would be complete" (Sampier, 2008c, p. A1). In a most striking moment, defense lawyer Marc Wolfe questioned McCarron on the stand about her daughter's murder. The exchange was reported in the *Journal Star* as follows:

> (DEFENSE LAWYER) WOLFE: When you were suffocating your daughter, did you think you were killing her?"
> MCCARRON: No.

WOLFE: Who did you think you were killing?
MCCARRON: Autism.

(Sampier, 2008c, p. A1)

On January 17, 2008, Dr. McCarron was convicted of the murder of her daughter in the first degree and was given a life sentence of thirty-six years in prison.

Making Sense of Murder

My interest in the re/telling of these stories of violence is not, at least strictly speaking, a search for quick or easy origins. I do not, in other words, attempt to empirically decipher who or what is responsible for the violence enacted against these three children. My critique—an interpretive one—resists the (persistent, seductive, collective) desire for moral clarity in favor of an analysis of the ways violence is functioning in culture—how this violence is made possible and even how it is framed as necessary. Rather than attempting to isolate an underlying cause, these instances of violence against autistic people must be read as an immediate cause for concern, an observation that demands that we—all of us 'living with autism' and so all of us who belong to and participate in the making of culture—look again to the cultural meanings we are collectively making of autism and nonautism and the relationship between the two. I suggested earlier that the conceptualization of autism as some pathological 'thing' that is not 'lived' but 'lived with'—where this 'living with' is understood, implicitly, as something done by *both* individuals and collectives—is animating dominant enactments of autism advocacy in this contemporary moment. I suggested, too, that this *animus* is generating significant ideological and material consequences. Let us examine this further and in relation to the stories of violence detailed above.

In the media coverage of the Dawes, Peng, and McCarron trials, autism was never considered as a life. To the contrary, it was narrated—in the newspaper headlines and in the articles that followed them, from the defense strategies to those of the prosecution, from the perpetrators' confessions to witness testimonials to the judges' final pronouncements—as nothing more than life's unfortunate and undesirable condition, a condition, moreover, that discursively served the purpose of rendering thinkable the seemingly unthinkable: the act of murdering one's own child. Indeed, autism, conceived of as life's unfortunate and undesirable condition, became a central way of understanding and indeed making sense of the seemingly nonsensical act of infanticide. The murders of Jason Dawes, Scarlett Chen, and Katie McCarron were transformed by the media and by the courts into nothing more than unfortunate and undesirable outcomes of the unfortunate and undesirable condition of living with autism.

Let us note, for example, how—and to what end—these three stories seem to revolve around the biomedical 'fact' that all victims 'had' autism. Autism anchored these stories and became a kind of *leitmotif* tying together and making sense of a narrative of violence. Newspaper headlines announcing the murders and, later, those that charted the trial and the convictions almost always made mention of Jason, Scarlett, and Katie's autism—"Mom killed autistic girl . . ."; "Mom jailed for killing autistic daughter"; "Boy's death vents despair over autism"; "Daughter's murder puts focus on toll of autism"; and so on—and the articles that followed them place autism at the center of the act of violence. According to the *Herald*, Dawes was a mother who looked at her autistic son's future with "despair" (Lamont, 2004a, para. 23). The *Star* framed Peng as "a mother increasingly frustrated with caring for her autistic daughter" (Small, 2007, p. A8). Likewise, the *Journal Star* described McCarron as "a woman obsessed with curing her daughter's autism" (Sampier, 2008c, p. A1). Desperation. Frustration. Obsession. The very motives of murder are understood as revolving around and contingent upon the shared 'fact' that both victim and perpetrator were 'living with' autism. And yet, most astonishingly (or perhaps, given our cultural orientation to autism, not astonishing at all), the relentless referencing of Jason, Scarlett, and Katie's autism was seldom—if ever—evoked, at least in the mainstream media, to argue that these three children were in fact victims of systemic oppression or targets of disability hate crimes. In order for their deaths to be conceived of as such, Jason, Scarlett, and Katie's autism must have first been conceived of as integrally bound up with who these children were and how they lived. It was not. Instead, autism was understood in these stories of violence along the dominant lines of a culture 'against' autism, a culture that commits itself, over and over again, to the belief that autism is some pathological condition of life, some 'thing' that is somehow fundamentally separate from life and some 'thing' that, in the name of life, must be fixed, cured, eliminated, lessened.

Autism as the Origin of Pathology

In chapter 1, I touched briefly upon the normative structures sur-rounding the role of the 'good' mother. As many feminist scholars have argued, the mother most often appears against a naturalized moral back-drop that figures motherhood as the "supreme calling" of the woman—a "happy achievement, a heavenly blessing, a womanly profession, the con-summate feminine achievement" (Barnett, 2006, p. 411). It is against this normative background of the good mother who loves, protects, nurtures, and cares for her children that narratives of the 'bad' (and sometimes the 'mad') mother appears. Rebecca Hyman writes: "cases of maternal infanticide are gripping because they seem to violate an inher-ent natural law, calling into question the essentialist notion that women are endowed with a nurturing maternal instinct" (Hyman, 2004, p. 192). When we come face to face with a (seeming) departure from mothering nature—when we are forced to confront a defiance of the presumed nat-ural state where mothers would not and could not harm their children—it grips us, and we require further explanation. The unnatural abomina-tion of infanticide, in other words, requires an etiological origin story. For example, when Andrea Yates famously drowned her five small chil-dren in Texas in 2001, many etiological explanations were offered, rang-ing from stories of her bad moral character (she was often characterized as 'evil' or as a 'monster'), to stories of her religious fanaticism (she was described as a fervent Christian who believed god told her to kill her children), to stories of her biomedical status and history of madness (she was described as 'mentally ill' exhibiting acute psychosis brought on by postpartum depression) (Hyman, 2004).

With respect to the McCarron, Peng, and Dawes murders, autism was cast as the primary explanatory origin story. Indeed, media cover-age of the three murders and the trials that followed frequently treated a pathological condition of autism as the only backstory of the murders that seemed to matter. News stories reporting on the murders and their trials referenced autism's red flag signs and symptoms, its genetic predis-positions, the numbers it has 'claimed,' and the frequency of its 'hits.' Reporting on the Jason Dawes case, Leonie Lamont of the *Sydney Morn-ing Herald* writes: "The Autism Council of Australia estimates there are 43,000 people in [New South Wales] with the disorder, including 11000 children and teenagers. Worldwide there [is] an epidemic in the num-bers of children born with autism spectrum disorder" (Lamont, 2004a, para. 18). "Classic symptoms include lack of eye contact, trouble with social interactions, repetitive behavior and a rigid reliance on routines," states an article from the *Chicago Tribune* reporting on the Katie McCarron murder; the article continues, "in more severe cases, children are extremely difficult to manage, sometimes causing injury to themselves and others" (Breslin, 2006, para. 10). Indeed, in all three stories, the moment the children were first diagnosed with autism was implicitly put forward as a marker of the beginning of the events that ended in their murder. If Peng's motive for killing Scarlett was frustration, for example, it was a frustration that had its origins in Scarlett's diagnosis of autism: "The same afternoon Scarlett was diagnosed," reports the *National Post*, "frustrated by her daughter's disruptive behaviour, Peng pushed her daughter's head underwater in the family bathtub" (Friday, 2010, p. A11). Similarly, if McCarron's motive for killing Katie was an obsession with curing her autism, it was an obsession that began with Katie's diagnosis. In the words of McCarron herself: "I cried hard when she first got her (autism) diagnosis. Then I stopped crying. I was always trying to figure out how to cure it" (Sampier, 2008c, p.A1). Autism was implicitly understood, in other words, as the beginning of the end of the lives of the three children: the impetus for violence and the underlying reason for the trials.

It might be argued that autism was only one of many origin stories evoked to explain the murders of Jason, Scarlett, and Katie. In some sense, this is true. Dawes, Peng, and McCarron were each, for example, differentially positioned in terms of their social class, and so in terms of the resources they had at their disposal. While Dawes was described as working tirelessly to care for her son and to secure him resources, McCarron was framed as having excellent resources and access to all the 'right' kinds of therapies. Madness was another explanatory story put forward in each of the cases. All three defendants were described as experiencing severe depression leading up to the murders. Neither dismissing the material distinctions of Dawes, Peng, and McCarron's differential experiences of social class and/or madness nor forgetting the ways in which these distinctions are, invariably, structured in inequitable and oppressive ways, we must also note, however, how such differences only came to matter as secondary characteristics flowing from and exacerbated by an underlying condition of living with autism. Social class was understood as meaningful only insofar as it differentially impacted each family's ability to provide rehabilitative/curative therapies for their children. Experiences of madness were narratively framed as effects of autism—a perspective that is supported in a great many empirical studies such as Piven et al.'s (1991) "Psychiatric Disorders in the Parents of Autistic Individuals"—which postulates a higher prevalence of affective disorders in parents of autistic children, a prevalence that is attributed, in part, to "the stress of raising a handicapped child" (p. 477)—but also in more commonsensical speculations. Such commonsense understandings of autism as 'naturally' and self-evidently depressing is evident in the following statement from a local Australian newspaper covering the Dawes murder: "Frustration, stress and depression can become the norm for both autistic people and their carers" (Walker, 2004, p. 21). In some sense, autism came to be understood as the singular and underlying pathology that Dawes, Peng, and McCarron were 'living with.' The sole salient detail of the defendant's backstory and the only pertinent beginning point of the murder timeline was the biomedical diagnosis of autism, a diagnosis that was narrated in all cases as the (tragic) confirmation that what were once 'just lives'—just kids, just parents, just families—had become 'lives with' autism's pathology.

Autism as a Waning Spectrum of Life

The murder trial, at least in some sense, is charged with the task of reckoning with fatal acts of violence. It is, in other words, charged with piecing together and ultimately (re)telling the story of violence so as to appraise this story in relation to the normative rules of conduct—both written and unwritten—in a given social order. In this (Western neoliberal) social order, as I have argued in earlier chapters, the normative rule that rules all others is the rule of life. And it is this transcendent and vital(izing) rule that is functioning to govern the possibilities for collectively reckoning with the (autistic) lives and deaths of, among others, Jason Dawes, Scarlett Chen, and Katie McCarron. In the news reports of the murders and the ensuing murder trials, the meaning of 'life with autism'—conceived of as a condition of the life of the individual and of the collective—was at once made conditional to, and so obscured by, questions of autism's 'severity' and of the subsequent 'potential' of all life living 'with' it. This is evident in the three respective trials where the biomedical status of the victim—and his or her subsequent 'potential'— became a materially salient detail that was evoked, substantiated, contested, and debated over and again. Let us consider further this preoccupation not only with the victim's status as autistic but also with the collective fixation on the relative degree of severity of the autism that the victims (and the parents) were understood to have 'had' to 'live with.'

Ten-year-old Jason Dawes was described, time and again, in the papers and in the courts as having had 'severe' autism. His mother, Daniela Dawes, in the words of the judge presiding over her sentencing hearing, "was required to educate, feed, toilet, bathe, entertain and love" him (Lamont, 2004b, para. 10). Four-year-old Scarlett Chen, although diagnosed as 'mildly autistic,' was nonetheless framed as exhibiting some of autism's 'severe' symptoms. In the words of the judge presiding over Peng's retrial, Scarlett "still wasn't speaking" and would have "require(d) assistance for the rest of her life and would never function 'normally'" (Kennedy, 2010, p. GT7). Three-year-old Katie McCarron's autism, by contrast, was described over and again as 'not severe.' In Paul McCarron's words, "Katie was always a well-behaved little girl" and, according to the *Journal Star*, she "wasn't prone to kicking, screaming, biting or behavior sometimes associated with more severe autism cases" (Sampier, 2008a, p. A1).

Recalling the historical genealogy from chapter 1, with the 1994 release of the DSM-IV, autism was rearticulated as a spectrum of disorders of greater or lesser severity. This conceptual organization of autism as a graded spectrum of pathologies is all the more evident with the 2013 release of the DSM-5, which begins to move away from strict categorical diagnosis of autism (i.e., either one meets the diagnostic criteria of autism or not) and toward a more dimensional one (i.e., to what degree does one meet the criteria). Here, autism is not so much biomedically (and so dominantly) recognized as a coherent and/or consistent group of pathological signs and symptoms but is recognized rather as encompassing a spectral range of many different pathological referents anchored by oppositional (and correspondingly moral) poles of severity. Individuals 'living with' a so-called mild case of autism, then, are often hierarchically coded as living in a state of 'high functioning' (i.e., can function well in normative terms, can fit into normative culture, and are positioned as close to and can even pass as nonautistic). Meanwhile, on the other end of the spectrum, individuals 'living with' a 'severe' case of autism are most often understood to be living in a state of 'low functioning' (i.e., cannot function well in normative terms, cannot fit into normative culture, cannot or do not pass).

If autism is not a life but is—as per the dominant refrain of our culture—that which must be 'lived with;' if autism is not, in other words, conceived of as (integral to) a living person but is instead understood as a pathology that has become attached to this life, it follows that a person 'living with' autism is a person whose relative amount or quality of life is and can be determined through a calculus of autism's severity. The cultural logic of severity and functionality goes something like this: if a 'mild' autism (as pathology) becomes attached to life, this (inherently normative) life is mostly unafflicted and unaffected. In other words, normative life—unquestionably naturalized as inherently healthy and apolitically understood as at once good and desirable—is (at least mostly) unencumbered, permitted to thrive. However, as the 'severity' of autism's pathology increases, and as it increases its hold on life, (normative) life is understood to be ever more compromised: weakened, siphoned, lessened. Under such a logic, the relationship between autism and nonautism is split into a simple binary, with neither complexity nor nuance. Nonautism is hope where autism is hopelessness. Nonautism is life where autism is a life-draining pathology. What is more, as nonautism is understood to be life and autism representative of a negative spectrum of biopolitical death, the nonautistic life 'living with' autism—whether this is the life of the individual with autism or the individual or collective living with an individual living with autism—is reframed not only as a life tied to death, as we all invariably are, but as a life affixed to and with death. A life, in other words, that has lost the possibility of moving toward life (for further analysis on the hierarchy of autism functionality and notions of severity, see Brown, 2012; Yergeau, 2010; Sequenzia, 2012a; Sequenzia, 2012b; Baggs, 2005; Sinclair, 2012).

In the three cases detailed above, as each individual instance of autism was unquestionably evoked and defined—in both medical and moral terms—as a pathological threat to life of greater or lesser severity, the lives and deaths of the three children were understood and reckoned with—in the courts and in the media—in particular and contingent ways. While Katie's autism was repeatedly narrated as 'mild' and as minimally affecting her own (normative) life and the (normative) lives of those around her, Jason's and Scarlett's cases of autism were narrated in invasive and 'profound' terms. Jason and Scarlett's autism was understood as inhibiting them (and their respective parents, who 'lived with' them and their autism) from fitting in to the normative order of life: a vital and vitalizing order where parents ought not *be required to* bathe and toilet (and love!) their ten-year-olds and where children ought to be endowed with the promise of growing up to become 'fully' independent, productive, and consumptive adults. In other words, Jason and Scarlett's autism was framed and so understood as inhibiting and even draining their (otherwise normative) lives and the (otherwise normative) lives of their parents, families, and communities. Their lives 'with' autism, in other words, were understood as transgressing the liberal rule of life. Of course, mainstream autism advocacy organizations are often involved in producing and sustaining this dangerous understanding that life with autism is no life at all. This has been exemplified time and again throughout this book. It is a sentiment that was made especially clear in a recent op-ed by Autism Speaks cofounder Suzanne Wright in which she describes 'tragic' families with non-normative autistic children. Living with autism, she states, "these families are not living" (Autism Speaks, 2013).

Yet just as we are confronted with this rather bleak image of autism wasting away (normative) life—an image that represents a violation of the liberal demand for life—the spectral quality of this post-DSM-IV version of autism, which conceives it not as a static pathology but as a *fluid range of pathologies*, together with the mechanistic moral hierarchy of 'higher' or 'lower' 'functionality,' offers a hopeful (and of course lucrative) narrative of the possibility for an incremental recovery of 'life.' As mechanistic paradigms of higher or lower functionality promise the possibility for improvement (read: normalization), the moral hierarchy of the spectrum itself leads us to the understanding that life 'with' autism always can and ought to be actively moving along the gradations of difference toward the most vital pole of life without it. Under a rule of life, then, the only way for autism and nonautism to live together is if the pathology of autism is demonstrably moving along the spectrum toward the vital life of nonautism. This story of pathology and potentiality was crucial to the enactments of violence against Jason, Scarlett, and Katie and to the ways such violence was subsequently reckoned with and normalized.

Fixing Autism

Let us return, once again, to the stories of violence pieced together in the newspapers. Even as Jason Dawes was narrated as 'severely' autistic, his life was not, interestingly enough, understood to be, by virtue of the 'severity' of his autism, *ipso facto* without potential (Lamont, 2004a, para. 1). Rather, the narrative of his life and death tells the story of a life that had gradually *lost its vital potential.* Daniela Dawes was called a "crusader for her son," having "battled doggedly for years to get the educational, behavioural and medical support her son needed," moving the family around to secure the best treatments and services—treatments and services they "didn't get" (Lamont, 2004a, para. 24, 8). Jason was narrated as entering puberty at the time he was killed. No longer a 'time-rich' child, Jason was understood to be 'out of time.' According to the *Herald*, "when Jason was diagnosed with autism at 18 months, doctors had recommended he get 20 hours of early intervention help a week. All his parents could secure for him was three hours a week" (Lamont, 2004a, para. 16). By ten years old, Jason had outgrown the crucial 'window' of opportunity where his 'severe' autism might have been lessened by early intervention therapies. And so the child was, in the words of defense lawyer Roland Bonnici, "doomed" (Lamont, 2004a, para. 16). Jason's 'life with' autism had, in other words, become understood as fixed on the wrong end of the vital spectrum and his mother was understood as having to 'live with' the fixity of this ostensibly nonvital state. Said Judge Roy Ellis: "[Daniela Dawes] constantly lived with the fact that her son had lost his best chance of acquiring greater life skills because of the failure of authorities to provide appropriate intervention during his early formative years" (Lamont, 2004b, para. 10). And so Daniela Dawes, whose life and the life of her son came to be understood as being 'with' autism in a permanent way, was subsequently interpreted as having been 'driven' to commit a 'tragic' but nonetheless vital (life-saving) act of murdering her ten-year-old child—an act that, under a liberal rule of life, was coded as both reasonable and even as necessary (Lamont, 2004a, para. 1, 19).

Scarlett Chen's life, too, was framed as 'fixed' to and on the autism spectrum, although the narrative of this fixity differs in some ways from Jason's story above. Unlike Jason's autism, Scarlett's autism was described as 'mild' and, what is more, at only four-years-old, she was still young (Vincent, 2009, p. GT4). She was still in her so-called formative years. She had not, according to dominant biomedical discourse (at least, entirely) missed that crucial 'window' for early intervention where therapies might optimize life by lessening autism. According to the *Star*, "while Scarlett would never function normally, she was only mildly autistic and there was potential for major improvement" (Vincent, 2009, p. GT4). Yet even with a promise of life without autism—a unfulfillable promise that, as we shall see, is in and of itself a damaging and dangerous one—Scarlett's mother, Xuan Peng, was said to want a 'quick fix,' a rapid return to normalcy that Scarlett's doctor told her would never happen entirely (Small, 2008a, p. A16). On the day Scarlett was killed, Dr. Leung told the family "there was nothing to be done for the girl surgically," and that while "there are all kinds of programs" that might help move Scarlett toward the vital end of the spectrum, the "reality," he said, was that Scarlett would "always be developmentally delayed" (Small, 2008a, p. A16). According to the *Star*, "Scarlett would need assistance for the rest of her life and would never function 'normally'" (Kennedy, 2010, p. GT7).

For Xuan Peng, the 'reality' that her daughter could not be 'fixed'—and quickly—served to affix both Scarlett and her mother to a 'life with' autism, a shared life that was not understood to be moving forward along the moral and medical gradients of the spectrum (or, at least, was not understood as moving fast enough) toward the vital life of non-autism. Stuck to and with autism, Scarlett and her mother's shared life was framed as wasting and this version of life with autism—combined with the 'constant' non-normative demands made by Scarlett (and compounded, according to the judge, by the hot July weather!)—was too much to live with. "At her wits end after a day of bad news [that there would be no 'quick fix'] and the extreme stress of taking care of her autistic child," Xuan Peng, in the words of the Justice Ian Nordheimer, "simply" and "tragically" "snapped," pushing her daughter's head under the water and holding her there until she died (Friday, 2010, p. A11; Kennedy, 2010, p. GT7). This act of violence was, moreover, made sensical (normalized) as a 'tragic' but vital act that—reasonably and even necessarily—severed the tie between (normative or living) life and (non-normative or life draining) autism.

The story of the life and death of Katie McCarron presents us with still another permutation of the dangerous story of what happens when autism and nonautism are understood as 'fixed' together. Like Scarlett's autism, Katie's autism was described as 'not severe.' Katie was "always a well-behaved little girl"(Sampier, 2008a, p. A1). Compliant with the demands of normative conduct, she would never kick or scream or bite, according to her father, as is sometimes the case with more 'severe' cases of autism. And on top of already being understood as being at the 'good' or vital end of the autism spectrum, Katie's parents had the means to send a two-year-old, very 'formative' Katie to a top-notch out of state school where she received the latest therapeutic interventions. Said Karen McCarron, "I tried very hard to lessen the effects of autism." "I sent her to a very good school" (Sampier, 2008c, p. A1). According to her father and her extended family, Katie had been making great (normative) progress, hurriedly catching up to her developmental milestones. Paul McCarron did note that while Katie was still "developmentally behind for her age," at the age of three she had already "learned the alphabet, knew shapes and colors, and recognized various animals"

(Sampier, 2008a, p. A1). Yet, despite Katie's purported proximity to the markers and milestones of normativity, her mother saw a normative or nonautistic child that was 'unfixable' insofar as she was 'fixed' with and to her autism. And so Katie, too, was killed.

Most interestingly, unlike the ways in which the Dawes and Peng cases were received and reckoned with, the murder of Katie McCarron was not represented by the courts or in the newspapers as a condition of how severe or demanding or trying (her) autism was; Katie's autism was understood to be 'mild,' her behaviors were described as 'good,' palatable, approximating the norm. Neither was Katie's murder made to be a condition of the accessibility or availability of resources. Her family was privileged; they were white, wealthy, educated, and otherwise well-positioned to secure the earliest diagnoses and the best medical opinions. They had help in the home and access to the latest rehabilitation treatments. Early 'warning signs' were noticed in 'good time.' An early diagnosis of 'mild' autism was attained 'on time.' Early interventions were procured before it was 'too late.' The child was responding to these treatments and normative progress was being made. By all accounts, Katie was catching up to her milestones, moving toward normalcy.

Indeed, it was this portrait of a three-year-old child with autism who was rapidly moving in the right and vital direction of life without it that led many to conclude that—unlike, say, the violent acts of Xuan Peng and Daniela Dawes that were understood to be caused by autism—McCarron's act of killing her daughter had little to do with autism at all (Luciano, 2006, p. A1). In a statement to reporters, Katie's grandfather, Michael McCarron, said:

> I am positively revolted when I read quotes that would imply any degree of understanding or hint at condoning the taking of my granddaughter's life [. . .] [this is] a very straight-forward murder case. This was not about autism. [. . .] We're not dealing with desperation here. We're not dealing with 'we have to end this child's pain.' (Luciano, 2006, p. A1)

Yet vis-à-vis Karen McCarron's confession that explicitly describes her hate of autism, as well as her intent to kill it, how could this murder not be 'about autism'? It most certainly had everything to do with autism. As Michael McCarron moves to distance Katie's murder from an 'autism murder,' what is revealed is the implicit, taken-for-granted understanding that a murder motivated by autism is a murder that, at least in some sense, is understandable, condonable, necessary even. As I have already demonstrated in the introductory chapter with the analysis of the Autism Ontario press release following the deaths of Tony Khor and Jeremy Bostick, the violent logic of necessary violence is covertly (and sometimes overtly[4]) produced and sustained by mainstream autism advocacy initiatives. I move now to further explore this conceptual—and materially salient—split between 'necessary murders' and 'unnecessary' or 'murderous murders' with respect to a negative (life-draining) spectrum of autism.

'Almost Living,' 'Mostly Dead'

In his haunting chapter "Coming Face-to-Face with Suffering," Michalko (2002) grapples with meanings made of the life and death of Tracy Latimer, the twelve-year-old Canadian girl with cerebral palsy who was murdered by her father, Robert Latimer, in October of 1993. Tracy was described by the courts and the media, by her physicians and by her parents, as having had to 'live with' a 'severe' disability, a disability that caused her to experience severe pain (Michalko, 2002, p. 104). Because of the severity of Tracy's disability and pain, for Latimer himself, as well as for those who supported him, "killing Tracy was an 'act of mercy' and not a criminal act" (Michalko, 2002, p. 104). Throughout his chapter, Michalko reckons with how Tracy's death—her murder—was reckoned with by the parties involved and by the public at large. Moreover, he reveals how modes of reckoning with murder reflect the conditions under which Tracy's death became possible and, in the minds of many, acceptable. Michalko shows how Tracy's murder was, in other words, widely understood as a necessary murder and not as a murderous one, and he does this by revealing how our ways of making sense of death have everything to do with our ways of making sense of life.

The dominant sentiment surrounding the Latimer case was that this was a case about pain: 'severe' suffering. Yet Michalko's analysis of the event of Tracy's murder demonstrates otherwise. He writes:

> Contrary to all opinion about the Latimer case—that of the media, of the courts and of Latimer himself—his problem is not born of suffering. Latimer 'knows' suffering all too well and he can recognize it when he 'sees' it. For him, no mistake, Tracy was suffering. Latimer was equally firm in his knowledge of what to do about it—eliminate it.

For him, 'do the right thing', eliminate Tracy's suffering through the only available means, eliminate Tracy. Latimer had resolved the question of suffering, and what to do about it, long before Tracy's birth. (Michalko, 2002, p. 107)

The problem of Tracy's life and death was, according to Michalko, rather a problem of normalcy. Severely disabled, Tracy was also severely distanced from the vital and morally good pole of normality. He suggests that the lives of disabled people are governed and evaluated by a "rationality of opposites." Michalko writes: "thought of as the opposite of able-bodiedness, disability, and the lives of its people, is judged second-rate at best and unworthy at worst" (Michalko, 2002, p. 108). For Michalko, one portion of the trial transcript in particular was highly instructive in this regard. What follows is an excerpt of trial testimony given by Latimer's wife—and Tracy's mother—Laura Latimer as she was questioned by the defense:

DEFENSE LAWYER: As Tracy developed in her first year, was there any suggestion that Tracy would not live at home?
LAURA LATIMER: No.—when she was born? No.
DEFENSE LAWYER: What were your hopes for her at that stage?
LAURA LATIMER: When we very first took Tracy home we knew that she had brain damage but they said it might be very mild or it might be worse. We . . . had every hope that . . . she would be able to go to school but would just be maybe slow in school . . . We tried to treat her like a normal child . . . we tried to make her life as normal as we could.
DEFENSE LAWYER: How did you feel after Tracy died?
LAURA LATIMER: When I found Tracy I was happy for her . . . I was happy because she didn't have to deal with her pain anymore. After she died . . . I don't even know if I cried. Tracy's her birth was way, way sadder than her death . . . we lost Tracy when she was born and . . . that's when I grieved for her . . . I did all my grieving for her when she was little. We lost her then.
(Quoted in Michalko, 2002, pp. 105–106)

Tracy, according to her mother, was 'lost' not at the moment of her death—the moment she was killed—but at the moment she was born, the moment she was given life. Tracy was born 'with' cerebral palsy: she was born 'with' a permanent and pathologized 'brain damage.' Born 'with' 'severe' cerebral palsy, Tracy was, in Michalko's (2002) words, "born with-out the prerequisite condition of normalcy (nondamaged brain)" (p. 109). Born 'with' all of this, Tracy was also born into the understanding that her life was to be forever affixed to life's absence (death). Her parents "tried" to "treat her like a normal child" and "tried to make her life as normal as [they] could," but Tracy did or could not approximate normalcy. As per her mother's testimony, her vital life was expelled from the world the moment it entered it. Michalko concludes his analysis with the chilling observation, "the loss of normalcy and personhood—the loss of Tracy—occurred at her birth and her actual death was inevitable and anticlimactic. Robert Latimer killed his *already dead daughter*. As he said, no crime was committed; he did the right thing" (Michalko, 2002, p. 110).

Returning to my analysis of the Dawes, Peng, and McCarron cases, which I understand to be not individual and isolated cases but related disability-motivated murders, it becomes clear that these cases are bound to the Latimer case by a continuous logic. Much like the case of Tracy Latimer, the murders of Jason Dawes, Scarlett Chen, and Katie McCarron were also "governed and evaluated by a rationality of opposites" (Michalko, 2002, p. 108). In the three cases detailed, as per my analysis above, nonautism was made synonymous with hope and possibility, while autism came to be understood as hopelessness and limit. Where nonautism was conceived of as life, autism was made a life-draining pathology. Yet the vital/izing conceptual device of the autism spectrum, an organizational device that both allows and obliges us to think about autism[5] as a vital range of abnormalities of differing severities, and that was very much at the center of the three autism murder trials, reveals something of the governing power of an oppositional rationality.

As we have already seen, insofar as it is anchored by (hierarchical) poles of a nonvital, abnormal autism and a vital, normal nonautism, the autism spectrum (of life) supports and sustains such a 'rationality of opposites.' Yet in examining the three cases of violence against autistic people detailed above, this 'rationality of opposites' is doing something other than setting up the strict either/or way of knowing disabled life that Michalko correctly identifies was at work in the Latimer case (Michalko, 2002, p. 108). Tracy was born into the biomedical category of severe (nonvital) disability and so was born into death. Jason, Scarlett, and Katie were born into an autism *spectrum of life* where the nonvital limit of severe disability was but one of many intermediary possibilities of living and dying. The spectral quality of the autism spectrum is a conceptual device for organizing a range of autism severities. The spectrum[6] gives birth to a whole range of vital possibilities and nonvital limits within the category of autism itself: it inaugurates many small and incremental ways of living and, necessarily, many and incremental ways of dying. In this way, the autism spectrum inaugurates an array of new kinds of living people: people who 'live with' a pathological (life-threatening) autism. Not-yet living people who—depending on the severity of their (nonvital) signs of autism and the degree to which they (can) approximate the (vital) signs of nonautism or normalcy—become conceptually understood, variously, as 'almost living' or 'mostly dead.'

This subtle logic structured the autism murder cases of Dawes, Peng, and McCarron. Unlike the violent acts of Dawes or Peng, which were discursively naturalized as 'necessary murders' for they performed the vital function of preventing autism from further laying waste to (normative) life—acts that were rendered permissible by the courts and by the media accordingly—McCarron's act of violence was recognized as, unnaturally and so unjustifiably, taking life. In accordance with a liberal logic of life and its calculus of pathological severity, the fatal violence inflicted on Katie was judged to be characteristic of a nonvital or 'murderous violence.' It was understood, in other words, as a violence that was enacted in name of death and not life. While Peng and Dawes were framed and so understood as performing the vital act of releasing themselves and their 'almost dead' children from autism's morbid grip, McCarron was framed and so understood as taking the life of her 'almost living' child. Peng and Dawes were freed to resume their lives. Karen McCarron was sentenced to life in prison.

Because Karen McCarron's violent action (and Katie's subsequent death) was not naturalized, normalized, and so obscured as a tragic though logical outcome of life with autism, as were the actions of Peng and Dawes, this third case permits us—if not compels us—to think more and think again about how acts of violence directed against autistic people—acts of violence that are, quite evidently, endemic to our contemporary culture—are supported by hegemonic understandings of the meaning of 'life with autism.' Katie McCarron's murder, Karen McCarron's confession, and the ensuing murder trial make explicit the material danger of dominant contemporary understandings of 'life with autism' and, in so doing, better position us to glean an underlying story that is nearly obscured in the Dawes and the Chen murders and in our contemporary cultural backdrop out of which these cases of violence emerge and against which they are subsequently reckoned with. More specifically, what the lives and deaths of all three kids show us—and what the case of Katie McCarron makes explicit—is the danger in the dominant if not near monolithic cultural practice of representing and so understanding autism as, simply, some pathological thing one 'has' and the related promise that individuals and collectives living with autism might someday live without it.

Splitting Matter

"I wanted a life without autism." These were the words offered by Dr. Karen McCarron as she sat in her hospital room, as she recovered from her suicide attempt, as she confessed to the murder of her three-year-old girl. McCarron lived with a daughter who lived with autism. McCarron's daughter and life were 'with' autism, and she wanted a daughter and a life without it. "I tried very hard to get autism out of our lives," she said. She tried all the best therapies and interventions, she sent her to all the right schools. Yet, even still, she lived with a child, and so she lived a life, that was not 'indistinguishable' from other children and normal lives. Even after the schools and the therapies and the early interventions, in McCarron's eyes, her (otherwise normal, nonautistic) Katie was still 'with' autism: near normative in her behaviors, almost living—yet not quite. McCarron lived a 'life with' autism.

McCarron lived with all of this, but she also lived with more than this. She lived with a conception of her child that was given to her by her culture: where 'life with' autism is, as a given, life under threat. Not quite life at all. A culture that expresses, time and again, its hate of autism and its desire for its elimination: where a pathologized autism is split off from and made discontinuous with life. "I wanted a life without autism," said McCarron: a life, she meant, with 'just' a living Katie and not a Katie living 'with.' "I loved Katie very much," she said, "I hate the autism, so, so much. I hate what it has done." "I miss my daughter every day," echoed Peng, "I still love my daughter. I hate autism."

Beloved children split in two. A child-with: part child, part autism. A part to love and a part to hate. A part to cultivate and a part to eliminate. In this, our, culture, it has become possible to have individual bodies (as well as whole populations) split cleanly in two—part living people and part life-draining pathology. Such a cultural orientation did not force McCarron's (or Peng's or Dawes's) hand in killing her child, but it nonetheless provides the necessary conditions that continues to make this kind of violence possible and even—for those of us monitoring the headlines—normal. Born of our culture, the violence enacted against Katie, Scarlett, and Jason (and all of the people, named and unnamed, who belong to the growing column of violence) is a cultural problem, and so, to borrow again from Michalko, "a problem for all of us" (Michalko, 2002, p. 111).

Conclusion: Advocating Otherwise

The dominant ways we have of engaging in autism advocacy (i.e., by fighting autism, battling it, hating it, waging a war against it, and working to eliminate it) require us to think of autism, not as itself a way of living, but as that which must be 'lived with.' Dominant forms of autism advocacy are playing a key role in sustaining this culture. Autism, advocacy so often tells us, must be minimized and/or eliminated in the hopes of recuperating the presumed goodness/rightness of normative life. This story requires us to think of ourselves—collectively and individually—as cleanly split into autistic and nonautistic parts. Autism is here and not there, you and not me: it is some 'thing' and not 'someone,' a (invalid) brain, and not an (invalidated) identity. Such a parsing of life and nonlife, people and pathologies, promises that there *can* be life without autism, that if autism is eliminated, someone without autism will remain. As is painfully evident throughout this chapter, such a promise is as false as it is dangerous. Autism is not some a priori thing-in-the-world but is rather an interpretive device used to make sense of the bodies of actual people. As discourse inevitably marks the body and gives it shape and possibility, person and autism cannot be separated in any easy or straightforward way. Attending to Sinclair's (1993) words, cited several times throughout this book, autism is "a way of being. It is *pervasive*; it colors every experience, every sensation, perception, thought, emotion, and encounter, every aspect of existence" (np). And from this, he crucially reminds us, "it is not possible to separate the autism from the person—and if it were possible, the person you'd have left would not be the same person you started with" (p. 2). Returning now to the specific cases of violence explored in this chapter: Katie, Scarlett, and Jason were not 'people living with autism' but *living autistic people*. Fighting their autism meant fighting them, hating their autism was hating them, killing their autism killed them.

Discourse is material. The everyday ways we collectively talk and think about autism are involved in the "making of the meaning of people"

(Titchkosky, 2007, p.3). Dominant assumptions and articulations about the quality and character of autistic lives teach us about what autism is and can be and govern the terms of our collective and individual responses to autism. And this, I believe, brings us back to the central question of the book: the question of advocacy. Contemporary discourses of autism advocacy have become *the* dominant way of making sense of autism and nonautism and the relationship between these entwined categories of being. Through dominant practices of contemporary autism advocacy, we learn about what autism means and what it means to advocate.

Throughout this book, I have argued that we, as a culture, must better account for the danger of routine, taken-for-granted assumptions that are, as we have seen, complicit in creating and sustaining a violent culture 'against' autism. By attending, throughout this book, to some of the dominant discourses of autism that circulate in and through our culture and our lives, and by exposing the underlying logics that give these stories shape and coherence, my aim has been to better understand and further contest the ways autism violence is normalized today. Rather than rejecting the work of autism advocacy full stop, I am instead writing an appeal to all who advocate (including myself). Advocacy—a mode of relating that is absolutely and unavoidably premised on uneven power relations—is never simple, certain, nor self-evident. It is work that is (and ought to be) difficult: fraught with uncertainty and risk. In my view, these uncertainties, these risks, are not cause to abandon the essential work of advocacy. Instead, they represent an invitation for us (all) to endeavor to become more aware of the awarenesses we already have of autism and nonautism, to think again about our collective, cultural understandings of autism and about the material effects these understandings have on the bodies of people. It is my hope this book has offered some frameworks for further understanding the critical importance of this kind of (non-normative) advocacy work, frameworks that might better support and sustain those who seek to advocate differently and otherwise.

Notes

———— ꙮ ————

Introduction

1. This work is a study of dominant cultural understandings of autism. Making use of an extensive collection of contemporary autism/advocacy artifacts, my writing draws heavily on common or dominant cultural ideas, phrases and sayings: they are interwoven throughout my observations and analyses. I do this with the hope that I might draw the reader's attention to how dominant language influences the ways autism is perceived and what it means. My use of both single and double quotes throughout the book is an attempt to highlight this. Readers should note that I use double quotes to mark out direct quotations. I use single quotes to place particular emphasis on a common cultural colloquialism or concept, to draw the reader's attention to a specific part of quoted text, or to mark out words with special or unusual meaning.

2. See Baggs, 2012; Durbin-Westby, 2012; ASAN, 2012; and chapter 1 for further elaboration on the autistic self-advocacy movement and its premises.

Chapter 1

1. See, for example, the contemporary red flag posters featured in chapter 3 (figs. 2–4).

2. And, as I argue in the later half of this book, the health of the individual is still very commonly read as a sign of the health of the nation state.

3. Parents of autistic children are, still to this day, most often represented as eccentric university professors, scientists, researchers, artists, doctors, and so on. They are most commonly represented as middle class and white. This dominant narrative of autism as a middle-class disorder of the (white) West has, no doubt, much to do with the booming autism industrial complex—discussed in chapter 4—that depends on the incessant consumption of middle-class parents trying to 'fix' or 'develop' their kids.

4. For example, Dr. Bernard Rimland, advocate, father of an autistic son, and

founder of the first American autism advocacy organization, the (then) Autism Society of America (ASA), was instrumental in pushing forward a behaviorist research agenda (Hyvonen, 2004; Nadesan, 2005).

5. See chapter 4 for an examination of the very lucrative business of autism.

6. This statistic is constantly changing, with the most recent CDC report (2014) claiming that 1 in 68 children are autistic (CDC, 2014). For further discussion and analysis of autism statistics, see chapter 4.

7. As one autism 'expert', Dr. Jerry Kartzinel, states, "autism, as I see it, steals the soul from a child; then, if allowed, relentlessly sucks life's marrow out of the family members one by one" (McCarthy, 2007).

Chapter 2

1. A process, of course, that works both ways. As I will explore, the delimitation of the subject of the autistic advocated for to someone (afflicted) 'with' a pathological autism, functions to (re)enforce the limits of the role of the advocate.

2. I use the language of potentiality with respect to both the autistic body and the body of the advocate, as disciplinary processes are always invested in the body . . . becoming.

3. The appearance of a commercial advertisement on an advocacy poster advertising the signs of abnormal developmental is not mere happenstance. In chapter 4, I explore the entwined relationship between biomedical notions of human development and capitalist notions of economic development.

4. Where, twenty years ago, parents might have compared children's milestones with a friend or a neighbor, now parents are confronted by the developmental milestones of the kids of five hundred of their closest friends on Facebook, Twitter or Instagram.

5. As Diehl et al. show in their 2011 article "'Seeing Red: Color Selection as an Indicator of Implicit Societal Conceptions about the Autism Spectrum", the (mostly negative) visual rhetoric of the color red is often associated with autism on poster graphs.

6. For an insightful examination of the ways in which disabled children's play has been transformed by the field of developmental psychology as a instrument of surveillance, measurement, and evaluation, see Runswick-Cole and Goodley's (2009) article in *Disability and Society*, "Emancipating play: Dis/abled children and development and deconstruction."

7. See chapter 4.

Chapter 3

1. For more about the "difference that disability makes", see Michalko (2002).

2. Bob Wright—CEO of Autism Speaks, former vice chairperson and executive officer of General Electric, former chairperson and CEO of NBC Universal and Starbucks celebrity—is clearly one such 'good' advocate subject.

3. Declaring April 2 as autism awareness day "in perpetuity" suggests a commitment to having autism in our midst forever. Yet, the promise of contemporary autism advocacy discourses—including the discourse surrounding World Autism Awareness Day—is that autism can be lessened/treated if not eliminated/cured. This disjuncture, of course, begs the question: is the search for better treatments and/or cure for autism a perpetual one?

4. On April 2, 2010, the Dutch Autism Association rang the closing bell at the

NYSE Euronext Amsterdam, Autism-Europe rang the opening bell at NYSE Euronext Brussels and Paris, and the Federação Portuguesa de Autismo and the Associação Portuguesa para as Perturbações do Desenvolvimento e Autismo rang the closing bell at NYSE Euronext Lisbon (New York Stock Exchange, 2010).

5. The buildings that were lit up in blue included the Empire State Building, Madison Square Gardens, the Toys 'R' Us in Times Square, Fenway Park (Boston), and Sak's Fifth Avenue in the US, the World Trade Center in Bahrain, the CN Tower in Canada, and the Kingdom Center in Saudi Arabia (Autism Speaks, 2011d).

6. Recalling the historical genealogy of autism from chapter 2, which traced the existence of autism as an articulated and articulable category back not even sixty years, this might have been a bit of an exaggeration on Obama's part.

7. And, as Sharon Stephens (1995) points out, in an increasingly global and globalized world, "it is not only modern European national citizens who should have a particular sort of childhood, but populations around the world, in need of 'civilization' and 'development'" (p. 16).

8. As Jim Sinclair (1999) demonstrates in his piece 'Why I dislike person first language', and I discuss further in chapter 6, the phrase 'person with autism' plays an important role in supporting the dangerous biomedical presupposition that autism is somehow separate and separable from a person 'with' it.

9. It is interesting to note that this language of recovery has also used by different factions mainstream autism advocacy movements as a way to describe curing or overcoming autism. Key examples of how the language of recovery is put to use include: Catherine Maurice famous 1993 memoir *Let me Hear Your Voice: A Family's Triumph over Autism,* describes the process of 'recovering' her two autistic children through intensive behavioral therapy. The language of recovery continues to be used in the context of behaviorist treatment approaches (ABA and IBI therapies). Notions of recovery are heavily associated with the antivaccination movement and other pseudo-scientific approaches to 'curing' autism. It is, I think, equally interesting to note how contemporary economic discourses use the language and concepts of childhood development to articulate processes of recovery (i.e., the success/progress of the American Recovery and Reinvestment Act is measured in terms of the economy's "growth and development" and even in terms of its "recovery milestones") (Government of the United States of America, 2009c).

10. See Albrect's (1992) *The Disability Business: Rehabilitation in America.*

11. To class a particular therapeutic approach as 'government endorsed', 'scientific,' or 'evidence-based' is not suggest that it is inherently free of ethical and/or health concerns (e.g., at the time of this writing, electroconvulsive therapy remains FDA-approved).

12. For example: you might take a quiz about your child's behaviors with *AutismTest®,* or upload video footage to better track the progression of your child's 'symptoms' on *BehaviorTrackerPro®, Model Me Going Places®* provides slideshows of images depicting smiling children modelling "socially appropriate" behaviors, *Look in my Eyes®* is a game that rewards players for looking directly into the eyes of a person on the screen. Parents, teachers, and anyone who works with or lives with autism can download behavior modification tools such as *ABA Flashcards©, Teach Emotions©, Everyday Social Skills©,* and so on.

13. For a compelling discussion of "growing sideways", see Kathryn Bond Stockton's book *The Queer Child, or Growing Sideways in the Twentieth Century* (2010).

14. Recall, here, the functional importance of the simplified and therefore highly consumable fact in a neoliberal economy of that relies on, as we have seen, the existence of the untimely body to be made timely.

15. See chapter 5 for a full description of this PSA.

16. And it is clear that "understanding" here refers to the understanding of the nature of autism's problem, which must not be confused with greater understanding of autism as a way of being in the world, or understanding of autistic people.

17. Nowhere is this more clear than in the words of one parent: "Our son has been on a 4 year recovery journey that was not like a ramp but more like the stock market, with times of plateaus and regressions, usually preceding advancement" (Autism Speaks, 2010a).

18. This is reflected in growing numbers of autism advocacy organizations and sponsored events that invoke this temporality of the now. To name a few: "Defeat Autism Now", "Cure Autism Now" (now Autism Speaks), "Fund Autism Now", "Help Autism Now", "Beat Autism Now", the "ACT NOW" project, "Walk Now for Autism," and simply "Autism Now"!

Chapter 4

1. The act was reauthorized in 2011 under the Obama administration.

2. In 2010, in response to pressure from autistic self-advocates and their families, ASAN president Ari Ne'eman was appointed to the IACC. Since then, other autistic representatives have served on the committee. ASAN continues to pressure the IACC for more autistic representation.

3. And as Kathleen Seidel importantly notes in *Neurodiversity: A Weblog* (now offline): "We do not know whether the girl is afraid of the photographer, or whether she wishes to be photographed. We do not know whether she has been paid for the use of her image" (Seidel, 2005b, para. 8).

4. The notion of autism as captor permeates the "Getting the Word Out" campaign materials. For example, figure 9 displays a poster from the campaign featuring a young, shirtless boy seemingly cowering in the shadows with a gag over his mouth. Additionally, the typography used in the "Getting the Word Out" logo is reminiscent of the piece-meal composition of a ransom note.

5. Interestingly and most ironically, the NYU CSC's demand is the only demand made in these ransom notes.

6. In an Autism Speaks press release entitled "Do you want to be in a World Autism Video?", the organization makes an appeal to families who have autistic children to submit home video footage of themselves and their children for potential inclusion in Cuarón's film. The press release issues very detailed instructions (complete with sketched illustrations) as to what kinds of scenes the organization will accept. "We need three video clips per submission," the press release states, "The first clip is: A person on the spectrum wearing a plain white t-shirt filmed alone in a place that is special to your family. It can be a landmark (Eiffel Tower, Big Ben, etc.), skyline, town square, backyard, schoolyard, amusement area or somewhere else of your choosing, The second clip we need is: Have the same person stand in the same spot this time surrounded by family members. All the people in the shot should be wearing white T-shirts. Please film both shots in the same camera angle. The third clip we need is: Film closer angles of the family—interacting, smiling, holding hands, hugging etc." I highlight the carefully choreographed nature of the film so as to emphasize the extent to which meanings of autism are *made* in this and, indeed, any advocacy initiative (Autism Speaks, 2009b).

7. Recall, from chapter 2, the advocate is always figured (at least in dominant advocacy frames) as nonautistic. Within dominant frames of autism advocacy, the

autistic subject is constrained, denied the power to observe autism. The autistic subject is and can only ever be seen. Therefore, the figure of the autistic *self*-advocate does not and, indeed, cannot exist here. This is, of course, not to say that autistic self-advocates don't exist. Rather, the autistic self-advocate is denied cultural intelligibility, altogether effaced as either 'too autistic' to advocate or 'not autistic enough'.

8. In chapter 5, I conduct a more detailed analysis of this conflation of meaning.

9. Foucault emphasizes elsewhere that 'killing' can and must be broadly conceived. He writes: "when I say 'killing', I obviously do not mean simply murder as such, but also every form of indirect murder: the fact of exposing someone to death, increasing the risk of death for some people, or quite simply, political death, expulsion, rejection, and so on" (Foucault, 1997, p. 256).

10. This intermingling of frames is made most evident, for example, in a recent research initiative—led by Rutgers University psychology researcher Dr. Maggie Shiffrar and Dr. Kent Harber and funded by an almost half-million dollar research grant from the Department of Homeland Security—that studies autistic subjects "lack of empathy" (what the Rutgers press release refers to as autism's "lens devoid of emotion") as a way to develop better screening techniques to use for profiling potential terrorist subjects (Rutgers University, 2008).

Chapter 5

1. Recall, of course that, as articulated by Baggs (2012), Durbin-Westby (2012), and others, autistic notions of self-advocacy non-normatively presupposed an understanding of 'self' that is both individual and collective.

2. In chorus and in solidarity with other interested and implicated people who are noticing, documenting and organizing around these deaths on online forums and blogs such as Joel Smith's (2006) This Way of Life website (2006), Amanda Bagg's (2008) *Ballastexistenz* blog, Kristina Chew's (2009) *Autism Vox* blog, Michelle Dawson's (2011) online forum, The Misbehaviour of Behaviourists, and Kathleen Seidel's (2005a) Neurodiversity website.

3. This is almost a direct quote from famed behaviorist Ole Lovaas, who developed what is now referred to as the best practice therapeutic approach, Applied Behavioral Analysis. He said that intensive behavior therapy was necessary to ensure that autistic children became "indistinguishable from their normal friends" (Lovaas, 1987, p. 8). See chapter 2.

4. The dangerous logic of a necessary autism murder was, for example, directly evoked by the (then) senior vice president of Autism Speaks, Alison Tepper Singer, in the 2006 Autism Speaks fundraising documentary *Autism Every Day*. In the presence of her eight-year-old autistic child, Singer states that when faced with inadequate educational services and the related prospect of her daughter's lack of progress, murder became a viable option. In Singer's words: "I remember that was a scary moment for me when I realized I had sat in the car for about 15 minutes and actually contemplated putting [her child] in the car and driving off the George Washington Bridge. That would be preferable to having to put her in one of these schools." She goes on to say that it was only because of her other child that she did not do it (Autism Speaks, 2006a).

5. As I am exploring in my current project, the concept of 'spectrum' has been variously used (both formally and informally—in popular culture) as a way of metaphorizing/making sense of a great many so-called disorders and the people that they reference. Diagnostic categories like 'Obsessive compulsive disorder' and 'Fetal

Alcohol Disorder' have now broadened into 'Obsessive compulsive spectrum disorder' and 'Fetal Alcohol Spectrum Disorder', respectfully. Categories of 'Anxiety' and 'Depression' are mapped out as a spectrum. And the concept is now being used in reference to designations like 'Obesity', 'addiction', and 'eating disorder'.

6. I am currently exploring notions of dimensionality and spectrum in my current project.

Bibliography

———— ❧ ————

Abberley, P. (1987). The concept of oppression and the development of a social theory of disability. *Disability, Handicap & Society*, 2(1), 5–19.

ABC WISN. (November 19, 2008). Father accused of killing son served in Navy, former firefighter. Retrieved at: http://www.wisn.com/news/18019398/detail.html.

Agamben, G. (1999). On potentiality. In *Potentialities: Collected essays in philosophy* (pp. 177–84). Stanford: Stanford University Press.

Agamben, G. (2005). *State of exception*. Chicago: University of Chicago Press.

Albrecht, G. L. (1992). *The disability business: Rehabilitation in america*. Thousand Oaks, CA: Sage Publications.

Alphonso, C. (June 24, 2008). Rules urged for calming autistic children with blanket. *The Globe and Mail*, p. A9.

American Psychiatric Association. (2000). *Diagnostic and statistical manual of mental disorders* (4th ed., text rev.). Washington, DC: American Psychiatric Association.

American Psychiatric Association. (2013). *Diagnostic and statistical manual of mental disorders* (5th ed.). Washington, DC: American Psychiatric Association.

Arnup, K. (1994). *Education for motherhood: Advice for mothers in twentieth-century Canada*. Toronto: University of Toronto Press.

ASAN. (2007). An Urgent Call to Action: Tell NYU Child Study Center to Abandon Stereotypes Against People with Disabilities. Autistic Self Advocacy Network [press release]. Retrieved at: http://autisticadvocacy.org/2007/12/tell-nyu-child-study-center-to-abandon-stereotypes.

ASAN. (2012). *And straight on until morning: Essays on autism acceptance*. Washington, DC: The Autistic Press.

Asperger, H. (1991). Autistic psychopathology in childhood. In U. Frith (ed.), *Autism and asperger syndrome* (pp. 37–39). New York: Cambridge University Press.

Attfield, E., and Morgan, S. H. (2006). *Living with autistic spectrum disorders: Guidance for parents, carers, and siblings* (illustrated ed.). London: Paul Chapman.

Attwood, T. (2008). *The complete guide to asperger's syndrome*. London: Jessica Kingsley Publishers.

Aubrecht, K. (2010). Rereading the ontario review of the roots of youth violence report: The relevance of fanon for a critical disability studies perspective. In M. Simmons (ed.), *Fanon & education: Thinking through pedagogical possibilities* (pp. 55–78). New York: Peter Lang.

Autism Association of Western Australia. (2007). *Living with autism: Practical strategies for supporting people with autism spectrum disorders.* Subiaco, W.A.: Autism Association of Western Australia.

Autism Awareness Australia. (2010). *Autism awareness public service announcement* [video file]. Retrieved at: http://www.autismawareness.com.au.

Autism Genome Project. (2011). Research techniques [web page]. Retrieved at: http://www.autismgenome.org/research/researchtechniques.htm.

Autism Ontario. (2007). Red flags for autism [poster]. Retrieved at: http://www.autismontario.com/client/aso/ao.nsf/Durham/Red+Flags+for+Autism.

Autism Ontario. (2009). Ontario community grieves loss of boy with autism [media release]. Retrieved at: http://www.autismontario.com/Client/ASO/AO.nsf/object/media+release+Oct+26+re+mississauga/$file/media+release+Oct+26+re+mississauga.pdf.

Autism Society of America. (2005a). Getting the word out [web page]. Retrieved at: http://www.gettingthewordout.org.

Autism Society of America. (2005b). Autism 101, Getting the word out [web page]. Retrieved at: http://www.gettingthewordout.org/101.php.

Autism Society of America. (2013). Autism Society's Response to Autism Speaks Blog. Retrieved at: https://web.archive.org/web/20131117060943/http://www.autism-society.org/news/autism-society-response.html.

Autism Society of America (Ventura County Chapter). (n.d.). Possible signs of autism [poster]. Retrieved at: http://www.vcas.info/VCAS/Downloads_files/Possible%20Signs.pdf.

Autism Society Canada. (2004). *Canadian autism research agenda and canadian autism strategy: A white paper.* Toronto: Autism Society Canada. Retrieved at: http://www.autismsocietycanada.ca/DocsAndMedia/ASC_Internal/finalwhite-eng.pdf.

Autism Speaks. (2005). NBC networks to focus on autism [media release]. Retrieved at: http://www.autismspeaks.org/inthenews/naar_archive/nbc_networks_focus_on_autism.php.

Autism Speaks. (2006a). *Autism Every Day* [film]. Dir. Lauren Thierry.

Autism Speaks. (2006b). Learn the signs campaign [web page]. Retrieved at: http://www.autismspeaks.org/whatisit/learnsigns.php.

Autism Speaks. (July 25, 2007). Starbucks now serving Autism Speaks' freshly brewed thought of the day [press release]. Retrieved at: http://www.autismspeaks.org/press/starbucks_thought.php.

Autism Speaks. (2008a). CNN announces global coverage for first world autism awareness day [media release]. Retrieved at: http://www.autismspeaks.org/inthenews/cnn_waad.php.

Autism Speaks. (2008b). World autism awareness day [media release]. Retrieved at: http://www.autismspeaks.org/inthenews/world_autism_awareness_day_coverage.php.

Autism Speaks. (2009a). Yoko Ono shows her support for autism speaks at the United Nations [media release]. Retrieved at: http://www.autismspeaks.org/inthenews/waad_2009_yoko_ono.php.

Autism Speaks. (2009b). Do you want to be in a world autism video? [web page]. Retrieved at: http://www.autismspeaks.org/inthenews/autism_video_project.php.

Autism Speaks. (2009c). $100 million challenge kicks off global 'decade for autism' [press release]. Retrieved at: http://www.autismspeaks.org/press/world_focus_on_autism_2009.php.

Autism Speaks. (2009d). Bob and Suzanne Wright on the new CDC prevalence numbers [video file]. Retrieved at: http://www.youtube.com/user/AutismSpeaksVids#p/u/31/fZcKP_OknDw.

Autism Speaks. (2010a). IAN research report: Family stress [news item]. Retrieved at: http://www.autismspeaks.org/inthenews/ian_findings_family_stress_part_1.php.

Autism Speaks. (2010b). *Autism Speaks strategic plan for science 2009–2011*. Retrieved at: http://www.autismspeaks.org/docs/strategic_plan/AS_Strategic_Plan_2009_2011.pdf.

Autism Speaks. (2010c). Times have changed [public service announcement]. Retrieved at: http://www.autismspeaks.org/whatisit/ad_council_campaign.php.

Autism Speaks. (2011a). Autism tissue program (ATP) [web page]. Retrieved at: http://www.autismtissueprogram.org/site/c.nlKUL7MQIsG/b.5183271/k.BD86/Home.htm.

Autism Speaks. (2011b). Autism genetic resource exchange (AGRE) overview [web page]. Retrieved at: http://agre.autismspeaks.org/site/c.lwLZKnN1LtH/b.5002149/k.E3CE/Overview.htm.

Autism Speaks. (2011c). About world autism awareness day, World Autism Awareness Day [web page]. Retrieved at: http://www.worldautismawarenessday.org/site/c.egLMI2ODKpF/b.3917077/k.186A/About_World_Autism_Awareness_Day.htm.

Autism Speaks. (2011d). Light it up blue [web page]. Retrieved at: http://www.lightitupblue.org.

Autism Speaks. (2012a). Cost of Autism Summit [web page]. Retrieved at: http://www.autismspeaks.org/science/science-news/%E2%80%98costs-autism%E2%80%99-summit.

Autism Speaks. (2012b). As autism soars: nobody is left untouched [web page]. Retrieved at: http://www.autismspeaks.org/blog/2012/04/04/autism-soars-no-one-left-untouched.

Autism Women's Network. (2012). *Autism Women's Network* [blog]. Retrieved at: http://autismwomensnetwork.org.

Autistic Self Advocacy Network (ASAN). (2011). Mission statement [web page]. Retrieved at: http://www.autisticadvocacy.org.

Auton (Guardian ad litem of) v. British Columbia (Attorney General). (2004). Supreme Court of Canada. 78, 3 S.C.R. 657.

Baggs, A. (2005). Getting the truth out [web page]. Retrieved at: http:www.gettingthewordout.org.

Baggs, A. (2007). In My Language. [video file]. Retrieved at: https://www.youtube.com/watch?v=JnylM1hI2jc

Baggs, A. (2008). Ballastexistenz [web page]. Retrieved at: http://ballastexistenz.autistics.org.

Baggs, A. (2012). The meaning of self-advocacy. In Julia Bascom (ed.), *Loud Hands: Autistic People, Speaking*. Washington, DC: ASAN.

Baker, A., and Hughes, C. J. (February 5, 2010). Mother held in death of boy, 8, at luxury hotel. *New York Times*. Retrieved at: http://www.nytimes.com/2010/02/06/nyregion/06hotel.html.

Barnes, C. (1998). The social model of disability: A sociological phenomenon ignored by sociologists? In T. Shakespeare (ed.), *The disability reader: Social science perspectives* (pp. 65–78). London: Cassell Academic.

Barnes, C., Oliver, M., and Barton, L. (2002). *Disability studies today*. Cambridge, UK: Malden, MA: Polity Press and Blackwell Publishers.

Barnett, B. (2006). Medea in the media. *Journalism*, 7(4), 411.

Baron-Cohen, S. (1997). *Mindblindness: An essay on autism and theory of mind*. Cambridge, MA: MIT Press.

Baron-Cohen, S. (2001). Theory of mind in normal development and autism. *Prisme*, 34, 174–83.

Bascom, Julie (ed.). (2012). *Loud Hands: Autistic People Speaking*. Washington, DC: Autistic Self Advocacy Network.

Bell, C. (2006). Introducing white disability studies. In L. Davis (ed.), *The disability studies reader* (pp. 275–82). New York: Routledge.

Ben-Moshe, L. (2011). Disabling incarceration: Connecting disability to divergent confinements in the USA. *Critical Sociology*. doi:10.1177/0896920511430864.

Bergland, R. L. (2000). *The national uncanny: Indian ghosts and American subjects*. Hanover, NH: University Press of New England.

Berlant, L. G. (1997). *The queen of America goes to Washington city: Essays on sex and citizenship*. Durham, NC: Duke University Press.

Berry, J. F. (December 30, 2006). Woman gets prison for child's killing in 2002. *The Press Enterprise*, p. B01.

Bettelheim, B. (1972). *The empty fortress: Infantile autism and the birth of the self*. New York: Free Press.

Biklen, D., and Attfield, R. (2005). *Autism and the myth of the person alone* (illustrated ed.). New York: NYU Press.

Black, E. (2003). *War against the weak eugenics and America's campaign to create a master race*. New York: Basic Books.

Bolton, M. Morgan (February 21, 2007). As family buries son, quest for justice begins; autistic teen died last week while in care of workers who now face manslaughter charges. *Times Union*, p. A1.

Borum, R. (2004). *Psychology of terrorism*. Tampa: University of South Florida.

Boyden, J. (1997). Childhood and the policy makers: A comparative perspective on the globalization of childhood. In A. James and A. Prout (eds.), *Constructing and reconstructing childhood: Contemporary issues in the sociological study of childhood* (pp. 187–226). Washington, DC: Falmer Press.

Boyle, D. (Director). (2002). *28 days later* [motion picture]. United Kingdom: 20th Century Fox.

Briggs, C. L., and Hallin, D. C. (2007). Biocommunicability: The neoliberal subject and its contradictions in news coverage of health issues. *Social Text*, 25(493), 43.

Broderick, A. (2011). Autism as rhetoric: Exploring watershed rhetorical moments in applied behavior analysis discourse. *Disability Studies Quarterly*, 31(3), n.p.

Broderick, A., and Ne'eman, A. (2008). Autism as metaphor: Narrative and counternarrative. *International Journal of Inclusive Education*, 12, 5(6), 459–76.

Brooks, M. (October 5, 2009). More kids have autism than thought: US study. Reuters. Retrieved at: http://www.reuters.com/article/2009/10/05/us-kids-autism-idUSTRE59446N20091005.

Brown, L. (2013). *Autistic Hoya* [blog]. Retrieved at: http://www.autistichoya.com/

Brown, L. (2013). Honoring the dead. Autistic Hoya [web page]. Retrieved at: http://www.autistichoya.com/2013/03/honoring-dead.html

Brown, L. (2012a). So high functioning (sarcasm). Autistic Hoya [web page]. Retrieved at: http://www.autistichoya.com/2012/09/so-high-functioning-sarcasm.html

Brown, L. (2012b). There's something wrong with you. Autistic Hoya [web page]. Retrieved at: http://www.autistichoya.com/2012/01/theres-something-wrong-with-you.html.

Brown, L. (2011a). Advocacy and ableism. Autistic Hoya [web page]. Retrieved at: http://www.autistichoya.com/2011/12/advocacy-and-ableism.html

Brown, L. (2011b). What is self-advocacy? Autistic Hoya [web page]. Retrieved at: http://www.autistichoya.com/2011/07/what-is-self-advocacy.html

Brown, L. (2011c). The significance of semantics: Person first language, why it matters. Autistic Hoya [web page]. Retrieved at: http://www.autistichoya.com/2011/08/significance-of-semantics-person-first.html.

Buescher, A.V., et al. (2014). Costs of autism spectrum disorders in the United Kingdom and the United States. *JAMA Pediatrics*, 168(8), 721–28.

Burke, K., Gendar, A., and Moore, R. (November 23, 2006). 'I terminated the life of my autistic son.' *New York Daily News*, p. 8.

Burke, P. (1997). *Gender shock: Exploding the myths of male and female*. New York: Anchor Books.

Burman, E. (1994). *Deconstructing developmental psychology*. London, New York: Routledge.

Burman, E. (2008). *Developments: Child, image, nation*. New York: Routledge.

Bush, G. W. (2001). Remarks following a meeting with the National Security team [speech]. In *Public papers of the presidents of the United States, July 1 to December 31, 2001*. Washington, DC: Government Printing Office.

Bush, G. W. (2004). Remarks on the anniversary of operation Iraqi freedom [speech]. In *Public papers of the presidents of the United States, January 1 to June 30, 2004*. Washington, DC: Government Printing Office.

Butler, J. (1993). *Bodies that matter: On the discursive limits of sex*. New York: Routledge.

Butler, J. (1999). *Gender trouble: Feminism and the subversion of identity*. New York: Routledge.

Butler, J. (2004a). *Precarious life: The powers of mourning and violence*. New York: Verso.

Butler, J. (2004b). *Undoing gender*. New York: Routledge.

Butler, J. (2009). *Frames of war: When is life grievable?* New York: Verso.

Canguilhem, G. (1991). *The normal and the pathological*. New York: Zone Books (original work published 1966).

Carey, B. (February 9, 2007). Study puts rate of autism at 1 in 150 U.S. children. *New York Times*. Retrieved at: http://www.nytimes.com/2007/02/09/health/09autism.html.

Carson, L. (September 8, 2010). Firefighters in Columbia discover woman's body, injured man. *Baltimore Sun*. Retrieved at: http://proquest.umi.com/pqdweb?did=2132752051&sid=5&Fmt=3&clientId=12520&RQT=309&VName=PQD.

Castells, M. (2009). *The rise of the network society: Information age, economy, science, and culture v.1* (2nd ed.). Malden, MA: Blackwell Publishers.

CBC News. (September 29, 2009). Dad in murder-suicide had sought help for autistic son. Retrieved at: http://www.cbc.ca/news/health/story/2009/09/29/edmonton-murder-suicide-confirmed.html.

CBC News. (October 9, 2009). Man despaired over moving autistic son, wife says. Retrieved at: http://www.cbc.ca/news/health/story/2009/10/09/edmonton-wife-speaks-lack-of-support-autistic-boy.html.

CBC News. (October 26, 2009). Mother charged with autistic son's death. Retrieved at: http://www.cbc.ca/news/canada/toronto/story/2009/10/26/mississauga-homicide.html.

CBS Chicago. (February 1, 2012). Family furious after Calumet city police shoot, kill boy with autism. Retrieved at: http://chicago.cbslocal.com/2012/02/01/boy-15-shot-dead-by-police-in-calumet-city.

Centers for Disease Control and Prevention (CDC). (2006). *Prevalence of the autism spectrum disorders (ASDs) in multiple areas of the United States, 2000 and 2002.* Washington, DC: US Department of Health and Human Services. Retrieved at: http://www.cdc.gov/ncbddd/autism/documents/AutismCommunityReport.pdf.

Centers for Disease Control and Prevention (CDC). (2010). *Prevalence of the autism spectrum disorders (ASDs) in multiple areas of the United States, 2004 and 2006.* Washington, DC: US Department of Health and Human Services. Retrieved at: http://www.cdc.gov/ncbddd/autism/states/ADDMCommunityReport2009.pdf.

Centers for Disease Control and Prevention (CDC). (2012). *Prevalence of autism spectrum disorders (ASDs) among multiple areas of the United States.* Washington, DC: US Department of Health and Human Services. Retrieved at: http://teacch.com/news/12_231272A_CommunityReport._complete.pdf.

Centers for Disease Control and Prevention (CDC). (2014). *Prevalence of autism spectrum disorder among children aged 8 years—Autism and Developmental Disabilities Monitoring Network, 11 sites, United States, 2010.* Washington, DC: US Department of Health and Human Services. Retrieved at: http://www.cdc.gov/mmwr/preview/mmwrhtml/ss6302a1.htm.

Çevik, K. (2012). The Autism Wars [website]. Retrieved at: http://theautismwars.blogspot.ca.

Charlton, J. (2000). *Nothing about us without us: Disability oppression and empowerment.* Los Angeles: University of California Press.

Chen, M. (2012). *Animacies: Biopolitics, racial mattering, and queer affect.* Durham, NC: Duke University Press.

Chew, K. (2009). Autism Vox [web page]. Archived at: http://blisstree.com.

Chew, K. (2007). Kidnapped by autism: Making noise about "Ransom Notes." Autism Vox [web page]. Retrieved at: http://www.blisstree.com/2007/12/08/mental-health-well-being/kidnapped-by-autism-making-noise-about-ransom-notes.

Churchill, D. (July 19, 2001). Family still waiting for answers to how autistic man died. *The Hamilton Spectator,* p. A9.

Cimera, R. E., and Cowan, R. J. (2009). The costs of services and employment outcomes achieved by adults with autism in the US. *Autism,* 13(3), 285.

Clare, E. (1999). *Exile and pride: Disability, queerness, and liberation.* Cambridge, MA: SouthEnd Press.

Clare, E. (2001). Stolen bodies, reclaimed bodies: Disability and queerness. *Public Culture,* 13(3), 359–65.

CNN. (2010). Mother to 911—'I killed my kids' [video file]. Retrieved at: http://www.youtube.com/watch?v=deH6VPjQIP8.

Connell, J. (2007). How I wrote the "song of the red flag." In A. Green and J. Branfman (eds.), *The big red songbook* (pp. 367–70). Chicago: Charles H. Kerr.

Connor, S. (June 10, 2010). Breakthrough brings fresh hope for families living with autism. *Dublin Herald.* Retrieved at: http://www.herald.ie/lifestyle/health-beauty/breakthrough-brings-fresh-hope-for-families-living-with-autism-2215041.html.

Corker, M., and French, S. (eds). (1999). *Disability discourse.* Philadelphia: Open University Press.

Corker, M., and Shakespeare, T. (eds). (2002). *Disability/postmodernity: Embodying disability theory.* New York: Continuum.

Crenshaw, M. (2000). The psychology of terrorism: An agenda for the 21st century. *Political Psychology,* 21(2), 405–20.

Cuarón, A. (2009). *I am autism* [video file]. New York: Autism Speaks.

Daily Mail. (August 5, 2011). 'She was going to kill me too,' says ex-husband of psychiatrist who shot her autistic 'Too Fat for 15' son before turning the gun on herself. Retrieved at: http://www.dailymail.co.uk/news/article-2022360/I-die-says-ex-husband-psychiatrist-shot-son-turning-gun-herself.html.

Darabont, F. (Director). (2010). *The walking dead* [motion picture]. United States of America: HBO.

Davidson, J., and Orsini, M. (eds). (2013). *Worlds of autism: Across the spectrum of neurological difference*. Minneapolis: University of Minnesota Press.

Davis, D. L. (2007). *The secret history of the war on cancer*. New York: Basic Books.

Davis, K. (March 2, 2009). Police: Chesapeake woman killed herself, autistic grandson. *Viginian-Pilot*. Retrieved at: http://hamptonroads.com/2009/03/police-chesapeake-woman-killed-herself-grandson-drug-overdose.

Davis, L. J. (1995). *Enforcing normalcy: Disability, deafness, and the body*. New York: Verso.

Davis, L. J. (2002). *Bending over backwards: Disability, dismodernism, and other difficult positions*. New York: New York University Press.

Davis, L. J. (2006). *The disability studies reader* (2nd ed.). New York: Routledge.

Dawson, M. (2003). Bettelheim's worst crime: Autism and the epidemic of irresponsibility. No autistics allowed: Explorations in discrimination against autistics [web page]. Retrieved at: http://www.sentex.net/~nexus23/md_01.html.

Dawson, M. (2005). The word is out about autism: Canada in the era of autism advocacy. No autistics allowed: Explorations in discrimination against autistics [web page]. Retrieved at: http://www.sentex.net/~nexus23/naa_sen.html.

Dawson, M. (2008a). ABA success stories: Gender disturbed children desperately need treatment. The autism crisis: Science and ethics in the era of autism politics [web page]. Retrieved at: http://autismcrisis.blogspot.com/2008/11/aba-success-stories.html.

Dawson, M. (2008b). No autistics allowed: Explorations in discrimination against autistics [web page]. Retrieved at: http://www.sentex.net/~nexus23/naa_02.html.

Dawson, M. (2011). The misbehaviour of behaviourists [online forum]. Retrieved at: http://www.quicktopic.com/27/H/vJvhV4fDnBgw7.

Delhi, K. (1994a). Fictions of the scientific imagination: Researching the Dionne quintuplets. *Journal of Canadian Studies*, 29(4), 86–110.

Dehli, K. (1994b). They rule by sympathy: The feminization of pedagogy. *The Canadian Journal of Sociology/Cahiers Canadiens De Sociologie*, 19(2), 195–216.

Dehli, K. (2008). Coming to terms: Methodological and other dilemmas in research. In K. Gallagher (ed.), *The methodological dilemma: Creative, critical, and collaborative approaches to qualitative research* (pp. 46–66). New York: Routledge.

DeMyer, M. K., Hingtgen, J. N., and Jackson, R. K. (1981). Infantile autism reviewed: A decade of research. *Schizophrenia Bulletin*, 7(3), 388.

Diament, M. (September 25, 2009). Groups outraged over video released by Autism Speaks. Disability Scoop [web page]. Retrieved at: http://www.disabilityscoop.com/2009/09/25/autism-speaks-video/5541.

Diehl, J. J., et al. (2011). Seeing red: Color selection as an indicator of implicit societal conceptions about the autism spectrum. *Disability Studies Quarterly*, 31(3), n.p.

Dillon, K. M. (1995). *Living with autism: The parents' stories* (illustrated ed.). Boone, NC: Parkway Publishers.

Dillon, M., and Reid, J. (2009). *The liberal way of war: Killing to make life live*. New York: Routledge.

Dininny, S. (July 11, 2006). Boy, 15, gets 26 years in friend's death; Evan Savoie was 12 when playmate was stabbed, beaten. *Columbian*, p. C2.

Diprose, R. (1995). A 'genethics' that makes sense. In V. Shiva and I. Moser (eds.), *Biopolitics: A feminist and ecological reader on biotechnology* (illustrated ed.) (pp. 162–74). London: Palgrave Macmillan.

Dolnick, E. (1998). *Madness on the couch: Blaming the victim in the heyday of psychoanalysis.* New York: Simon & Schuster.

Douglas, P.N. (2013). As if you have a choice: Autism mothers and the remaking of the human. *Health, Culture and Society* 5(1): 167–81.

Douthit, R. (Executive Producer). (2009). Jenny Mccarthy and Jim Carrey discuss autism; medical experts weigh in [television program]. Retrieved at: http://transcripts.cnn.com/TRANSCRIPTS/0904/03/lkl.01.html.

Dowdie, J. E. (Director). (2008). *Quarantine* [motion picture]. United States of America: Screen Gems.

Durbin-Westby, P. (2012). I am not a self-advocate [blog]. Retrieved at: http://paulacdurbinwestbyautisticblog.blogspot.ca/2012/11/i-am-not-self-advocate.html.

Dylan, B. (1978). No time to think. On *Street legal* [CD]. California: Columbia.

Easter Seals. (2008). Easter seals study sheds new light on parents' life-long fears, anxieties and critical supports needed to raise a child with autism [press release]. Retrieved at: http://www.easterseals.com/site/PageServer?pagename=ntl_pr_autism_study.

Edelman, L. (2004). *No future: Queer theory and the death drive.* Durham, NC: Duke University Press.

Erevelles, N. (1996). Disability and the dialectics of difference. *Disability & Society,* 11(4), 519–38.

Erevelles, N. (2002). Material citizens: Critical race theory, disability studies, and the politics of education. *Disability, Culture, and Education,* 1(1), 5–26.

Erevelles, N. (2011). Color of violence: Reflecting on gender, disability and race in wartime. In Kim Q. Hall (ed.), *Feminist disability studies* (pp. 117–37). Bloomington: Indiana University Press.Ericson, R. V. (2007). *Crime in an insecure world.* Cambridge, UK: Polity.

Ericson, R. V., and Doyle, A. (2003). Introduction. In R. V. Ericson and A. Doyle (eds.), *Risk and morality* (pp. 13–21). Toronto: University of Toronto Press.

Evans, B. (2010). Anticipating fatness: Childhood, affect and the pre-emptive 'war on obesity.' *Transactions of the Institute of British Geographers,* 35(1), 21–38.

Fagan, T. K. (1987). Gesell: The first school psychologist. Part I. The road to Connecticut. *School Psychology Review,* 16(1), 103–107.

Fairbanks, A. (April 18, 2009). Tug of war over costs to educate the autistic. *The New York Times.* Retrieved at: http://www.nytimes.com/2009/04/19/education/19autism.html.

Falco, M. (April 2, 2009). Progress is slow in the war against autism. CNN Health. Retrieved at: http://articles.cnn.com/2009–04–02/health/autism.update_1_mmr-vaccine-autism-spectrum-disorders-vaccines-cause-autism?_s=PM:HEALTH.

Falco, M. (March 28, 2014). Autism rates now 1 in 68 U.S. children: CDC. CNN. Retrieved at: http://www.cnn.com/2014/03/27/health/cdc-autism.

Farr, S. (November 10, 2009). Man fatally shoots autistic son, then himself. *Philadelphia Daily News,* p. 11.

Feinstein, A. (2010). *A history of autism: Conversations with the pioneers* (illustrated ed.). Malden, MA: John Wiley and Sons.

Fernand, D. (May 21, 2006). A mother's leap of love. *Sunday Times,* p. 3.

Ferrell, A. (June 7, 2004). Charge dropped against Renee Britt. *The Post and Courier,* p. B1.

Finkelstein, V. (1998). Emancipating disability studies. In T. Shakespeare (ed.), *The disability reader: Social science perspectives* (pp. 28–49). London: Cassell.

First Signs Inc. (2010). First signs ASD video glossery [web page]. Merrimac, MA: First Signs Inc. Retrieved at: http://www.firstsigns.org.

Fitzpatrick, M. (2008). *Defeating autism: A damaging delusion.* New York: Taylor & Francis.

Foucault, M. (1970). *The order of things: An archaeology of the human sciences.* New York: Tavistock Publications Limited.

Foucault, M. (1972). *The archaeology of knowledge.* New York: Pantheon Books.

Foucault, M. (1975). *The birth of the clinic: An archaeology of medical perception.* New York: Vintage Books.

Foucault, M. (1979). *Discipline and punish: The birth of the prison.* New York: Vintage Books.

Foucault, M. (1980). *Power/knowledge: Selected interviews and other writings 1972–1977.* New York: Pantheon Books.

Foucault, M. (1983). On the genealogy of ethics: An overview of work in progress. In H. Dryfus and P. Rabinow (eds.), *Michel Foucault: Beyond structuralism and hermeneutics, 2nd ed.* (pp. 229–52). Chicago: University of Chicago Press.

Foucault, M. (1984). Nietzsche, Genealogy, History In P. Rabinow (ed.), The *Foucault Reader* (pp. 76–100). Toronto: Random House Canada.

Foucault, M (1988). Technologies of the self. In Ed. L. Martin, H. Gutman and P. H. Hutton *Technologies of the self: A seminar with Michel Foucault* (pp.16–49). MA: University of Massachusetts Press.

Foucault, M. (1990). *The history of sexuality, volume I: An introduction.* New York: Random House.

Foucault, M. (1995). *Discipline and punish: The birth of the prison* (2nd ed., reprint, illustrated ed.). New York: Random House of Canada.

Foucault, M. (1997). *Society must be defended: Lectures at the collège de france, 1975–76.* New York: Picador.

Foucault, M. (2001). *Madness and civilization: A history of insanity in the age of reason* (2nd ed.). New York: Routledge.

Foucault, M. (2003). *Abnormal: Lectures at the collège de france, 1974–1975.* London: Verso.

Foucault, M. (2006). *History of madness.* Oxon: Routledge.

Foucault, M. (2009). *Security, territory, population: Lectures at the collège de france.* New York: Palgrave Macmillan.

Fox, M. (December 18, 2009). With autism at 1 in 110 kids, treatment in demand. Reuters. Retrieved at: http://in.reuters.com/article/2009/12/18/us-autism-usa-snapanalysis-idINTRE5BH43720091218.

Freehling, A. (February 18, 2001). Living with autism: Disorder disconnects kids from world. *Daily Press.* Retrieved at: http://articles.dailypress.com/2001–02–18/news/0102150192_1_raleigh-s-mother-secretin-gel.

Friday, T. (June 16, 2010). Mother admits to drowning autistic child. *National Post,* p. A11.

Frith, C. D., and Frith, U. (1999). Interacting minds: A biological basis. *Science,* 286(5445), 1692–95.

Frith, U. (1990). *Autism: Explaining the enigma.* Hoboken, NJ: Wiley-Blackwell.

Frith, U., and Happé, F. (1999). Theory of mind and self-consciousness: What is it like to be autistic? *Mind & Language,* 14(1), 1–22.

Gallahue, P., and Messing, P. (December 6, 2003). Drowned by mom; Brooklyn artist kills daughter, 20, in tub: Cops. *New York Post,* p. 7.

Ganz, M. L. (2007). The lifetime distribution of the incremental societal costs of autism. *Archives of Pediatrics and Adolescent Medicine*, 161(4), 343.

Garland-Thomson, R. (1996). *Extraordinary bodies: Figuring physical disability in american culture and literature*. New York: Columbia University Press.

Garland-Thomson, R. (2011). Misfits: A feminist materialist disability concept. *Hypatia*, 26(3), 591–609.

Garris, M. (Director). (1994). *The stand* [TV mini series]. United States of America: ABC.

Geier, M. R., and Geier, D. A. (2003). Neurodevelopmental disorders after thimerosal-containing vaccines: A brief communication. *Experimental Biology and Medicine*, 228(6), 660.

Gernsbacher, M. A., Dawson, M., and Hill Goldsmith, H. (2005). Three reasons not to believe in an autism epidemic. *Current Directions in Psychological Science*, 14(2), 55–58.

Gesell, A. (1922). The village of a thousand souls. In M. Sanger (ed.), *The pivot of civilization in historical perspective: The birth control classic* (pp. 132–36). Seattle: Inkling Books (original work published 1913).

Gill, C. (November 16, 2010). Mother killed autistic son, 12 by making him drink bleach. *Daily Mail*, p. 30.

Gilman, S. L. (1985). *Difference and pathology: Stereotypes of sexuality, race, and madness*. Ithaca, NY: Cornell University Press.

Gilman, S. L. (1993). *Freud, race, and gender*. Princeton, NJ: Princeton University Press.

Gilroy, P. (2000). *Against race: Imagining political culture beyond the color line*. Cambridge, MA: Harvard University Press.

Gladwell, M. (2002). *The tipping point: How little things can make a big difference*. Boston: Back Bay Books.

Gleason, M. L. (1999). *Normalizing the ideal: Psychology, schooling, and the family in postwar Canada*. Toronto: University of Toronto Press.

Goffman, E. (1963). *Stigma: Notes on the management of spoiled identity*. New York: Prentice Hall.

Goldstein, S., and Eiserer, T. (July 23, 2010). Irving mother accused of killing children is on suicide watch. *Dallas Morning News*. Retrieved at: http://www.dallasnews.com/news/crime/headlines/20100723-irving-mother-accused-of-killing-children-is-on-suicide-watch-at-jail.ece.

Goodley, D. (2010). *Disability studies: An interdisciplinary introduction* (illustrated ed.). London: SAGE Publications.

Goodley, D., and Runswick-Cole, K. (2010). Emancipating play: Dis/abled children, development and deconstruction. *Disability & Society*, 25(4), 14.

Government of the United States of America. (2009a). President Obama announces recovery act funding for groundbreaking medical research [press release]. Retrieved at: http://www.whitehouse.gov/the_press_office/President-Obama-Announces-Recovery-Act-Funding-For-GroundingBreaking-Medical-Research.

Government of the United States of America. (2009b). Remarks by the president on the American recovery and reinvestment act [speech]. Retrieved at: http://www.whitehouse.gov/the_press_office/Remarks-by-the-President-on-the-American-Recovery-and-Reinvestment-Act-at-the-National-Institutes-of-Health.

Government of the United States of America. (2009c). Timeline/milestones. US Recovery and Reinvestment Act [web page]. Retrieved at: http://www.recovery.gov/About/Pages/timeline.aspx.

Graham, L., and Slee, R. (2008). Inclusion? In S. L. Gabel and S. Danforth (eds.), *Dis-*

ability & the politics of education: An international reader (illustrated ed.) (pp. 453–76). New York: Peter Lang.

Green, A. H. (1997). Perspectives on a puzzle piece. National Autistic Association. (Original work published 1987.) Retrieved at: http://www.nas.org.uk/nas/jsp/polopoly.jsp?a=2183&d=364.

Grinker, R. R. (2008). *Unstrange minds: Remapping the world of autism*. New York: Basic Books.

Gross, Z. (2012). Metaphor stole my autism: The social construction of autism as separable from personhood and its effect on policy, funding and perception. In Julia Bascom (ed.), *Loud hands: Autistic people speaking* (pp. 179–91). Washington, DC: Autistic Self Advocacy Network.

Guerry, Y. (April 2, 2008). Living with autism in the UK. BBC. Retrieved at: http://news.bbc.co.uk/2/hi/uk_news/7326323.stm.

Gupta, S. (2007). Behind the veil of autism. *Paging Dr. Gupta*. CNN. Retrieved at: http://www.cnn.com/HEALTH/blogs/paging.dr.gupta/2007/02/behind-veil-of-autism.html.

Hacker, F. J. (1978). *Crusaders, criminals, crazies: Terror and terrorism in our time*. New York: Bantam Books.

Hacking, I. (2009a). How we have been learning to talk about autism: A role for stories. *Metaphilosophy*, 40(3–4), 499–516.

Hacking, I. (2009b). Autistic autobiography. *Philosophical Transactions of the Royal Society B: Biological Sciences*, 364(1522), 1467–73.

Hall, S. (2007). The spectacle of the other. In S. Hall (ed.), *Representation: Cultural representations and signifying practices* (pp. 223–90). Thousand Oaks, CA: Sage Press.

Haraway, D. J. (1991). *Simians, cyborgs, and women: The reinvention of nature, part 7* (2nd ed., reprint, illustrated ed.). London: Free Association Books.

Hardt, M., and Negri, A. (2001). *Empire*. Cambridge, MA: Harvard University Press.

Harp, B (2007). One more for NYU child study center. Square 8: Squawk About Disability and Society [webpage]. Retrieved at: http://aspergersquare8.blogspot.ca/2007/12/one-more-for-nyu.html#links

Harp, B. (2012). *Unpuzzled* [blog]. Retrieved at: http://unpuzzled.net.

Harvey, D. (2007). *The limits to capital*. New York: Verso.

Hassan, R. (2009). *Empires of speed: Time and the acceleration of politics and society*. Boston: Brill Academic Publishers.

Hassert, D., and White, R. (February 24, 2007). Short trial; swift, long sentence. *Cincinnati Post*, p. A13.

Heilker, P., and Yergeau, M. (2011). Autism and rhetoric. *College English*, 73(5), 485–97.

Helliwell, C., and Hindess, B. (2005). The temporalizing of difference. *Ethnicities*, 5(3), 414–18.

Hench, D. (April 29, 2010). Autistic man's dad decided to end it all; police say Daniel McLatchie left a note expressing fear about his son's future care before the murder-suicide. *Portland Press Herald*, p. B1.

Henriques, J., et al. (eds). (1998). *Changing the subject: Psychology, social regulation, and subjectivity*. New York: Routledge.

Higgins, M. (November 19, 2006). Family sues city, home in death of autistic man. *Chicago Tribune*, p. 2.

Hill, A., Ross, B., and Mosk, M. (November 30, 2012). Death at school: Parents fight back against deadly discipline. *ABC News*. Retrieved at: http://abcnews.go.com/Blotter/death-school-autism-parents-fight-back-deadly-discipline/storynew?id=17841322#.UeVtkj7wJgI.

Horgan, J. (2005). *The psychology of terrorism*. New York: Routledge.

Housemarque. (Developer). (2010). *Dead nation* [video game]. United States of America: Sony Computer Entertainment.

Houston Chronicle. (March 9, 2000). Child Restrained, Dies. Retrieved from ProQuest Newsstand. (Document ID: 50895677).

Houston, R. A., and Frith, U. (2000). *Autism in history: The case of Hugh Blair of Borgue* (illustrated ed.). Malden, MA: Wiley-Blackwell.

Hudson, R. A. (1999). *The sociology and psychology of terrorism: Who becomes a terrorist and why.* Washington, DC: Library of Congress. Retrieved at: http://www.loc.gov/rr/frd/pdf-files/Soc_Psych_of_Terrorism.pdf.

Huffman, T., and Keung, N. (March 2, 2005). Mom charged with murder; daughter, 4, drowned in tub last year; arrest 'so unexpected' husband says. *Toronto Star*, p. B01.

Hughes, B., and Paterson, K. (1997). The social model of disability and the disappearing body: Towards a sociology of impairment. *Disability & Society*, 12(3), 325–40.

Hyman, R. (2004). Medea of suburbia: Andrea Yates, maternal infanticide, and the insanity defense. *Women's Studies Quarterly*, 32(3/4), 192–210.

Hyvonen, S. L. (2004). *Evolution of a parent revolution: Exploring parent memoirs of children with autism spectrum disorders* [PhD dissertation]. Berkeley, CA: Wright Institute Graduate School of Psychology.

I Am Autism Speaks. (2009). I am autism speaks [video file]. Retrieved at: http://www.youtube.com/watch?v=yU2paLv1MGE&feature=player_embedded.

Ice-Pick Lodge. (Developer). (2006). *Pathologic* [video game]. Russia: Gamersgate.

Jackman, T., and McCrummen, S. (July 15, 2006). Ex-Bush aide fatally shoots son, himself. *The Washington Post*, p. B1.

James, P. D. (2006). *The children of men*. New York: Vintage Books.

Järbrink, K., Fombonne, E., and Knapp, M. (2003). Measuring the parental, service and cost impacts of children with autistic spectrum disorder: A pilot study. *Journal of Autism and Developmental Disorders*, 33(4), 395–402.

Jarsma, P., and Welin, S. (2012). Autism as a natural human variation: Reflections on the claims of the neurodiversity movement. *Health Care Analysis*, 20(1), 20–30.

Jaslo, R. (March 19, 2012). Mothers of autistic children earn 56% less income, study says. CBSNews. Retrieved at: http://www.cbsnews.com/news/mothers-of-autistic-children-earn-56-less-income-study-says

Johnston, J. (November 5, 2005). The mother who loved her son to death. *Daily Mail*, p. 38.

Juicy Juice. (2009). [web page]. Retrieved at: http://www.juicyjuice.com.

Kafer, A. (2013). Feminist, queer, crip. Bloomington: Indianna University Press.

Kalla, D. (2005). *Pandemic.* New York: Tom Doherty Associates.

Kane, W., and Bulwa, D. (March 8, 2012). Sunnyvale mom kills autistic son, self, police say. *San Francisco Chronicle*. Retrieved at: http://www.sfgate.com/crime/article/Sunnyvale-mom-kills-autistic-son-self-police-say-3388400.php.

Kanner, L. (1935). *Child psychiatry.* Springfield, IL: CC Thomas.

Kanner, L. (1943). Autistic disturbances of affective contact. *Nervous Child*, 2(2), 217–30.

Kanner, L. (1949). Problems of nosology and psychodynamics in early childhood autism. *American Journal of Orthopsychiatry*, 19(3), 416–26.

Karoliszyn, H., Parascandola, R., and Paddock, B. (December 7, 2010). Strangling at S.I. psych center probed. *New York Daily News*, p. 24.

Kegley, J. (April 20, 2010). Mother wants answers in autistic son's death while in police custody. *Lexington-Herald*. Retrieved at: http://www.kentucky. com/2010/04/20/1230733/mother-wants-answers-in-sons-death.html.

Kennedy, B. (June 15, 2010). Mother 'snapped' and drowned autistic daughter. *Toronto Star*, p. GT7.

Kennedy, B. (June 16, 2010). 'I won't kill another baby, I won't,' woman promises before release. *Toronto Star*, p. GT7.

Kennedy, J. F. K. (1963). UNICEF appeal. John F. Kennedy presidential library and museum [speech]. Retrieved at: http://www.jfklibrary.org/Research/Ready-Reference/JFK-Miscellaneous-Information/Appeal-UNICEF.aspx.

Kirby, D. (December 4, 2008). The pentagon: A voice of reason on vaccines and autism? *Huffington Post*. Retrieved at: http://www.huffingtonpost.com/david-kirby/the-pentagon—a-voice-of_b_148490.html.

Klar-Wolfund, E. (2008). The mismeasure of autism: The basis for current autism advocacy. In W. Lawson (ed.), *Concepts of normality: The autistic and typical spectrum* (illustrated ed.) (pp. 104–29). Philadelphia: Jessica Kingsley Publishers.

Knapp, M., Romeo, R., and Beecham, J. (2009). Economic cost of autism in the UK. *Autism*, 13(3), 317.

Kogan, M. D., et al. (2009). Prevalence of parent-reported diagnosis of autism spectrum disorder among children in the US, 2007. *Pediatrics*, 124(5), 1395–1403.

KRCR News Channel 7. (August 3, 2010). Man arrested in death of brother. Retrieved at: http://www.krcrtv.com/news/24497879/detail.html.

Kuhn, R. (2004). Eugen Bleuler's concepts of psychopathology. *History of Psychiatry*, 15(3), 361–66.

Kuhn, T. S. (1962). *The structure of scientific revolutions*. Chicago: University of Chicago Press.

Kumari Campbell, F. (2005). Legislating disability: Negative ontologies and the government of legal identities. In S. Tremain (ed.), *Foucault and the government of disability* (pp. 108–32). Ann Arbor: University of Michigan Press.

Kumari Campbell, F. (2009). *Contours of ableism: The production of disability and abledness* (illustrated ed.). New York: Palgrave Macmillan.

Lamont, L. (June 1, 2004). When love is not enough. *Sydney Morning Herald*. Retrieved at: http://www.smh.com.au/articles/2004/05/31/1085855494917.html.

Lamont, L. (June 3, 2004). Dawes 'has suffered too much.' *Sydney Morning Herald*. Retrieved at: http://www.smh.com.au/articles/2004/06/02/1086058923624. html.

The Lancet. (2010). Retraction—ileal-lymphoid-nodular hyperplasia, non-specific colitis, and pervasive developmental disorder. Retrieved at: http://press.thelancet. com/wakefieldretraction.pdf.

Lane, H. (2006). Constructions of deafness. In L. Davis (ed.), *The disability studies reader* (2nd ed.) (pp. 153–71). New York: Routledge.

Latour, B. (1993). *We have never been modern*. Cambridge, MA: Harvard University Press.

Lavin, C., and Russill, C. (2010). The ideology of the epidemic. *New Political Science*, 32(1), 65–82.

Lebensztejn, J. C. (1988). Framing classical space. *Art Journal*, 47(1), 37–41.

Lewallen, E. (2008). A history of a stick figure. *Words are pictures too [blog]*. Retrieved at: http://wordsarepicturestoo.wordpress.com/2008/01/22/see-you-at-ignite-2.

Linton, S. (1998). *Claiming disability: Knowledge and identity*. New York: New York University Press.

Lister, R. (2003). Investing in the citizen-workers of the future: Transformations in citizenship and the state under new labour. *Social Policy and Administration*, 35(5), 427–43.

London School of Economics and Political Science. (June 10, 2014). Autism is the most costly medical condition in the UK. Retrieved at: http://www.lse.ac.uk/newsAndMedia/news/archives/2014/06/Autism.aspx.

Long, G. (June 19, 2007). Woman enters plea in toddler's murder. *WOWK News*. Retrieved at: http://wowktv.com/story.cfm?func=viewstory&storyid=25336.

Longmore, P. (2013). Heaven's special child: The making of poster children. In L. Davis (ed.), *Disability Studies Reader* (4th ed.) (pp. 34–41). New York: Routledge.

Lovaas, O. I. (1987). Behavioral treatment and normal educational and intellectual functioning in autistic children. *Journal of Consulting and Clinical Psychology*, 55(1), 3–9.

Lowery, D. (July 5, 2002). Mother convicted in murder of autistic child. *Savannah Morning News*, p. 14A.

Makin, K. (June 10, 2004). Fighting autism too costly, top court told court told. *Globe and Mail*, p. A10.

Mallett, R., and Runswick-Cole, K. (2012). Commodifying autism: The cultural contexts of 'disability' in the academy. In D. Goodley, B. Hughes, and L. Davis (eds.), *Disability and social theory: New developments and directions* (pp. 33–51). Basingstoke, UK: Palgrave Macmillan.

Martinez, E. (August 7, 2009). Mom starved disabled daughter to death, say cops. *CBS News*. Retrieved at: http://www.cbsnews.com/8301–504083_162–5197894–504083.html.

Marx, K. (1933). *The civil war in France*. New York: International Publishers.

Masser, M., and Creed, L. (1984). Greatest love of all [recorded by Whitney Houston]. On *Whitney Houston* [CD]. USA: Arista Records. (Original work published 1977.)

Mbembe, A. (2003). Necropolitics. *Public Culture*, 15(1), 11–40.

McCarthy, J. (2007). *Louder than words: A mother's journey in healing autism*. New York: Penguin.

McCarthy, J. (2009). *Mother warriors: A nation of parents healing autism against all odds*. New York: Penguin Group USA.

McCarthy, J., and Kartzinel, J. (2010). *Healing and preventing autism: A complete guide* (reprinted). New York: Penguin Group USA.

McGee, M. (2012). Neurodiversity. *Contexts*, 11(3), 12–13.

McGhee, T. (June 8, 2010). Murder charge for mom of infant; the counselor told police she tried three times to smother her son because she feared he was autistic, an affidavit says. *Denver Post*, p. A1.

McGuire, A. (2012). Representing autism: A sociological examination of autism advocacy. Atlantis: Critical Studies in Gender, Culture and Social Justice. 35.2: 62–71.

McGuire, A. (2010). Disability, non-disability and the politics of mourning: Reconceiving the 'we.' *Disability Studies Quarterly*, 30(3/4): np.

McGuire, A. E., and Michalko, R. (2011). Minds between us: Autism, mindblindness and the uncertainty of communication. *Educational Philosophy and Theory*, 43(2), 162–77.

McHenry v. PacificSource Health Plans, 643 F. Supp. 2d 1236. (Dist. Court, D. Oregon 2009).

McLuhan, M. (2001). *Understanding media: The extensions of man* (critical ed.). Corte Madera, CA: Ginko Press.

McMartin, P. (April 23, 2007). Living with autism. *Vancouver Sun*. Retrieved at: http://www2.canada.com/vancouversun/features/autism/index.html.

McRuer, R. (2006). *Crip theory: Cultural signs of queerness and disability* (illustrated ed.). New York: NYU Press.

McRuer, R. (2012). Cripping queer politics, or the dangers of neoliberalism. *S & F Online*, 10(1/2). Retrieved at: http://sfonline.barnard.edu/a-new-queer-agenda/cripping-queer-politics-or-the-dangers-of-neoliberalism.

Meekosha, H. (2011). Decolonizing disability: Thinking and acting globally. *Disability and Society*, 26(6), 667–82.

Mercer, D. (January 5, 2008). Mom charged in autistic girl's death headed to trial. *Sauk Valley Media*. Retrieved at: http://www.saukvalley.com/articles/2008/01/05/news/state/84958348793076.txt?__xsl=/print.xsl.

Meyer, N. (June 11, 2014). MIT researcher's new warning: At today's rate, half of all U.S. children will be autistic (by 2025). AltHealth Works [website]. Retrieved at: http://althealthworks.com/2494/mit-researchers-new-warning-at-todays-rate-1-in-2-children-will-be-autistic-by-2025/#sthash.SeqMNtNV.dpuf.

Michalko, R. (1998). *The mystery of the eye and the shadow of blindness*. Toronto: University of Toronto Press.

Michalko, R. (1999). *The two-in-one: Walking with Smokie, walking with blindness*. Philadelphia: Temple University Press.

Michalko, R. (2002). *The difference that disability makes*. Philadelphia: Temple University Press.

Mikami, S. (Creator). (1997). *Resident evil* [video game]. Japan: Capcom.

Mills, S. (2003). *Michel Foucault*. New York: Routledge.

Minh-ha, T. T. (1992). *Framer framed* (illustrated ed.). New York: Routledge.

Mitchell, B. (May 21, 2008). 10-Year term sought in starvation of sister, 23; autistic woman resembled a skeleton. *The Toronto Star*, p. A4.

Mitchell, B., and Wilkes, J. (October 27, 2009). Accused mother 'loved son so much.' *The Toronto Star*. Retrieved at: http://www.thestar.com/news/crime/article/716555—accused-mother-loved-son-so-much.

Mitchell, D. T. (2002). Narrative prosthesis and the materiality of metaphor. In S. L. Snyder, B. J. Brueggeman, and R. Garland Thomson (eds.), *Disability studies: Enabling the humanities* (pp. 15–30). New York: Modern Language Association of America.

Morss, J. R. (1990). *The biologising of childhood: Developmental psychology and the darwinian myth*. Hove, UK: Lawrence Erlbaum Associates.

Murkoff, H. E., Eisenberg, A., and Hathaway, S. E. (1981). *What to expect when you're expecting*. New York: Workman Publishing.

Murray, S. (2008). *Representing autism: Culture, narrative, fascination*. Liverpool, UK: Liverpool University Press.

Murray, S. (2011). *Autism*. London: Routledge.

Nadesan, M. H. (2002). Engineering the entrepreneurial infant: Brain science, infant development toys, and governmentality. *Cultural Studies*, 16(3), 401–32.

Nadesan, M. H. (2005). *Constructing autism: Unravelling the 'truth' and understanding the social*. New York: Routledge.

National Autism Association. (2009). New government report shows autism now affects one in 91 [press release]. Retrieved at: http://www.nationalautismassociation.org/press100609.php.

National Autism Association. (2010). Never give up [public service announcement]. Retrieved at: http://www.nationalautismassociation.org.

National Autistic Society. (2008). Autism is [poster].

National Post. (July 29, 2003). Autistic student killed in three-hour gang attack. p. A14.

Ne'eman, A. (2010). The future (and the past) of autism advocacy, or why the ASA's magazine, the advocate, wouldn't publish this piece. *Disability Studies Quarterly*, 30(1): np.

Neisser, U. (1976). *Cognition and reality: Principles and implications of cognitive psychology.* San Francisco: W. H. Freeman.

Nelson, J. (October 15, 2004). Rialto woman sentenced for her brother's death. *Inland Valley Daily Bulletin.* Retrieved from ProQuest Newsstand. (Document ID: 986493211).

Newcastle Herald. (May 26, 2009). Starvation murder trial: Girl was autistic. Retrieved at: http://www.theherald.com.au/news/local/news/general/starvation-murder-trial-girl-was-autistic/1522550.aspx#.

New York Stock Exchange. (2010). NYSE Euronext celebrates third annual world autism awareness day and autism awareness with first-ever global bell ringing [press release]. Retrieved at: http://www.euronext.com/fic 000/056/271/562715.pdf.

New York University Child Study Center. (2007a). Ransom notes campaign [web page]. Retrieved at: www.aboutourkids.org/about_us/public_awareness.

New York University Child Study Center. (2007b). Millions of children held hostage by psychiatric disorders [press release]. Retrieved at: http://www.aboutourkids.org/files/news/press_room/assets/ransom_notes_release.pdf.

New York University Child Study Center. (2008). A message regarding the 'ransom notes' public awareness campaign [media release]. Retrieved at: http://www.miwatch.org/documents/Ransomnotescampaignwithdrawn.pdf.

O'Keefe, E. (December 6, 2006). Congress declares war on autism. ABC News. Retrieved at: http://abcnews.go.com/Health/story?id=2708925&page=1.

Oliver, M. (July 23, 1990). The individual and social models of disability [paper presented at Joint Workshop of the Living Options Group and the Research Unit of the Royal College of Physicians]. Retrieved at: http://disability-studies.leeds.ac.uk/files/library/Oliver-in-soc-dis.pdf.

Oliver, M. (1996). *Understanding disability: From theory to practice.* New York: Palgrave Macmillan.

Oller, J. W., and Oller, S. D. (2009). *Autism: The diagnosis, treatment, & etiology of the undeniable epidemic.* Sudbury, MA: Jones & Bartlett Learning.

Overboe, J. (1999). Difference in itself: Validating disabled people's lived experience. *Body and Society,* 5(4), 17–30.

Park, A. (June 9, 2014). The lifetime cost of autism tops $2 million per person. *Time.* Retrieved at: http://time.com/2849264/the-lifetime-cost-of-autism-tops-2-million-per-person.

Pastor, A., and Pastor, D. (Director). (2009). *Carriers* [motion Picture]. United States of America: Paramount Vantage.

Payne, S. G. (1995). *A history of fascism, 1914–1945.* Madison: University of Wisconsin Press.

Petersen, W. (Director). (1995). *Outbreak* [motion picture]. United States of America: Warner Bros.

Peterson, I. (July 11, 2002). New Jersey reviews and fines long-term care center after an autistic boy, 14, dies. *New York Times.* Retrieved at: http://select.nytimes.com/gst/abstract.html?res=F50B14FA39540C728DDDAE0894DA404482.

Peterson, N. (2008). Autism speaks [photograph] Retrieved at: http://www.flickr.com/photos/mrn8/2212219989.

Picard, A. (April 3, 2007). Autism a lifelong burden, study shows: Because few adults with the disorder can work, the economic costs continue. *Globe and Mail,* p. A13.

Pinion-Whitt, M. (October 19, 2010). Crestline deaths result of murder-suicide. *The Sun.* Retrieved at: http://proquest.umi.com/pqdweb?did=2167034581&sid=16&Fmt=3&clientId=12520&RQT=309&VName=PQD.

Piven, J., et al. (1991). Psychiatric disorders in the parents of autistic individuals. *Journal of the American Academy of Child & Adolescent Psychiatry,* 30(3), 471–78.

Porter, J. I. (1997). Foreword. In D. T. Mitchell and S. L. Snyder (eds.), *The body and physical difference: Discourses of disability (pp. xiii–xiv).* Ann Arbor: University of Michigan Press.

Post, J. M. (2008). *The mind of the terrorist: The psychology of terrorism from the IRA to al-Qaeda* (illustrated, reprint ed.). New York: Palgrave Macmillan.

Powell, B. (March 15, 2008). Mom jailed for killing child; husband and mother of mentally unstable woman claim she's innocent of drowning autistic girl. *Toronto Star,* p. A12.

Puar, J. K. (2007). *Terrorist assemblages: Homonationalism in queer times.* Durham, NC: Duke University Press.

Razack, S. (1998). *Looking white people in the eye: Gender, race, and culture in courtrooms and classrooms.* Toronto: University of Toronto Press.

Razack, S. (2008). *Casting out: The eviction of Muslims from western law and politics.* Toronto: University of Toronto Press.

Refrigerator Mothers. (2003). [Motion Picture]. Chicago: Kartemquin Films.

Reich, W. (1998). *Origins of terrorism: Psychologies, ideologies, theologies, states of mind* (illustrated, reprint ed.). Washington, DC: Woodrow Wilson Center Press.

Ritter, J. (May 23, 2005). Families confront stiff cost of autism. *Chicago Sun-Times,* p. 26.

Robertson, S., and Ne'eman, A. Autistic acceptance, the college campus, and technology: Growth of neurodiversity in society and academia. *Disability Studies Quarterly,* 28(4), n.p.

Rones, N. (July 19, 2009). Living with autism: "Losing my little boy." *Redbook Magazine.* Retrieved at: http://www.redbookmag.com/kids-family/advice/living-with-autism-0208.

Rose, N. (1989). *Governing the soul: The shaping of the private self* (2nd ed., revised, illustrated ed.). New York: Free Association Books. (Original work published 1989.)

Rose, N. (1999). *Powers of freedom: Reframing political thought.* Cambridge, MA: Cambridge University Press.

Rose, N. (2007). *The politics of life itself: Biomedicine, power, and subjectivity in the twenty-first century.* Princeton, NJ: Princeton University Press.

Rosenwasser, B., and Axelrod, S. (2002). More contributions of applied behavior analysis to the education of people with autism. *Behavior Modification,* 26(1), 3–8.

Ross, D. S., and Jolly, K. A. (2006). *That's life with autism: Tales and tips for families with autism.* Philadelphia: Jessica Kingsley Publishers.

Rubin, J. (January 27, 2011). Jury awards family $1.7 million; fired LAPD officer is found to have been reckless in killing man. *Los Angeles Times,* p. AA7.

Rubin, J. (March 5, 2011). Police commission overrules chief, says LAPD shooting was wrong. *Los Angeles Times.* Retrieved at: http://articles.latimes.com/2011/mar/05/local/la-me-shooting-20110305.

Rutgers University. (2008). Rutgers psychology researcher examines connections between vision and movement as they relate to perceived threats and to autism [press release]. Retrieved at: http://news.rutgers.edu/medrel/news-releases/2008/10/rutgers-psychology-r-20081008.

Rutter, M. (2000). Genetic studies of autism: From the 1970s into the millennium. *Journal of Abnormal Child Psychology,* 28(1), 3–14.

Salomon, M. (Director). (2008). *The andromeda strain* [TV mini series]. United States of America: A&E Network.

Sampier, K. (January 8, 2008). 'She wanted the autism gone': Prosecution lays out case in McCarron trial; girl's father says condition wasn't severe. *Peoria Journal Star*, p. A1.

Sampier, K. (January 10, 2008). 'Wish Katie were dead': Mother-In-Law testifies McCarron claimed she would prefer daughter to have cancer over autism. *Peoria Journal Star*, p. B1.

Sampier, K. (January 11, 2008). 'I hated the autism so, so much': Jury in McCarron trial hears confession tape; defense begins presenting its case. *Peoria Journal Star*, p. A1.

Saramago, J. (1999). *Blindness* (reprint ed.). San Diego, CA: Houghton Mifflin Harcourt.

Savarese, D. J. (2010). Communicate with me. *Disability Studies Quarterly*, 30(1), n.p.

Scelfo, J., and Kantrowitz, B. (December 7, 2006). Families cheer as autism bill passes. *Newsweek*. Retrieved at: http://www.asasb.org/AutismBill.cfm.

Schram, J., and Bain, J. (July 30, 2010). Pressure got to suicide-slay ma. *New York Post*, p. 17.

Science Daily. (April 3, 2007). Autism costs society an estimated $3 million per patient, according to report. Retrieved at: http://www.sciencedaily.com/releases/2007/04/070403112757.htm.

Seidel, K. (2005a). *Neurodiversity: A weblog* [blog]. Retrieved at: http://neurodiversity.com/weblog.

Seidel, K. (2005b). Getting the truth out about autism. *Neurodiversity: A weblog* [blog]. Retrieved at: http://neurodiversity.com/weblog/article/51/

Sequenzia, A. (2012a). Non speaking, low functioning. In Julia Bascom (ed.), *Loud hands: Autistic people speaking* (pp. 107-108). Washington, DC: Autistic Self Advocacy Network.

Sequenzia, A. (2012b). Non speaking autistic speaking [blog]. Retrieved at: http://nonspeakingautisticspeaking.blogspot.ca.

Sequenzia, A. (2012c). Why autism speaks hurts us. In Julia Bascom (ed.), *Loud hands: Autistic people speaking* (pp. 192-193). Washington, DC: Autistic Self Advocacy Network.

Shapiro, J. (1994). *No pity: People with disabilities forging a new civil rights movement.* New York: Broadway Books.

Shildrick, Margrit, and Price, Janet. (1998). Uncertain thoughts on the dis/abled body. In M. Shildrick and J. Price (eds.), *Vital signs: Feminist reconfigurations of the bio/logical body (pp. 224–49).* Edinburgh: Edinburgh University Press.

Shockley, P. (January 4, 2010). DA: Father pondered killing son weeks before the slaying. *Daily Sentinel.* Retrieved at: http://proquest.umi.com/pqdwebdid=1931926511&sid=20&Fmt=3&clientId=12520&RQT=309&VName=PQD.

Shorter, E. (2005). *A historical dictionary of psychiatry.* New York: Oxford University Press.

Sibley, K. (2015). Radical Neurodivergence Speaking [blog]. Retrieved at: http://timetolisten.blogspot.ca/.

Siddique, H. (2014). Study says cost of autism more than cancer, strokes and heart disease. *The Guardian.* Retrieved at: http://www.theguardian.com/society/2014/jun/09/autism-costs-more-cancer-strokes-heart-disease.

Simons, A. (July 10, 2009). Charges expected in boy's killing. *Star Tribune*, p. A1.

Simons, M. (2006). Learning as investment: Notes on governmentality and biopolitics. *Educational Philosophy and Theory*, 38(4), 523–40.

Sinclair, J. (1993). Don't mourn for us. *Our Voice: The Newsletter of Autism*, 1(3). Retrieved at: http://www.grasp.org/media/mourn.pdf.

Sinclair, J. (1999). Why I dislike 'person first' language. Jim Sinclair [web page]. Retrieved at: http://www/jimsinclair.org/person_first.htm.

Sinclair, J. (2012). Autism Network International: The development of a community and its culture. In Julia Bascom (ed.), *Loud hands: Autistic people, speaking*. Washington, DC: ASAN.

Small, P. (November 21, 2007). Mom killed autistic girl: Crown. *Toronto Star*, p. A8.

Small, P. (February 7, 2008). 'Quick fix' wanted for girl: MD says. *Toronto Star*, p. A16.

Small, P. (February 28, 2008). Mother drowned autistic girl, court told. *Toronto Star*. Retrieved at: http://www.thestar.com/article/307710.

Smith, J. (2006). Murder of autistics. This way of life [web page]. Retrieved at: http://www.geocities.ws/growingjoel/murder.html.

Smith, K. (September 19, 2008). Woman gets 10 years in death of autistic boy, 5. *Arizona Daily Star*. Retrieved at: http://www.accessmylibrary.com/coms2/summary_0286-35212975_ITM.

Smith, L. (August 26, 2005). Autistic boy, 5, dies after US therapy. *The Times*, p. 21.

Snyder, S. L., and Mitchell, D. T. (2006). *Cultural locations of disability*. Chicago: University of Chicago Press.

Solomon, A. (2008). The autism rights movement. *New York Magazine*. Retrieved at: http://nymag.com/news/features/47225.

Soteropoulos, J. (December 18, 2002). Stepmother to stand trial in man's death; Audrey McDaniels withheld food from Brahim Dukes, 18, who was autistic, prosecutors said. *Philadelphia Inquirer*, p. B5.

Spackman, B. (1996). *Fascist virilities: Rhetoric, ideology, and social fantasy in Italy*. Minneapolis: University of Minnesota Press.

Stahl, R. (2008). A clockwork war: Rhetorics of time in a time of terror. *Quarterly Journal of Speech*, 94(1), 27.

Stephens, S. (1995). Children and the politics of culture in late capitalism. In *Children and the politics of culture* (pp. 3–50). Princeton, NJ: Princeton University Press.

Stephenson, J., Harp, B., and Gernsbacher, M. A. (2011). Infantilizing autism. *Disability Studies Quarterly*, 31(3), n.p.

Stockton, K. B. (2009). *The queer child, or growing sideways in the twentieth century* (illustrated ed.). London: Duke University Press.

Szasz, T. (1995). Idleness and lawlessness in the therapeutic state. *Society*, 32(4), 30–35.

Szasz, T. S. (2010). *The myth of mental illness: Foundations of a theory of personal conduct* (revised, annotated ed.). Toronto: Harper Collins. (originally published, 1974)

Tager-Flusberg, S., Baron-Cohen, S., and Cohen, D. J. (1993). An introduction to the debate. In S. Tager-Flusberg, S. Baron-Cohen, and D. J. Cohen (eds.), *Understanding other minds: Perspectives from developmental cognitive neuroscience* (pp. 3–9). Oxford: Oxford University Press.

Tambar, J. (October 25, 2009). Mississauga mother charged in autistic son's murder. *The Toronto Star*. Retrieved at: http://www.thestar.com/news/gta/crime/article/716070—mississauga-mother-charged-in-autistic-son-s-murder.

Taylor, A. (June 4, 2009). Disabled lad killed in attack. *The Sun*, p. 6.

Telegraph-Herald. (August 16, 2006). Conviction upheld for man who killed boy at church; self-described minister suffocated the autistic boy during what prosecutors called an exorcism. P. D6.

Timimi, S., Gardner, N., and McCabe, B. (2010). *The myth of autism: Medicalising men's and boys' social and emotional competence* (illustrated ed.). Basingstoke, UK: Palgrave Macmillan.

Titchkosky, T. (2001). Disability: A rose by any other name? People-first language in Canadian society. *Canadian Review of Sociology/Revue Canadienne de Sociologie*, 38(2), 125–40.

Titchkosky, T. (2007). *Reading and writing disability differently: The textured life of embodiment*. Toronto: University of Toronto Press.

Titchkosky, T. (2011). *The question of access: Disability, space, meaning*. Toronto: University of Toronto Press.

Titchkosky, T., and Aubrecht, K. (2009). The anguish of power: Remapping mental diversity with an anticolonial compass. In S. R. Steinberg, K. Tobin, and A. Kempf (eds.), *Explorations of educational purpose, Vol. 8: Breaching the colonial contract* (pp. 179–99). New York: Springer.

Titchkosky, T., and Michalko, R. (2009). *Rethinking normalcy: A disability studies reader.* Toronto: Canadian Scholars Press.

Toronto Star. (April 15, 2011). Mom sentenced 8–10 years for withholding son's cancer drugs. Retrieved at: http://www.thestar.com/news/world/article/975288—mom-sentenced-8–10-years-after-withholding-son-s-cancer-drugs?bn=1.

Tran, M., and Anton, M. (July 31, 2002). Stress pushed man to kill autistic son, self, says family. *Los Angeles Times*, p. B6.

Tremain, S. (2001). On the government of disability. *Social Theory and Practice*, 27(4), 617–36.

Tremain, S. (2008). The biopolitics of bioethics and disability. *Journal of Bioethical Inquiry*, 5(2/3), 101–106.

Tremain, S. (2010). Biopower, styles of reasoning, and what's still missing from the stem cell debates. *Hypatia: A Journal of Feminist Philosophy*, 25(3), 577–609.

Tremain, S. (2012). Review essay of *Racism and Sexual Oppression in Anglo-America: A Genealogy* by Ladelle McWhorter and *The Faces of Intellectual Disability: Philosophical Reflections* by Licia Carlson. *Hypatia: A Journal of Feminist Philosophy*, 27(2), 440–45.

Turtle Rock Studios. (Developer). (2008). *Left 4 dead* [video game]. United States of America: Valve Corporation.

US Department of Health and Human Services. (1999). *Mental health: A report of the surgeon general.* Retrieved at: http://www.surgeongeneral.gov/library/mental-health/home.html.

Venables, S. (November 26, 2006). Psychologist researcher into autism who overturned the theory that it was a reaction to bad parenting. *The Independent*. Retrieved at: http://www.autism.com/all_rimland_london.asp.

Vincent, D. (December 30, 2009). New trial for dead girl's mom. *Toronto Star*, p. GT4.

Virilio, P. (1986). *Speed and politics*. Los Angeles: Semiotext(e).

Wald, P. (2008). *Contagious: Cultures, carriers, and the outbreak narrative*. Durham, NC: Duke University Press.

Walkerdine, V. (1998). Developmental psychology and the child-centered pedagogy: The insertion of piaget into early education. In J. Henriques, W. Hollway, C. Urwin, C. Venn, and V. Walkerdine (eds.), *Changing the subject: Psychology, social regulation, and subjectivity* (pp. 153–202). New York: Routledge.

Wallis, C. (November 6, 2009). 'I am autism': An advocacy video sparks protest. *Time Magazine*. Retrieved at: http://www.time.com/time/health/article/0,8599,1935959,00.html.

Walsh, P. (January 11, 2010). Disabled man dies of injuries after being restrained at work. *Star Tribune*. Retrieved at: http://www.startribune.com/local/west/81135252.html?source=error.

Watts, I. E., and Erevelles, N. (2004). These deadly times: Reconceptualizing school violence by using critical race theory and disability studies. *American Educational Research Journal*, 41(2), 271.

Weiss, R. (February 8, 2007). 1 in 150 children in US have autism, new survey finds. *Washington Post*. Retrieved at: http://www.washingtonpost.com/ac2/wp-dyn/comments/display?contentID=AR2007020801883.

Wendell, S. (2006). Toward a feminist theory of disability. In L. Davis (ed.), *The disability studies reader* (2nd ed.) (pp. 153–71). New York: Routledge.

Wilkinson, M. (April 19, 2007). Three found guilty of murder. *Oxford Mail*. Retrieved at: http://www.oxfordmail.co.uk/news/1338831.print.

Williams, D. (1995). *Somebody, somewhere: Breaking free from the world of autism*. New York: Three Rivers Press.

Winfrey, O. (2007). Living with autism. *Oprah Winfrey Show* [TV episode]. Retrieved at: http://www.oprah.com/world/Living-with-Autism

WoodTV (ABC News). (July 6, 2012). Mom charged in death of son with autism. Retrieved at: http://www.woodtv.com/dpp/news/local/sw_mich/mom-held-in-death-of-adult-autistic-son#.T_fjVrrE-Cc.twitter.

Wright, S. (2013). Autism Speaks to Washington: A call to action. *Autism Speaks* [blog]. Retrieved at: http://www.autismspeaks.org/news/news-item/autism-speaks-washington-call-action.

Wynberg et al. v. Ontario. (2006). Ontario Supreme Court of Justice. C4342.

Yergeau, M. (2010). Circle wars: Reshaping the typical autism essay. *Disability Studies Quarterly*, 30(1), n.p.

Yergeau, M. (2013). Clinically significant disturbance: On theorists who theorize theory of mind. *Disability Studies Quarterly*, 33(4), n.p.

York University. (2010). Taking aim at autism from many angles [press release]. Retrieved at: http://www.yorku.ca/yfile/archive/index.asp?Article=15613.

Younge, M. (2001). Foreword. In M. Corker and T. Shakespeare (eds.), *Disability/postmodernity: Embodying disability theory (pp. xii–xiv)*. London: Continuum.

Zennie, M. (June 13, 2013). Desperate mother and godmother 'killed severely autistic boy, 14, by stabbing him multiple times in the chest.' *Daily Mail*. Retrieved at: http://www.dailymail.co.uk/news/article-2340710/Alex-Spourdalakis-Autistic-boy-14-killed-mother-godmother-removed-hospital.html.

Zisk, A. (2012). I hid. In *Loud hands: Autistic people speaking*. Washington, DC: Autistic Self Advocacy Network.

Index

ableism, 3, 17, 33; biopolitics and, 176, 178; systems of oppression and, 18, 41, 50, 80, 201. *See also* murders of autistic/disabled people; violence against autistic people

abnormalcy, 54, 167, 180, 220; 1930s and 1940s research, 31–36; cognitivist views, 49–50; as deviant double, 84; embodied, 68–69, 71, 75–76, 79, 81, 93–96; gaze not possible, 93–94; Lovaas's influence, 45; proliferation of categories, 142, 165

absent referent, 95

advocacy. *See* autism advocacy; autistic self-advocacy

advocacy epidemic, 55, 59–60

advocacy subjects. *See* subject positions

advocate-warrior, 157–58, 172, 176, 180–81

Agamben, Giorgio, 103, 130–31, 132

Akhter, Faryaal, 200

Akhter, Zain, 200

Aleshire, Timothy, 199

"Amanda Baggs Controversy" blog, 14

American Recovery and Reinvestment Act, 116, 125

anachronistic humans, 79–80

And Straight on Till Morning: Essays on Autism Acceptance (ASAN), 8

anthropomorphization of autism, 151, 153–54, 180

any-bodies, 85, 93, 96–98, 111

apologies, depoliticization of, 159–61

Applied Behavioral Analysis (ABA), 44–46, 101, 229n3 (ch. 5)

The Arc, 183

Aristotle, 130–31, 132

artifacts, 19–20; Starbucks cups, 103–9, 117, 128, 134

Asperger, Hans, 30, 31–32, 33–34, 36

Aspies for Freedom (AFF), 62

Auriemma, Angelica, 196

autism: 'bad' bodies and brains, 44–46, 51, 77, 81, 90–91, 95–96, 108–9; business of, 125, 126-130; as commodity fetish, 107; as condition, 30–31; as cost, 1, 19, 120-121, 126, 141, 167; as cultural crisis, 8–11; as cultural outlaw, 25, 146; as disorder-in-need-of-order, 5, 32, 43, 59–60; as exclusively white middle-class, 40–41, 225n3 (ch. 1); as a happening, 142; historical genealogy, 27–28, 212; as interpretive category, 21–23; as life-draining, 175–76, 213, 218, 220, 222; as mode of thinking, 29; as origin of pathology, 209–11; as relational, 11, 18–19, 21–23, 58, 68, 105, 165; as

natural, concept of, 77
Nazi death camps, 36, 39
Nazi eugenics, 33–34
Ne'eman, Ari, 8, 11, 62, 64, 155, 158, 228n2 (ch. 3)
negative ontology, 173
Negri, Antonio, 140–41
Neisser, Ulric, 49
neoliberalism, 53; autism as threat to, 24–25, 111–12, 120; categories of race, queerness, and disability, 131–32; child as 'time-rich,' 120, 124; freedom, rhetoric of, 114–15, 122–23; market timing, 109–11; temporality of the 'now,' 119–20, 133, 142–43, 228n18 (ch. 3); time and, 105–6, 112–13, 115–16. *See also* liberalism
neurodivergence, 59
neurodiversity, politics of, 58–60
Neurodiversity: A Weblog (Seidel), 228n3 (ch. 4), 229n2 (ch. 5)
neurodiversity movements, 43, 155, 158
neuroimaging technologies, 49
neuroplasticity, 50, 51
neuroscience, 46–50
neutral debate rhetoric, 159–61
New York University Child Studies Center Ransom Notes campaign, 64, 152–55, 159–60, 185
news headlines, 120–21, 135
nonautism, 58, 68; binary with autism, 71, 90–91, 207, 213–14, 216, 224; as hope and possibility, 213, 219–20; life as condition of, 121, 191–93
nonhumanness, autism as state of, 24, 48, 90–91, 101
non-neurotypicality, 59
non-normative advocacy, 58, 65–66
Nordheimer, Ian, 216
normalization, 9, 20, 24, 28, 92; behaviorist, 44–46; discipline-normalization, 89–90; psychiatry's focus on child, 75–76
normativity, 94, 147, 217; extranormativity, 179; as homeland, 182–84; non-normativity, 29, 65–66, 102. *See also* gaze, normalizing
nostalgia, 140
Not Dead Yet, 195
"nothing about us without us," 60

'now,' 119–20, 130, 133, 142–43, 228n18 (ch. 3)
nurture, 36–37

Obama, Barack, 117–18, 122, 125, 126, 134; outbreak narrative, 116, 138; on spread of autism, 137–38
observing, acts of, 31–32
odds, 135–39, 149, 188
"On Potentiality" (Agamben), 130–31, 132
online writing, 18
Ono, Yoko, 170
"Ontario Community Grieves Loss of Boy with Autism" (Autism Ontario), 3–6, *4, 9*, 15
oppression, 101; bodies and, 16–17; multiple, interlocking, 18, 41, 50, 79–80, 93, 111, 201
The Order of Things (Foucault), 70
outbreak narrative, 116, 138–39

panoptic visibility, 91–93
pathologization, 28, 31–32, 43; of enemy figure, 177–82; of mothering, 36–41
pathology: autism as origin of, 209–11; becoming aware of autism as, 53–55; fluid range of, 214; moving, 141, 181
patriotism, 181
Pediatrics, 139
Peng, Xuan, 203–5, 210–11, 215–16
Peoria Journal Star, 205–6, 208, 212
"Personal Pathway Model" to terrorism, 179
person-first language, 187–90, 227n9 (ch. 3)
"Perspectives on a Puzzle Piece" (Green Allison), 41–43
Pinckney, Tiffany, 197
Piven, J., 211
Poirier, Gabriel, 198
policymaking, 64
political naming, 59
Porter, James I., 95
potentiality, rhetoric of, 45, 54, 77, 81, 84, 94–95, 100, 122; impotentiality, 130–32; murder of autistic people and, 202, 211–17; risk-benefit potentials, 130–33
Poussin, Nicolas, 161–62, *163*

power: circulation of, 71–72; narrative
and, 11–14; as productive/transfor-
mative, 72, 91; of social model of
disability, 16; tactics of, 28. *See also*
biopolitics/biopower
power relations, 19, 23, 27, 224; subject
positions and, 68–69, 72–73
prevalence, 104, 112, 133–35, 137, 139
"Prevalence of the Autism Spectrum
Disorders (ASDs) in Multiple Areas
of the United States 2004 and 2006,"
134–35
Price, Janet, 16
problem-in-need-of-response, 5, 10, 32,
43, 59–60
product, autism as, 107
products, developmental, 88
pseudoscience, 56, 127
"Psychiatric Disorders in the Parents of
Autistic Individuals" (Piven), 211
psychoanalysis, 36, 44, 47
Puar, J. K., 107, 177
puzzle metaphor, 68, 191, 192–93

racial hygiene, 32, 34
racialized body, 79–80
racism: exclusion of nonwhite mothers,
40–41; as fragmentation, 173–74; war
as, 173
Ransom Notes campaign (New York
University Child Studies Center), 63,
152–55, 159–60, 185
rationality of opposites, 219–20
reason, 76–77
recovery, discourse of, 116, 125, 214,
227n9 (ch. 3)
red flag metaphor, 67, 96, 149
red flag warning signs, 24, 54–58, 67–
102; Autism Ontario poster, 81–83,
82, 86–87, 93, 99, 101; awareness
campaigns, 56–57, 93–94; beware,
96–98, 193; biomedicine, 87–93;
border-crossing nature of, 81, 84, *86*;
National Autistic Society poster, 83–
85, *85*, 87; red color, 98–100, 226n5
(ch. 2); underdevelopment, rhetoric
of, 68, 77, 81, 85, 99, 101; violence
toward autistics and, 200; wariness,
94–96, 193
'refrigerator' mother, 38–39, 40
Refrigerator Mothers (film), 41

regimes of truth, 70, 74
registries, 183–84
regulation, 97, 107, 165
Reid, 166, 170, 172
relatedness, 17–18
reproductive interference, 35
resistance, 15, 58–59, 62–63, 65;
depoliticization of, 159–61; to gaze,
93
responsive advocacy, 3, 8
Richter, Zach, 62
Rimland, Bernard, 46, 225–26n4 (ch.
1)
'Ripper' figure, 151
risk-benefit potentials, 130–33
Robertson, Scott Michael, 60, 63
Rochester, Rylan, 200
Rose, Nikolas, 75–76, 87–88, 122
Runswick-Cole, Katherine, 107, 128
Russill, C., 139

Safe Minds, 57
Sampier, Kevin, 205
Santorum, Rick, 144
scales, developmental, 75–76, 87–88,
226n4 (ch. 1)
schizophrenia, 29–30
schooling, as intervention, 76–77, 100
Schwartz, Phil, 62
scientific discourse, 70–71
Second Annual World Focus on Autism,
155
security response, 141, 168, 177, 193;
normative homeland, 182–84
"'Seeing Red': Color Selection as an
Indicator of Implicit Societal Conceptions about the Autism Spectrum"
(Diehl et al.), 226n5 (ch. 2)
Seidel, Kathleen, 62, 228n2, 229n2 (ch.
5)
self-determination rights, 183
September, 11, 2001, 177
Sequenzia, Amy, 62
services and supports, call for as
response to murders, 5, 7, 214–15
severity, discourse of, 1–2, 211–14
sexism, 36–41
Shakespeare, Tom, 17
Shaw, Eric D., 179
Shestack, John, 146
Shiffrar, Maggie, 229n10 (ch. 4)